SYSMOD - The Systems Modeling Toolbox, 3rd edition

Pragmatic MBSE with SysML

Tim Weilkiens

SYSMOD - The Systems Modeling Toolbox, 3rd edition

Pragmatic MBSE with SysML

Tim Weilkiens

ISBN 978-3-9818529-8-1

/MBSE4U

Publishing on the Pulse of the Markets

MBSE4U is a publishing house for books about MBSE. They are intended to be regularly updated to align the content with the highly dynamic systems engineering domain.

Contents

About MBSE4U

Publishing on the Pulse of the Market

MBSE4U is a publishing organization for model-based systems engineering books that are regularly updated to follow the dynamic changes in the MBSE community and the markets.

MBSE4U has published the following books:

- Tim Weilkiens. SYSMOD - The Systems Modeling Toolbox - Pragmatic MBSE with SysML. 3rd edition. 2020.
- Tim Weilkiens. The New Engineering Game. 2019.
- Benjamin Weinert. Ein Framework zur Architekturbeschreibung von sozio-technischen maritimen Systemen. 2018. (German Edition)
- Christian Neureiter. A Domain-Specific, Model Driven Engineering Approach for Systems Engineering in the Smart Grid. 2017.
- Tim Weilkiens. Variant Modeling with SysML. 2016.

Please let us know if you want to write a book to be published by MBSE4U (info@mbse4u.com). We have a lean publishing process to reward the authors well for providing their valuable MBSE knowledge to the community.

About Tim Weilkiens

I am a consultant and trainer, author, publisher, lecturer, executive board member of the German consulting and training company oose, and active member of the OMG and INCOSE organizations. I wrote parts of the initial SysML specification, and I am still active in the ongoing work on SysML. I am involved in many MBSE activities, and you can meet me at many conferences on MBSE and related topics.

As a consultant, I have advised many companies in different domains. The insights into their challenges are one source of my experience that I share in my books and presentations.

I have written many books about modeling, including *Systems Engineering with SysML* (Morgan Kaufmann, 2008) and *Model-Based System Architecture* (Wiley, 2015). I am the editor of the pragmatic and independent MBSE methodology SYSMOD – the Systems Modeling Toolbox.

You can contact me at tim@mbse4u.com and read my blog about MBSE at www.mbse4u.com.

History and Outlook

This chapter gives a brief overview of the SYSMOD version's history and an outlook on future planned changes.

SYSMOD Versions

- 4.2 Third edition of the book *SYSMOD - The Systems Modeling Toolbox. MBSE4U. 2019*
  - Added chapter "Engineering for the Planet"
  - Added SYSMOD Methods: "Analyze the Problem", "Model Risks", "Specify Test Cases", and "Model the Test Architecture"
  - Added SYSMOD Adoption Process
  - Added a chapter about the adoption of MBSE
  - Added a chapter about a brief introduction to SysML 1.6
  - Mapping ISO 15288 to SYSMOD
  - New OCL constraints for SYSMOD stereotypes (*«continuousUseCase»*)
  - New StakeholderKindCategory: Other
  - Updated to SysML 1.6
  - Some minor typos and updates
- 4.1 Second edition of the book *SYSMOD - The Systems Modeling Toolbox. MBSE4U. 2016*
- 4.0.2 Actor stereotypes specialize SysML Block
- 4.0.1 Fixed some typos and minor changes

- 4.0 First edition of the book *SYSMOD - The Systems Modeling Toolbox. MBSE4U. 2015*
- 3.0 Third edition of the German book *Systems Engineering mit SysML/UML. dpunkt-Verlag. 2014*
- 2.0 First edition of the English book *Systems Engineering with SysML/UML. Morgan Kaufman. 2008*
- 1.0 First publication of SYSMOD in the German book *Systems Engineering mit SysML/UML. dpunkt-Verlag. 2006*

SYSMOD Outlook

- More behavior descriptions in architecture models
- More tools for on-site workshops to elaborate SYSMOD Products
- Functional safety modeling
- Methods for Collaborative Engineering
- MBSE and Digital Twins, Data Analytics, Artificial Intelligence, and Machine Learning
- Configuration Management
- Framework Evaluation of MBSE Methodologies for Practitioners (FEMMP)
- Description of SYSMOD using the Essence framework

Preface

Many years ago, I bundled modeling methods and practices to the Systems Modeling Toolbox (SYSMOD). At the same time, I worked together with other MBSE experts on the first version of SysML 1.0 [SysML07]. SYSMOD is a discovery and not an invention. It consists of already well-known methods and practices. I am more an editor than an author of SYSMOD and collected practices, transferred some of them from other disciplines to the systems engineering discipline, and described the links between the practices to combine them to a methodology. Nowadays, SYSMOD is used in many industrial projects worldwide.

In 2006, I published SYSMOD in the German book *Systems Engineering mit SysML/UML* (dpunkt) and 2008 in the English edition *Systems Engineering with SysML/UML* [We08]. The third edition of the German book was published in 2014 [We14]. Besides SYSMOD, the books provide a comprehensive description of the SysML. To release more regular updates, in 2015, I published the first edition of a book specifically on the SYSMOD methodology. You are currently holding the book in your hands (or have it stored on your device or cloud).

This third edition of the book includes additional methods about problem analysis, risk management, and testing, a chapter about SysML, and a chapter about the adoption of MBSE in an organization.

The SYSMOD Method Analyze the Problem (section 4.5) is about an explicit rethinking of the problem statement: “Are we solving the right problem with the system?”.

The methods Specify Test Cases (section 4.15) and Model the Test Architecture (section 4.21) add the important verification and validation aspect to the SYSMOD methodology. You find a more detailed list of the changes in the history section above.

I appreciate any feedback on the book. You can reach me by email: tim@mbse4u.com. This book is considered to be an eBook. However, a print version of the book is also available.

I like to write books in a gender-fair language. On the other hand, I avoid cluttering the flow of reading by always using both genders in the same sentence. Therefore, I only used one gender where it was not appropriate to use gender-neutral language. Feel free to replace the gender with your favorite one wherever it is appropriate.

I thank my colleagues at my company for long profound discussions about MBSE.

I thank NoMagic for their support. I created the SysML diagrams in this book with their modeling tool Cameo Systems Modeler.

If you need MBSE training or consulting services, feel free to contact me. My company - the consultancy oose - provides professional MBSE training and coachings, for example, to introduce MBSE in your organization.

Tim Weilkiens, July 2020.

tim@mbse4u.com

1. SYSMOD - The Systems Modeling Toolbox

SYSMOD is the abbreviation for Systems Modeling Toolbox and an MBSE methodology with a strong focus on the individual methods. The modeling language and tools come second. Processes in SYSMOD are guidelines and no strict rules. It is more important to master the craftsmanship than to follow a process.

SYSMOD works perfectly together with the OMG Systems Modeling Language (OMG SysML) [SysML19]. SysML is a general-purpose modeling language for systems engineering and a worldwide standard. It is not mandatory to do SYSMOD with SysML. As a default, however, I would always recommend this combination.

Process, Method, and *Methodology* are common terms with many different meanings. SYSMOD follows the definitions given by James N. Martin [Ma96]:

"A Process is a logical sequence of tasks performed to achieve a particular objective. A process defines "WHAT" is to be done, without specifying "HOW" each task is performed."

"A Method consists of techniques for performing a task, in other words, it defines the "HOW" of each task."

Based on Jeff Estefan [Es08], a *Tool* facilitates the accomplishment of the methods, and a *Methodology is a consistent set of related processes, methods, and tools.*

SYSMOD uses an extended version of this definition to explicitly include humans: A methodology is a collection of processes, Methods, Products, Roles, and tools.

The tools are a set of applications, servers, interfaces, and so on, which form the System Modeling Environment (SME).

The SYSMOD toolbox consists of three main artifact kinds:

- The SYSMOD Products are significant artifacts of the systems development like requirements or the architecture descriptions.
- The SYSMOD Methods are best practices on how to create an SYSMOD Product.
- The SYSMOD Roles are work descriptions of a person. A Role is responsible for SYSMOD Products and a primary or additional performer of SYSMOD Methods.

The following figure 1.1 depicts the relationships between SYSMOD Methods, Products, and Roles.

A Role is part of 0..* methodologies, is responsible for 1..* Methods, and supports 0..* Methods as a co-worker.

A Method is part of 0..* methodologies and has precisely one Role that is responsible for the Method and some Roles as additional performers. Each Method requires 0..* Products as inputs and produces 1..* Products as outputs. Exactly one Role is responsible for a Product. A Product is part of 0..* methodologies.

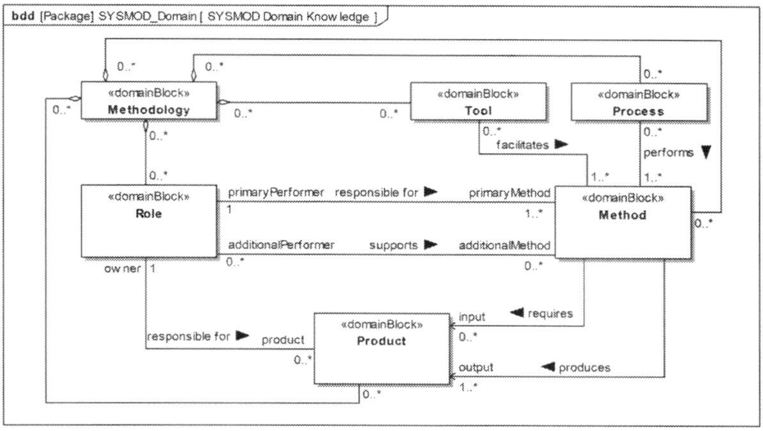

Figure 1.1: Main SYSMOD Artifact Kinds

A process is part of 0..* methodologies and performs 1..* methods. A tool is also part of 0..* methodologies and facilitates 1..* Methods.

A methodology is a collection of processes, Methods, Products, Roles, and tools.

The SYSMOD Infrastructure Process (figure 3.3), SYSMOD Analysis Process (figure 3.4), and the SYSMOD Architecture Process (figure 3.5) demonstrate a typical logical order of execution of the SYSMOD Methods. In practice, a project typically uses a customized set of methods in a different order, and with many iterations and loops.

Before the book starts with the main SYSMOD content, the next chapter 2 solicits your attention to a critical topic. Our planet is in bad shape, and I assume all of you would like to have a good life for yourself, your family, your descendants, and all the life around you. It is quite evident that we must actively do something to make that happen. We engineers must also take responsibility. Chapter 2 deals with the responsibility of each individual engineer and channeling engineering power for the planet.

Since the SYSMOD Processes provide a good overview of the toolbox, I start to describe SYSMOD with the process chapter. Next, follows the chapters about the SYSMOD Methods, Products, and Roles. Each chapter lists the elements with a brief description.

The Guidances chapter provides practical explanations of how to do the modeling of the SYSMOD Methods and Products.

Examples are always helpful for a better understanding. The Examples chapter demonstrates the application of SYSMOD with a fictitious example. Since a book is a book and a model is a model, the examples chapter can only provide some views on the overall model. The example as a model is available as part of the SYSMOD plugin (see www.mbse4u.com).

Chapter 9 presents the SysML profile for SYSMOD. It describes the stereotypes that are necessary to apply the SYSMOD concepts to a model.

Chapter 10 describes how to define a customized MBSE Methodology using SYSMOD.

Chapter 11 is about more MBSE Tools and opens additional drawers of the MBSE toolbox and presents some helpful patterns and other practices for MBSE.

Chapter 12 provides a brief introduction to the OMG Systems Modeling Language (SysML) Version 1.6.

In the annex, you find a mapping of SYSMOD to the ISO15288 processes.

2. Engineering for the Planet

Engineers build great systems that save lives, protect the environment, provide energy, safety, mobility, economic development, convenience, and many more. But they also build systems that kill and harm people, destroy our environment, and do other bad things.

The people who use such systems take the primary responsibility, but the engineers who built the systems also take part in it. They have the expertise and can influence solutions to ensure a more sustainable future.

We are facing more and more global challenges like climate change, increasing world population, pandemics, environmental destruction, or the possibility of an asteroid impact.

Engineering power makes the impossible possible. Engineers brought humans to the moon, which is still unbelievable, but it was much more unthinkable in the 1960ies. The Chinese built a dam that slows down the earth's rotation. Regardless of if all this is good or bad, it is extremely powerful.

Regarding the critical situation of our planet, we must channelize the power of engineering for a worth living future. Besides large planet-saving projects and heroic deeds, it is also about the many small micro-decisions and actions of each engineer in the world that, in total, will move us in the right direction.

Let *Engineering for the Planet* be part of the engineering mindset, a mandatory part of standards and policies, and part of the engineer's toolbox full of methods & tools.

SYSMOD, for example, provides an actor element *Planet Environment* associated with tasks about sustainability analysis, and an actor category *«environmentalImpact»*. See section 7.8 about how to use the Planet Environment.

X4Planet is an organization to focus on global resources experts on saving the planet. The X stands for any domain like engineering or organizational consulting. Join the community and do your part. Following X4Planet on social media is a good starting point. See www.x4planet.org for more information.

3. SYSMOD Processes

Processes are valuable, but of higher value is the craftsmanship of MBSE with a well-filled toolbox of methods, patterns, and tools. Although I initially called SYSMOD the Systems Modeling Process, my understanding of SYSMOD is now that it is a Systems Modeling Toolbox.

The SYSMOD Processes presented in this chapter are only a description of one useful logical order of execution of the SYSMOD Methods. I assume that in practice, the SYSMOD Processes are never performed as specified here. The order and the collection of methods are in each project different. In particular, you should not mix up the logical order and the timely order. The logical order does not imply a waterfall process. SYSMOD is independent of a waterfall or agile approach. The execution is an orthogonal aspect, and both approaches are possible with SYSMOD, whereby I prefer an agile approach.

Figure 3.1 shows the SYSMOD Processes and the primary SYSMOD Roles that perform the embedded SYSMOD Methods. The following figures depict the details of the processes, including the logical order of execution of the SYSMOD Methods.

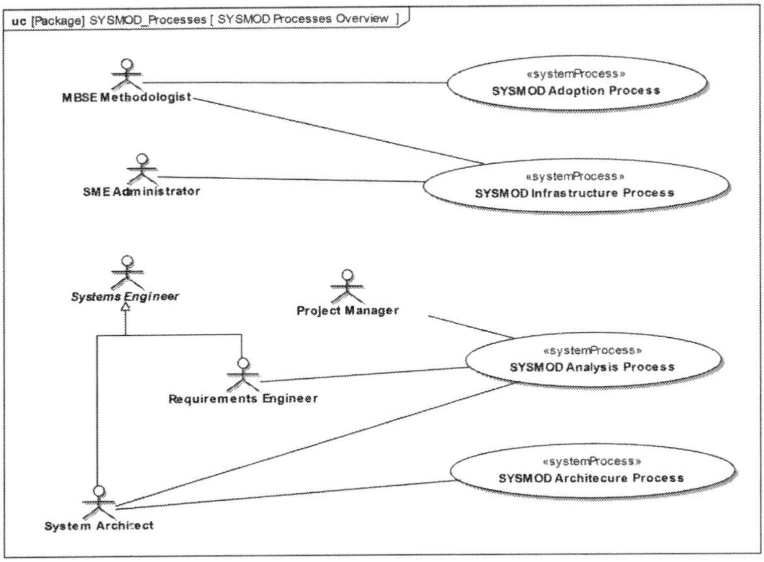

Figure 3.1: SYSMOD Processes

Figure 3.2[1] shows the SYSMOD MBSE Adoption Process (SMAP), including the Methods and the flow of the Products from and to the Methods.

SMAP uses SYSMOD itself to define a customized MBSE Methodology for a project or organization. The system of interest in SMAP is the MBSE Methodology.

Chapter 10 provides more details about SMAP and how you can use the Methods to develop an MBSE Methodology.

[1]: A larger version of the diagram is available at www.mbse4u.com/sysmod-figures.

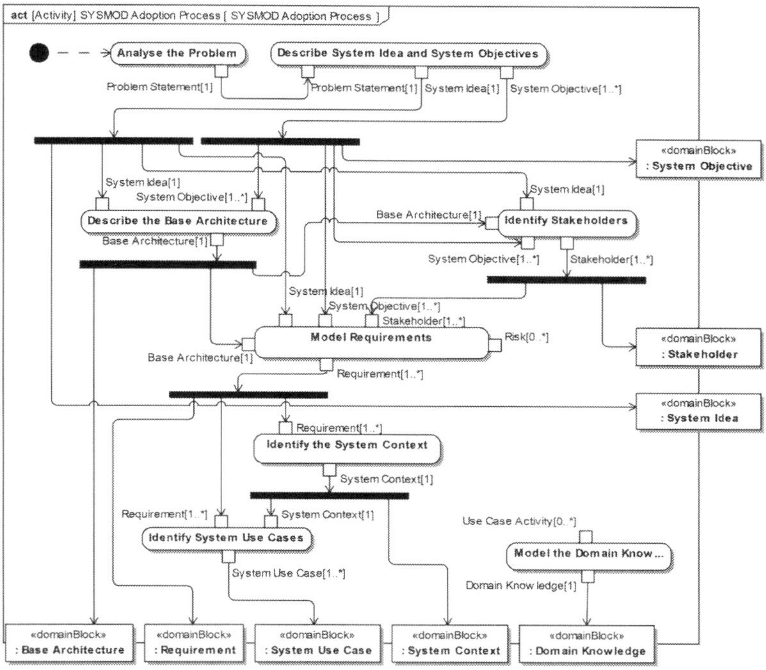

Figure 3.2: SYSMOD MBSE Adoption Process (SMAP)

Figure 3.3 shows the SYSMOD Infrastructure Process. The following Products are the results of the process:

- 5.1 MBSE Methodology
- 5.2 System Modeling Environment (SME)
- 5.3 MBSE Training

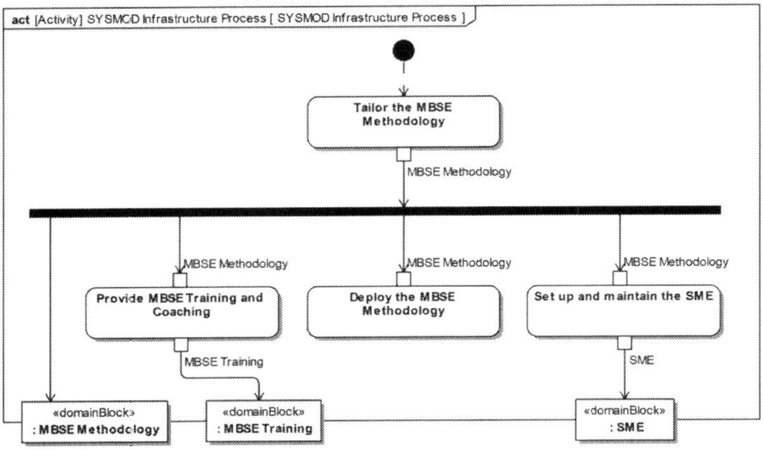

Figure 3.3: SYSMOD Infrastructure Process

Figure 3.4 shows the SYSMOD Analysis Process. It looks similar to the MBSE Adoption Process. The system of interest is now the product we want to develop and not the MBSE Methodology.

The following Products are the results of the process:

- 5.7 Base Architecture
- 5.15 Domain Knowledge
- 5.10 Requirements
- 5.9 Risks
- 5.8 Stakeholders
- 5.11 System Context
- 5.5 System Idea
- 5.6 System Objectives
- 5.13 System Processes
- 5.12 System Use Cases
- 5.14 Use Case Activities

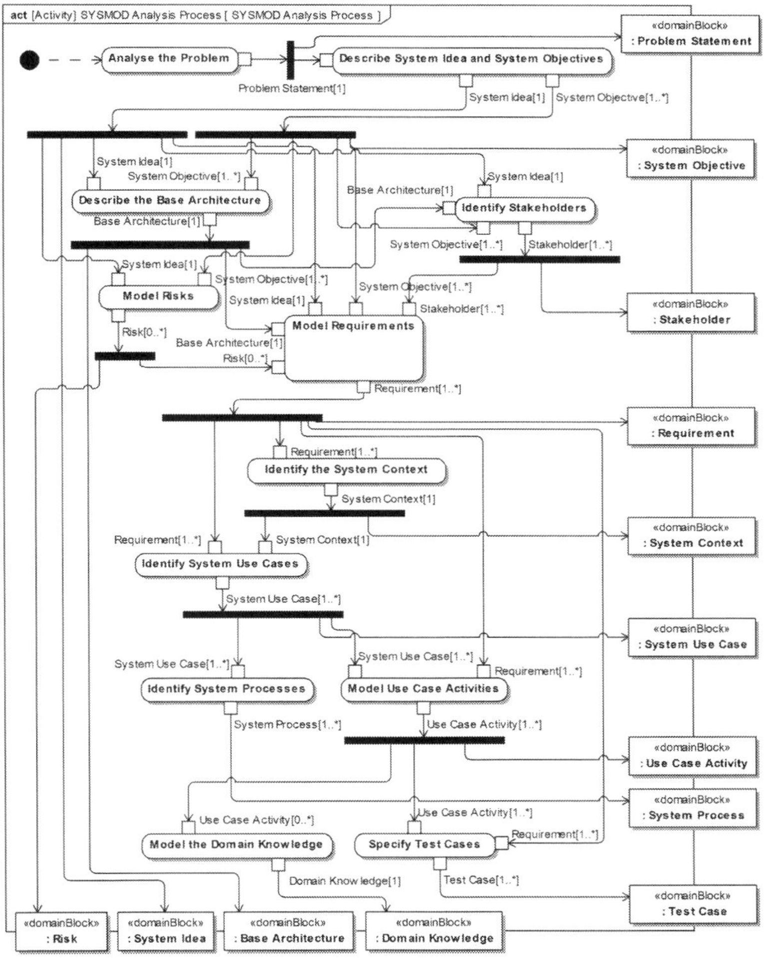

Figure 3.4: SYSMOD Analysis Process

Figure 3.5 shows the SYSMOD Architecture Process. The following Products are the results of the process:

- 5.20 Logical Architecture
- 5.21 Product Architecture
- 5.22 Scenarios
- 5.23 System States

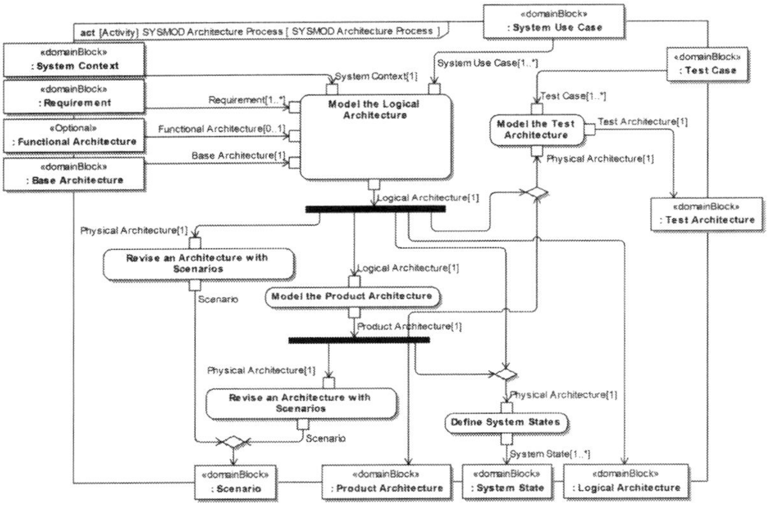

Figure 3.5: SYSMOD Architecture Process

A valuable supplement of SYSMOD is the Functional Architectures for Systems method (FAS). See section 11.2 for a brief description of FAS. You find a detailed description of the FAS method in the book *Model-Based System Architectures* [We15].

Figure 3.6 shows how SYSMOD integrates the FAS method. It lies between the analysis and the architecture methods. Inputs of the FAS method are the Use Case Activities from the SYSMOD Analysis Process, and the output of the FAS method - the functional architecture - is an optional input for the SYSMOD Architecture Process. See Model Logical Architecture in section 4.17 about how to use a functional architecture for the development of physical architectures.

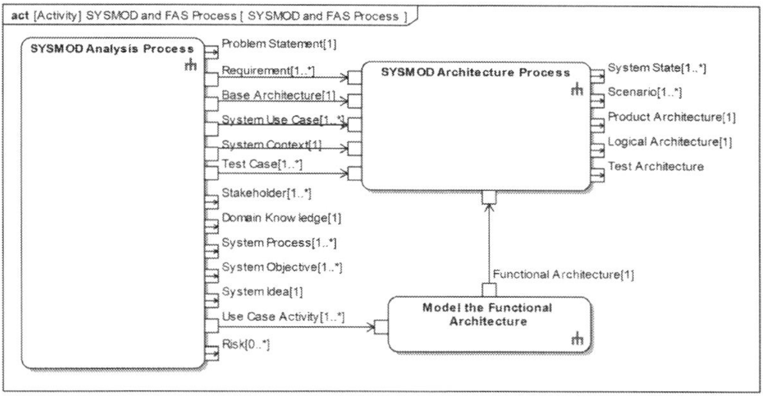

Figure 3.6: SYSMOD and FAS

Of course, SYSMOD Methods and Products can be used in the context of an ISO 15288 inspired process landscape. Appendix A provides a mapping of the ISO 15288 processes to the SYSMOD Methods.

4. SYSMOD Methods

The SYSMOD Methods are a collection of tasks to create significant artifacts for the systems development (see SYSMOD Products in chapter 5).

Below is the list of SYSMOD Methods in a logical order according to the SYSMOD Processes (see chapter 3):

- 4.1 Tailor the MBSE Methodology
- 4.2 Set up and maintain the SME
- 4.3 Deploy the MBSE Methodology
- 4.4 Provide MBSE Training and Coaching
- 4.5 Analyze the Problem
- 4.6 Describe the System Idea and the System Objectives
- 4.7 Describe the Base Architecture
- 4.8 Identify Stakeholders
- 4.9 Model Risks
- 4.10 Model Requirements
- 4.11 Identify the System Context
- 4.12 Identify System Use Cases
- 4.13 Identify System Processes
- 4.14 Model Use Case Activities
- 4.15 Model the Domain Knowledge
- 4.16 Specify Test Cases
- 4.17 Model the Functional Architecture
- 4.18 Model the Logical Architecture
- 4.19 Model the Product Architecture
- 4.20 Revise an Architecture with Scenarios
- 4.21 Define System States
- 4.22 Model the Test Architecture

4.1 Tailor the MBSE Methodology

Tailor a given MBSE Methodology to the specific needs of an organization or project.

Purpose

Adapting the MBSE Methodology to the specific needs of the engineering project avoids useless overhead on engineering tasks that have no real value to the project and Stakeholders.

Description

An MBSE Methodology is a collection of Processes, Methods, Products, Roles, and tools. A predefined MBSE Methodology like SYSMOD does not fit one-to-one to an organization or project. Some steps need to be more emphasized, others are superfluous and can be skipped, and some engineering artifacts are not even covered by the methodology and need to be added. That is not a lack of methodology. The tailoring is a standard task before you apply the methodology to your projects.

You can use SYSMOD itself to elaborate your needs for a methodology and to derive the methods. In this case, the MBSE Methodology itself is the system of interest. See chapter 10 on how to use SYSMOD to develop an MBSE Methodology.

Relationships

Primary Performer	6.2 MBSE Methodologist
Inputs	None
Outputs	5.1 MBSE Methodology
ISO 15288 Process	A Infrastructure Management

Further Information

- The SYSMOD Processes in chapter 3 are an example of a consistent and defined set of Products, Methods, and Roles.
- Chapter 10 describes the MBSE Adoption Process.

4.2 Set up and maintain the SME

Configure the modeling tools and create a System Modeling Environment (SME) for the project or organization.

Purpose

Provide a suitable SME to perform the tailored MBSE Methodology.

Description

The core of the SME is a SysML modeling tool. Although there are other systems engineering modeling languages available, SysML is the de facto standard, and you need good arguments not to use it.

Out-of-the-box, a SysML modeling tool provides the whole set of SysML model elements as well as some extensions defined by the tool vendor or other standards.

It is necessary to enable methodology-specific extensions to use a SysML modeling tool for a tailored MBSE Methodology. Additionally, you should remove superfluous model elements from the toolbox and add convenience functions to provide a more convenient user experience.

If required, model libraries must be made accessible, and toolchains to other tools like requirements management or simulation tools must be established.

Besides the SysML tool, other tools are typically part of the SME(#Product52SystemsModelingEnvironment). They must also be customized.

Relationships

Primary Performer	6.1 SME Administrator
Inputs	5.1 MBSE Methodology
Outputs	5.2 System Modeling Environment
ISO 15288 Process	A Infrastructure Management

Further Information

None

4.3 Deploy the MBSE Methodology

Deploy the customized MBSE Methodology in the organization.

Purpose

An MBSE Methodology must be actively deployed to be accepted and to be adopted by the organization.

Description

The deployment of the MBSE Methodology should enable the successful application of the MBSE Methodology. The methodology should not be introduced in one step; instead, define intermediate goals. For example, according to the levels SYSMOD1 to SYSMOD3 in the SYSMOD Model Purpose Model (section 11.3). Think big and start small.

Deploying MBSE is a change process that needs time to be successfully adopted by the organization. But, typically, time is a rare good in projects. They do not have the time to play around with new methodologies and sandbox projects. The projects must use methods and tools effectively and valuable from the early beginning.

Keep an eye on the value/effort relation whereby the relation includes several perspectives: the short-term project perspective, the long-term organization perspective, and the human perspective of the engineers who do the job.

It is essential to integrate new methods as a mandatory part of the engineering process. Projects discard optional parts as soon as the schedule is getting tough what is always the case. If they are necessary, make sure that the steps are applied productively in the project, including taking the learning curve into account.

Relationships

Primary Performer	6.2 MBSE Methodologist
Inputs	5.1 MBSE Methodology
Outputs	None
ISO 15288 Process	A Infrastructure Management

Further Information

None

4.4 Provide MBSE Training and Coaching

Train the MBSE Methodology and related modeling languages and tools as well as provide coaching for assistance to apply the MBSE Methodology.

Purpose

Anyone who plays a role in the MBSE Methodology and, to a certain extent, also the Stakeholders of the project must know and be able to use the MBSE Methodology.

Description

People must be familiar with the MBSE Methodology, modeling languages, and modeling tools. You must differentiate between people who must be able to read the models and people who build the models. These are different skills whereby the reading skill is a subset of the building skill. Creating a model requires a much more in-depth knowledge than reading a model or understanding views of the model.

In addition to the training, you must provide consulting services for the projects to quickly resolve issues, remove hurdles, and get feedback from the projects. In the beginning, this can be done by external experts. In the long run, internal persons should take over continuous consultation. External experts are only used for particular topics, in exceptional cases, and for occasional reviews.

Relationships

Primary Performer	6.2 MBSE Methodologist
Inputs	5.1 MBSE Methodology
Outputs	None
ISO 15288 Process	A Human Resource Management

Further Information

None

4.5 Analyze the Problem

Purpose

Find out the real problem that should be resolved by the system. Sometimes it is not the initial problem statement, and the real problem must be identified by a profound analysis.

Description

An illustrative example of the importance of finding the real problem is the quote by Henry Ford: "If I had asked my customers what they wanted, they would have said a faster horse." The quote hits the point. Even if it is doubted that Henry Ford had really said this, it illustrates very well that the real problem to be solved and the real needs to be satisfied require a profound analysis.

Design Thinking is an approach to solve problems creatively with a particular focus on problem analysis. The origin of Design Thinking lies in the 1960s [Ar65]. An essential recent publication about Design Thinking is *Change by Design: How Design Thinking Transforms Organizations and Inspires Innovation* from Tim Brown [Br09], and *The Design Thinking Playbook* [Le18].

Design Thinking is well-known in the business and engineering domain and used as a standard method for around 15 years. The main drivers were the Stanford University, the company IDEO and the Hasso Plattner Institute.

Part of the Design Thinking process is the redefinition of the initial problem statement to find the real challenge that satisfies the needs of the stakeholders. Design Thinking does not ask what the users want, but what the users need.

The problem statement is co-developed with a prototype in an iterative process. A first problem statement leads to the first solution attempts that again clarify the problem statement, and so on. The user is always in the center of the Design Thinking process. Besides the visible problem, Design Thinking addresses also the invisible emotional needs of the user.

Reinhard Haberfellner et al. describe another approach with the problem-solving process (figure 4.1) [Ha19].

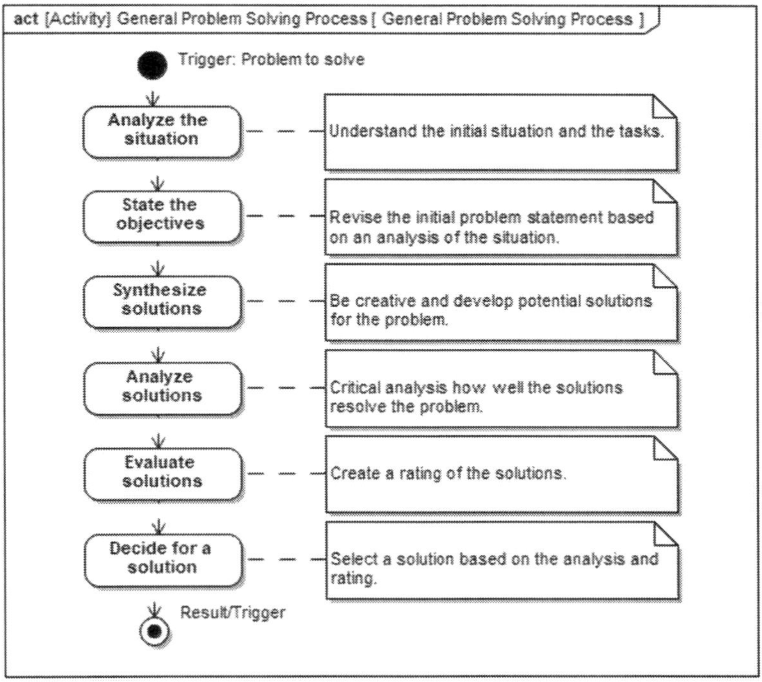

Figure 4.1: Problem Solving Process

The problem-solving process is based on the five steps of

problem-solving by John Dews, published in 1910 [De10]. The process starts with the analysis of the problem before it proceeds with the development of solutions.

The process in figure 4.1 looks sequential, but it depicts only the logical sequence and not the execution order, which includes lots of feedback cycles.

Two simple workshop tools to explore the problem space are the 6M and 5-Why methods. You find a description of these methods in chapter 11.

Relationships

Primary Performer	6.3 Project Manager
Inputs	None
Outputs	5.4 Problem Statement
ISO 15288 Process	A Business Mission Analysis

Further Information

- 7.2 How to Analyze the Problem
- 8.2 Example Problem Statement
- 11.11 Workshop Tool: 6M Method
- 11.12 Workshop Tool: 5 Why Method

4.6 Describe the System Idea and System Objectives

Describe the idea and objectives of the system.

Purpose

The System Idea and System Objectives need to be known to all participating parties so they can make the right decisions on the way to the final system. It is not to be taken for granted that all project members know the System's Idea and the System's Objectives. They must be actively communicated.

Description

If you know the objectives, you will find a solution even if some distances of your way are unknown, unsafe, or full of obstacles. If you do not know the objectives, but all the rules of your perfect development process, you will reach a destination that likely does not meet your requirements and needs.

The System Idea is the elevator pitch of your system. Every project member must have a common understanding of the basic notion of the system that can be told during an elevator ride: short, precise, concise, and unique.

The System Idea and System Objectives are part of the system model to communicate them and to link them with system artifacts like Requirements.

There are various sources for the System Idea and System Objectives. Be it a genius thought, a given contract, an output of product management work, or anything else. A Design Thinking process [Br09], or a Value Proposition Design [Os14] is a potential predecessor step.

Often, this SYSMOD Method about the System Idea and System Objectives only works up the somewhere given notion and objectives of the system artifacts for the communication inside the system development project teams. The outcome is stored or referenced in the system model.

Practical tools to work out the idea and the objectives in a workshop are the Product Box (section 11.8), the Product Vision Board by Roman Pichler [Pi16] (section 11.9), and the SAMS method with storyboards (section 11.10).

The Requirements for the system should support the objectives. The relationship in the model is a trace from the Requirements to the System Objectives. See section 8.4 Example System Objectives for an example of these relationships.

Relationships

Primary Performer	6.3 Project Manager
Inputs	5.4 Problem Statement
Outputs	5.5 System Idea, 5.6 System Objectives
ISO 15288 Process	A Business Mission Analysis

Further Information

- 7.3 How to Model the System Idea
- 7.4 How to Model the System Objectives
- 8.3 Example System Idea
- 8.4 Example System Objectives
- 11.8 Workshop Tool: Product Box

- 11.9 Workshop Tool: Product Vision Board
- 11.10 Workshop Tool: SAMS Method

4.7 Describe the Base Architecture

Define the given Physical Architecture at the project start that constrains the solution space.

Purpose

The Base Architecture defines the level of abstraction of the Requirements and provides the scope for innovation and architectural and technical decisions.

Description

Most Requirements already include some technical decisions. I have rarely seen absolute solution-free requirements. The Base Architecture defines the technical decisions that are already fixed at the beginning of a project. They are constraint requirements of the system.

A car has four wheels, an aircraft two wings. Typically, that is already set with the start of the project, and the engineers must not think of different solutions, and the system requirements are based on this architecture decisions. Although, it is, of course, possible to develop cars and aircraft with a different architecture. In that case, you need a different Base Architecture.

If the Base Architecture is more abstract, the solution space of the system opens. If the Base Architecture is more concrete, there is little space for innovation. A manufacturer who develops a new version of its product for the market every year has a concrete Base Architecture. It is the predecessor architecture of the previous version with some abstractions to open the solution space for minor improvements. A company that develops an entirely new product never seen before needs a very abstract Base Architecture.

The Base Architecture description can be reused for projects of similar systems.

Furthermore, the Base Architecture is an excellent source to spot potential for disruptive innovations. The Base Architecture covers concepts like "We have always done it that way?" and you can ask, "What if we change our common architectural approaches?". It can open up previously untouchable innovation potential.

Relationships

Primary Performer	6.5 System Architect
Inputs	5.5 System Idea, 5.6 System Objectives
Outputs	5.7 Base Architecture
ISO 15288 Process	A Business Mission Analysis

Further Information

- 7.5 How to describe the Base Architecture
- 8.6 Example Base Architecture

4.8 Identify Stakeholders

Identify all individuals and organizations that may have Requirements or an interest in the system.

Purpose

It is decisive for the success of the project that the concerns of all Stakeholders are sufficiently considered.

Description

The list of Stakeholders is initially elaborated in a workshop and continually reworked during the project. Typically, you can reuse the list of Stakeholders from a previous project. A further requirements analysis and system architecting digs up more Stakeholders.

The Stakeholders' concerns are a source for Requirements, and they are a source for needs that are not explicitly stated but are essential and must be considered by the system, respectively, the engineering team.

We document the name and the concerns of the Stakeholder and the contact information (such as email, availability) to be able to get in touch with them. To prioritize the long list of Stakeholders, we classify the priority and the effort to consider the Stakeholder. That enables a 2-dimensional prioritization (figure 4.2). You can assign each quadrant a different strategy on how to work with the Stakeholders.

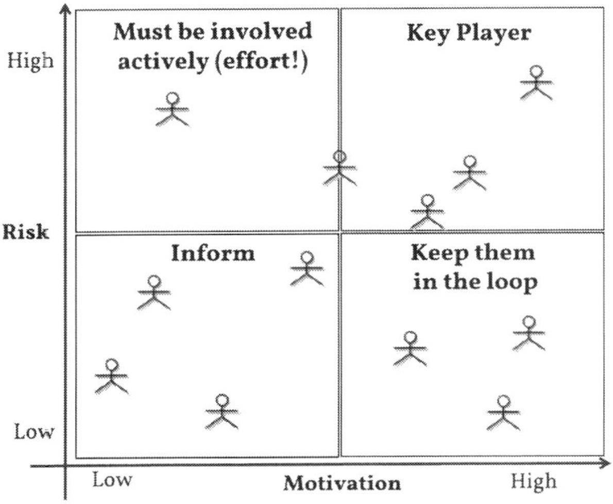

Figure 4.2: Stakeholder Prioritization Matrix

Relationships

Primary Performer	6.4 Requirements Engineer
Inputs	5.7 Base Architecture, 5.5 System Idea, 5.6 System Objectives
Outputs	5.8 Stakeholders
ISO 15288 Process	A Business Mission Analysis, A Stakeholder Needs and Requirements Definition

Further Information

- 7.6 How to model Stakeholders
- 8.5 Example Stakeholders

4.9 Model Risks

Specify the business, organizational, and technical Risks in the system model.

Purpose

The Risks specify the potential inability to achieve the System Objectives. They are linked to other model elements to provide traceability to and from the Risks.

Description

Risk Management is an important topic in itself and is only dealt with a small extent by SYSMOD. This SYSMOD Method *Model Risks* only specifies the Risks in the model and links them to other model elements, but does not cover the entire Risk Management process.

The System Idea and System Objectives inputs are intended for the initial setup of the Risks. Later, you will also derive Risks from the System Architectures, for example.

Relationships

Primary Performer	6.4 Requirements Engineer
Inputs	5.5 System Idea, 5.6 System Objectives
Outputs	Risks
ISO 15288 Process	Risk Management

Further Information

- 7.7 How to Model Risks
- 8.7 Example Risks

4.10 Model Requirements

Specify the Requirements in the system model.

Purpose

The Requirements are the contract between the System Engineers and the Stakeholders of the system.

Description

The Requirements specify the features of the system. Depending on the abstraction level covered by the system model (see Zigzag Pattern in section 11.6), the Requirements are stakeholder requirements or system requirements.

The Stakeholders are the source of the Requirements. You receive the requirements as documents, as an outcome of workshops, as a result of a discussion, in the form of a presentation, as defined requirements in a proprietary requirements management tool format, and so on.

Requirements in a SysML model can be the original requirements or proxies for requirements stored outside of the SysML model, for example, in a requirements management tool.

A Requirement can be the classical textual statement, or a formal modeled requirement expression, or a mix of both.

Relationships

Primary Performer	6.4 Requirements Engineer
Inputs	5.8 Stakeholders, 5.5 System Idea, 5.6 System Objective, 5.7 Base Architecture
Outputs	5.10 Requirements
ISO 15288 Process	A Stakeholder Needs and Requirements Definition, A System Requirements Definition

Further Information

- 7.7 How to model Requirements
- 8.8 Example Requirements

4.11 Identify the System Context

Identify all users and other external entities that interact with the system.

Purpose

The System Context defines the environment of the system that needs to be considered, the system boundary, and the interfaces of the system.

Description

The System Context depicts all elements from the environment of the system that interacts with the system. These elements are called system actors. The obvious ones are the users of the system and external systems with communication interfaces. Less obvious system actors, but equally important, are, for example, environmental effects like temperature or mechanical systems like the installation surface of the system. The SYSMOD Profile provides a list of system actor categories (section 9.2).

A special external entity is the Planet Environment. A Systems Engineer must consider the impact of the system of interest on the planet. The actor Planet Environment is an element in the SYSMOD Model Library (section 9.10) with the actor category EnvironmentalImpact. See section 7.8 about how to use the actor Planet Environment.

Besides the list of system actors, the System Context describes system interfaces and relevant flows of items between the system actors and the system.

The human actors and the humans or organizations behind the non-human actors are also Stakeholders of the system (section 4.6). Stakeholders that do not directly interact with the system are not part of the actor list. An actor always interacts with the system.

The System Architecture methods refine the System Context and add architecture-specific elements like interfaces. This part must be managed independently of the requirements-specific parts of the System Context to keep the problem space separate from the solution space.

Relationships

Primary Performer	6.4 Requirements Engineer
Inputs	5.10 Requirements
Outputs	5.11 System Context
ISO 15288 Process	A Business Mission Analysis, A Stakeholder Needs and Requirements Definition, A Architecture Definition

Further Information

- 7.8 How to model the System Context
- 8.9 Example System Context

4.12 Identify System Use Cases

Identify all services of the system provided for the actors and Stakeholders of the system.

Purpose

The System Use Cases are the services and the essential ends of a system. The system is developed and operated to achieve these services.

Description

The System Use Cases provide an outside-in view on the system functions from the perspective of the system actors. That supports the system development to build a system that satisfies the real needs of the system actors. An inside-out perspective on the functional requirements of a system can also lead to a system that satisfies all of them, but with the risk that they do not consider the usability needs of the users.

An illustrative example, in most cases, is remote controls for a projector (figure 4.3). They provide all required functions, but not from the perspective of the users. The remote control offers lots of buttons, and the primary use cases are hard to find.

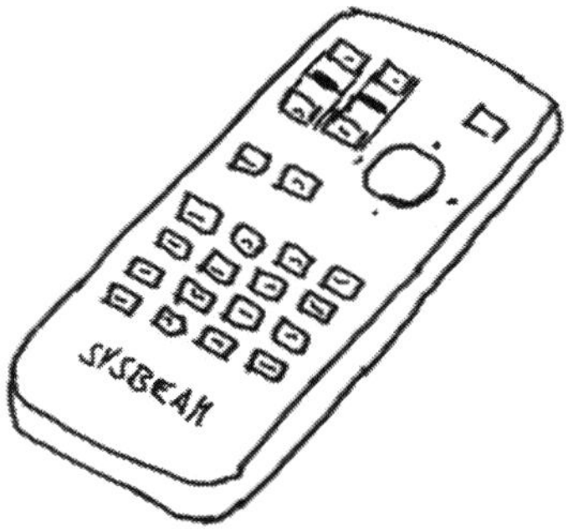

Figure 4.3: Remote Control

The System Use Case description should at least include

- the associated system actors
- the trigger that starts the use case
- the result of the use case
- a brief textual description (2-5 sentences)
- traceable paths to the non-functional requirements that are relevant for the use case
- traceable paths to the functional requirements that are covered by the use case

The set of use cases is a flat list without a hierarchy of super- and sub-use-cases. The Use Case Activities (section

5.13) specify the functional decomposition of the System Use Cases.

Relationships

Primary Performer	6.4 Requirements Engineer
Inputs	5.11 System Context, 5.10 Requirements
Outputs	5.12 System Use Cases
ISO 15288 Process	A Stakeholder Needs and Requirements Definition, A System Requirements Definition

Further Information

- 7.9 How to model System Use Cases
- 8.10 Example System Use Cases
- 11.10 Workshop Tool: SAMS Method

4.13 Identify System Processes

Describe the logical order of execution of the System Use Cases.

Purpose

The System Processes specify the valid logical orders of execution of the System Use Cases.

Description

Some System Use Cases can only be performed if another use case was performed before, or if the system is in a specific state. That can, for example, be defined by the pre- and postconditions of the use cases. A postcondition of one use case can satisfy the precondition of another use case.

A System Process makes such dependencies explicit. It can be a flow-oriented or a state-oriented description that specifies the execution order of use cases.

Relationships

Primary Performer	6.4 Requirements Engineer
Inputs	5.12 System Use Cases
Outputs	5.13 System Processes
ISO 15288 Process	A Stakeholder Needs and Requirements Definition, A System Requirements Definition

Further Information

- 7.10 How to model System Processes
- 8.11 Example System Processes

4.14 Model Use Case Activities

Model the behavior of the System Use Cases.

Purpose

The Use Case Activities specify the functional decomposition of the System Use Cases and, thus, the overall system in the problem space. They define the sequence of execution and object flow between the system functions.

Description

A System Use Case specifies, besides others, a name, a trigger, and a result. The Use Case Activity specifies the behavior of a System Use Case. The specification can be a rough description or an unambiguous and detailed specification of the included use case steps. The level of detail depends on the needs of your project.

Each step of a Use Case Activity is again specified with a Use Case Activity. The Use Case Activities that need no further refinements have no included steps. A use case step can also be called a system function.

A Use Case Activity includes the description of the input and output objects of the steps. The relationship of an output object of a step to an input of another step is called object flow.

The Use Case Activity can specify pre- and postconditions. The precondition must be true to trigger the System Use Case. The postcondition is true after the execution of the System Use Case.

It is a good practice to separate the use case steps that are responsible for the input and output of objects from and to the system actors from all the other steps. These input/output steps depend on interface technologies, which are, typically, more unstable than the core steps and less dependent on the specific domain.

Relationships

Primary Performer	6.4 Requirements Engineer
Inputs	5.12 System Use Cases, 5.10 Requirements
Outputs	5.14 Use Case Activities
ISO 15288 Process	A Stakeholder Needs and Requirements Definition, A System Requirements Definition

Further Information

- 7.11 How to model Use Case Activities
- 8.12 Example Use Case Activities

4.15 Model the Domain Knowledge

Define the terms of the domain from the perspective of the system.

Purpose

The Domain Knowledge defines the semantic and structure of the domain objects that are used by the system.

Description

The system has knowledge about objects of the domain. Imagine your system is a person, and you ask it about domain objects. For example

You: "Do you know the concept of an operator?"

System: "Yes. An operator is one of my users and has an ID, a name, and a list of active tasks."

You: "Do you know the concept of fire?"

System: "Yes. A fire has a severity value, position, and size."

The Domain Knowledge defines the knowledge of the system about the domain.

You can derive the domain objects from the object flow of the Use Case Activities. If an object is input or output of a system function, the system must know the concept of that object. Typically, the modeled Use Case Activities and the included objects flows are not complete. Therefore only parts of the Domain Knowledge could be directly be derived from them.

Especially if you separate the input/output steps of the Use Case Activities (see Model Use Case Activities), you get two kinds of domain objects:

1. The context objects are entities that are exchanged between the system and the system actors.
2. The system objects are domain objects that are used only inside the system.

The Domain Knowledge is also known as a *concept model* or a *data model* of the system.

Relationships

Primary Performer	6.4 Requirements Engineer
Inputs	5.14 Use Case Activities
Outputs	5.15 Domain Knowledge
ISO 15288 Process	A Stakeholder Needs and Requirements Definition, A System Requirements Definition

Further Information

- 7.12 How to model the Domain Knowledge?
- 8.13 Example Domain Knowledge

4.16 Specify Test Cases

Model the Test Cases that verify and validate the Requirements.

Purpose

The Test Cases close the loop from the system requirements to the Physical Architecture and system implementation via the Test Cases back to the system requirements.

Description

The Test Cases specify how to verify and validate that the system satisfies the Requirements. At the specification level, the Test Cases have a verify relationship to the Requirements and a dependency relationship to the architectural elements that are used in the test.

Figure 4.4 depicts the overall relationships in the context of the V model.

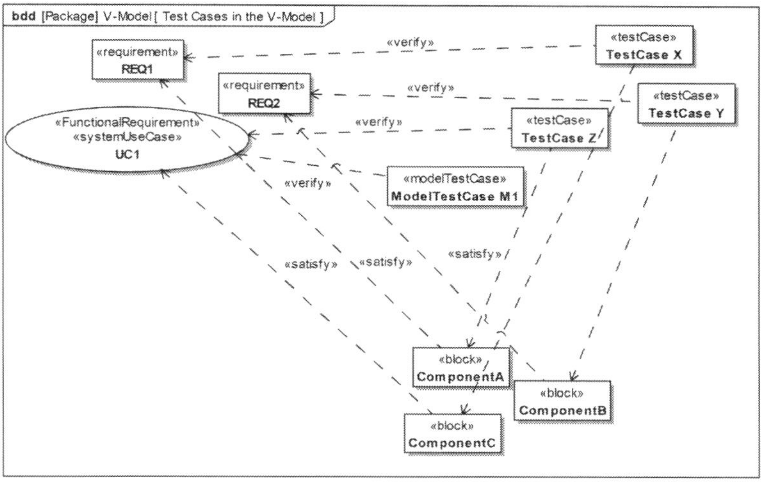

Figure 4.4: Test Cases in the V model

A special kind of a Test Case is the Model Test Case that verifies or validates that the model virtually satisfies the Requirements instead of the real system itself.

SYSMOD only considers the Test Cases on the system level. You also have Test Cases on the specific engineering disciplines levels (software test cases, and so on).

Relationships

Primary Performer	6.7 System Tester
Inputs	5.10 Requirements, 5.14 Use Case Activities
Outputs	5.16 Test Cases
ISO 15288 Process	A Verification, A Validation

Further Information

- 7.14 How to Specify Test Cases
- 8.14 Example Test Cases

4.17 Model the Functional Architecture

Model an architecture that is based only on functions.

Purpose

The Functional Architecture is independent of the technical implementation of the system, more stable across product families and generations, and is a guide to the derivation of a sustainable Physical Architecture.

Description

The modeling of a Functional Architecture is out of the scope of SYSMOD. The method and the product Functional Architecture are parts of the so-called FAS method. See the book *Model-Based System Architectures* for a detailed description of the FAS method [We15].

It is only mentioned here to emphasize this puzzle piece that perfectly fits SYSMOD to complete the picture.

Relationships

Primary Performer	6.5 System Architect
Inputs	5.14 Use Case Activities
Outputs	5.18 Functional Architecture
ISO 15288 Process	A Architecture Definition

Further Information

- 11.2 Functional Architectures for Systems (FAS)
- Website www.fas-method.org.
- Book: Model-Based System Architectures [We15].

4.18 Model the Logical Architecture

Model a Physical Architecture on a high abstraction level that satisfies the given Requirements.

Purpose

The Logical Architecture describes the technical concepts and principles of the system.

Description

The Logical Architecture is an abstract Physical Architecture. Thinking top-down in the development process, the Logical

Architecture is the first version of a Physical Architecture. It covers architectural and technical principles and concepts, for example, an electric motor, a valve, or a display as technical concepts. Further down in the intended top-down approach, the Product Architecture is then a concrete and more detailed specification of the concepts (section 5.21).

The Logical Architecture must conform to the Base Architecture. If strongly coupled, the Logical Architecture is a specialization of the Base Architecture. If loosely coupled, there are only allocate relationships between both architectures.

If you do not need a separate Logical Architecture, you can merge this step and the architecture with the Product Architecture. Finally, you have a Physical Architecture with logical and concrete product aspects.

Relationships

Primary Performer	6.5 System Architect
Inputs	5.12 System Use Cases, 5.11 System Context, 5.10 Requirements, 5.7 Base Architecture, 5.18 Functional Architecture
Outputs	5.20 Logical Architecture
ISO 15288 Process	A Architecture Definition

Further Information

- 7.14 How to model a Logical Architecture?
- 8.15 Example Logical Architecture

4.19 Model the Product Architecture

Model a concrete specification of the Physical Architecture.

Purpose

The Product Architecture is the most concrete specification of a Physical Architecture of the system of interest in the system model.

Description

The Product Architecture specializes the technical concepts and principles of the Logical Architecture. For example, an *Electric motor* in the Logical Architecture is specialized by an *Electric motor type 42X* in the Product Architecture, including a specification of the vendor, the size, the power consumption, and the mechanical, electrical, software interfaces, and other properties of interest.

If strongly coupled, the Product Architecture is a specialization of the Logical Architecture. If loosely coupled, there are only allocate relationships between both architectures.

In practice, you often do not have strictly separated Logical Architectures and Product Architectures. It is one single Physical Architecture that is a mix of both kinds: some parts cover technical concepts, other parts concrete specifications. The discriminator between the architecture kinds is the abstraction. You cannot measure abstraction, and therefore you cannot clearly define the border between the Logical Architecture and Product Architecture. It costs effort to separate the architectures explicitly. It should, therefore, only be done if it offers advantages and adds value to the project.

Relationships

Primary Performer	6.5 System Architect
Inputs	5.20 Logical Architecture
Outputs	5.21 Product Architecture
ISO 15288 Process	A Design Definition

Further Information

- 7.15 How to model a Product Architecture
- 8.16 Example Product Architecture

4.20 Revise an Architecture with Scenarios

Revise a System Architecture with usage scenarios.

Purpose

A Scenario maps a path through a Use Case Activity to an architecture and thereby tests if all necessary parts, structures, and interfaces are correctly defined.

Description

The Scenarios describe the collaboration of system parts to perform paths through the Use Case Activities. A path is one valid order of execution of the functions of a Use Case Activity. Each function is implemented by one or more parts and connections of the architecture.

The Scenario describes the messages that are sent from one part to another, which part performs which function and which connections between the parts are necessary.

Relationships

Primary Performer	6.5 System Architect
Inputs	5.19 Physical Architecture
Outputs	5.22 Scenarios
ISO 15288 Process	A Architecture Definition, A Design Definition

Further Information

- 7.17 How to Revise an Architecture with Scenarios
- 8.17 Example Scenarios

4.21 Define System States

Define the states, state transitions, and state-controlled functions of the system and parts of the system.

Purpose

The states and transitions of a system specifies the conditions of the whole system or parts of the system that constrain the execution of functions.

Description

A state describes a condition of the system or system part, for example, *active* or *maintenance mode*. It further specifies which functions can be performed in a state. A transition specifies the trigger and guard condition to switch from one state to another. They are specified by state machines

State machines can also be used to refine Requirements, for example, as the specification of a System Process (section 4.12).

Relationships

Primary Performer	6.5 System Architect
Inputs	5.19 Physical Architecture
Outputs	5.23 System States
ISO 15288 Process	A Stakeholder Needs and Requirements Definition, A System Requirements Definition, A Architecture Definition, A Design Definition

Further Information

- 7.18 How to model System States
- 8.18 Example System States

4.22 Model the Test Architecture

Model the setup of the test system and the system under test.

Purpose

The Test Architecture specifies the configurations of the test system, the system under test, and the environment to perform the Test Cases.

Description

Typically, you need a test system and additional actors to test your system. The Test Architecture specifies the setup of these elements. It can also specify the test system itself, i.e., the specification of the test system in a system model.

In any case, the Test Architecture consists of more than one test setup. For example, a setup for a user interaction test and another setup for a hardware-in-the-loop test (HIL).

If appropriate, you can apply variant modeling techniques to specify the different setups. See section 11.5 for more information about variant modeling and the VAMOS approach.

The OMG standard *UML Testing Profile (UTP)* can also be applied to a SysML model. It includes stereotypes to model test architectures like *SUT* (system under test), or *TestContext*. See www.omg.org/spec/UTP for more details.

Relationships

Primary Performer	6.7 System Tester
Inputs	5.19 Physical Architecture
Outputs	5.24 Test Architecture
ISO 15288 Process	A Verification, A Validation

Further Information

- 7.19 How to Model the Test Architecture
- 8.19 Example Test Architecture

5. SYSMOD Products

The SYSMOD Products are the outputs of the SYSMOD Methods. Typically, the Products are
created with SysML, but it can be any other modeling language that returns the appropriate elements. Text documents can also be the format of a product. However, in the latter case, it is not MBSE. I recommend the use of SysML.

Below is the list of SYSMOD Products in a logical order according to the SYSMOD Processes:

- 5.1 MBSE Methodology
- 5.2 System Modeling Environment (SME)
- 5.3 MBSE Training
- 5.4 Problem Statement
- 5.5 System Idea
- 5.6 System Objectives
- 5.7 Base Architecture
- 5.8 Stakeholders
- 5.9 Risks
- 5.10 Requirements
- 5.11 System Context
- 5.12 System Use Cases
- 5.13 System Processes
- 5.14 Use Case Activities
- 5.15 Domain Knowledge
- 5.16 Test Cases
- 5.17 System Architecture

5.1 MBSE Methodology

The MBSE Methodology is a consistent set of related Processes, Roles, Methods, Products, and tools.

Purpose

Even if you are an experienced systems engineer, you need guidance and structures for an effective application of MBSE in a complex engineering environment.

Main Description

The Roles, Methods, and Products are the toolbox. They are related to each other, as depicted in figure 1.1. The Processes define a useful logical execution order of the Methods and guide the Roles. The tools enable the effective implementation of the Methods.

Relationships

Responsibility	6.2 MBSE Methodologist
Output of Methods	4.1 Tailor the MBSE Methodology
Input of Methods	4.2 Set up and maintain the SME, 4.3 Deploy the MBSE Methodology, 4.4 Provide MBSE Training and Coaching
Example	SYSMOD

Representation

Text documents, reference cards, process models

5.2 System Modeling Environment (SME)

The SME represents the customized setup of the systems modeling tools.

Purpose

The SME must be customized to effectively facilitate the SYSMOD Methods and the daily work of the engineers and Stakeholders.

Description

In most cases, modeling tools cannot be used out-of-the-box. The SME is a set of modeling tools, configuration files, plugins, and so forth necessary to customize the tools for the MBSE Methodology.

A SysML modeling tool is the core of the SME. Of course, you could use a different modeling language than SysML, but you need good arguments not to use the widespread, worldwide standard.

Some typical customizations of the SME are:

- Enable access to model libraries.
- Load SysML profiles.
- Adapt the user interfaces of the modeling tools.
- Set up connections to other tools.
- Set up the configuration management for the model repositories.

Relationships

Responsibility	6.1 SME Administrator
Output of Methods	4.2 Set up and maintain the SME
Input of Methods	None
Example	None

Representation

Text documents, configuration files, other tool-dependent formats

5.3 MBSE Training

The MBSE Training deploys MBSE knowledge and skills to the SYSMOD Roles and Stakeholders of the MBSE Methodology.

Purpose

It is essential that knowledge and skills about the MBSE Methodology are communicated to the engineering teams and Stakeholders.

Description

The product MBSE Training represents not a single training, but all the different training sessions in different formats necessary to deploy MBSE. Mainly, they are performed to achieve the requested skills of the SYSMOD Roles. But also some Stakeholders of the engineering project must be trained in MBSE.

Relationships

Responsibility	6.2 MBSE Methodologist
Output of Methods	4.4 Provide MBSE Training and Coaching
Input of Methods	None
Example	None

Representation

On-site training, web-based training, handbook, and so forth.

5.4 Problem Statement

The Problem Statement is a clear and concise statement of an unwelcome situation that the system of interest should resolve.

Purpose

In engineering, we spend much focus and effort on the solution. It is essential not to forget the original problem to be resolved and to assure it is the right problem that is solved.

Description

The Problem Statement is a clear statement of the primary purpose that the system is intended to solve. It describes the gap between the current state and the desired state. It is a user-centric statement that starts with who is having the problem. Then, it describes the problem itself and the context of the problem, and finally, why it matters. Of course, you can change the order if it sounds better. Who, What, Where, and Why are the key questions answered by the Problem Statement.

The following is an example of a Problem Statement:

"Engineers must communicate a lot with other people in distributed teams, but would like to reduce the amount of traveling to save time and minimize the impact on the planet environment."

Design Thinking provides several methods of how to elaborate on a Problem Statement [Le18].

Relationships

Responsibility	6.3 Project Manager
Output of Methods	4.5 Analyze the Problem
Input of Methods	4.6 Describe the System Idea and the System Objectives
Example	8.2 Example Problem Statement

Representation

The SYSMOD stereotype *«system»* has a property *problemStatement* to store the text of the Problem Statement or references to external documents that cover the Problem Statement.

5.5 System Idea

The System Idea describes the core idea and leading features of the system.

Purpose

The System Idea is a brief description of the purpose of the system, including a list of the main features with a particular focus on the uniqueness of the system ("elevator pitch").

Description

The System Idea is the short answer to the questions *"What are you building and why are you doing this?"* and *"What is the value for the customer of the system?"*. This basic knowledge gets easily lost in all the details of a complex development project.

It is an elevator pitch for the system [Cr81].

Typically, the System Idea, as well as the System Objectives, are stored somewhere else in the documentation of the (product) management. In that case, the SYSMOD Product System Idea is a proxy for the source to establish a link to the engineering team.

Relationships

Responsibility	6.3 Project Manager
Output of Methods	4.5 Describe System Idea and System Objectives
Input of Methods	4.7 Describe the Base Architecture, 4.8 Identify Stakeholders, 4.10 Model Requirements
Example	8.3 System Idea

Representation

The SYSMOD stereotype *«system»* has a property *systemIdea* to store the text of the System Idea or references to external documents that cover the System Idea.

5.6 System Objectives

The System Objectives represent the main objectives of the vendor or owner of the system.

Purpose

The System Objectives are used to understand the rationale of the Requirements and to communicate the System Objectives to the developers of the system model.

Description

Like the System Idea, the System Objectives are typically documented outside of the development project in management documents. The SYSMOD System Objectives are a rework of those objectives specifically for the system development.

There are two kinds of objectives to be considered:

- Objectives directly related to the system. For example, *"Best system on the Market."*.
- Objectives directly related to the owner, operator, or vendor of the system. For example, *"To be the Market Leader (by offering this new system)."*.

Relationships

Responsibility	6.3 Project Manager
Output of Methods	4.5 Describe System Idea and System Objectives
Input of Methods	4.7 Describe the Base Architecture, 4.8 Identify Stakeholders, 4.10 Model Requirements
Example	8.4 System Objectives

Representation

- SysML requirements diagram, table or matrix
- SYSMOD stereotype *«objective»* (section 9.6)

5.7 Base Architecture

The Base Architecture is a description of the architectural and technical decisions that are preset at the project start.

Purpose

The Base Architecture documents architectural and technical constraints and sets the abstraction level for the system Requirements.

Description

The Base Architecture represents the system architecture that is already fixed before the project starts.

As a simple input for the project, the Base Architecture can be a sketch together with a brief textual description ("napkin architecture" or "beermat architecture").

As a more formal input, the Base Architecture is part of the system model in the form of block diagrams. The Base Architecture in the model could be strongly coupled with the Logical Architecture using the specialization relationship or loosely coupled by using the allocate relationship (see also section 11.7).

Relationships

Responsibility	6.5 System Architect
Output of Methods	4.7 Describe the Base Architecture
Input of Methods	4.8 Identify Stakeholders, 4.10 Model Requirements, 4.18 Model the Logical Architecture, 4.20 Revise an Architecture with Scenarios
Example	8.6 Base Architecture

Representation

- SysML block definition, internal block diagrams, and the underlying models
- SYSMOD stereotypes for Discipline-specific Elements (mechanical, electrical, software) (section 9.4).
- Text, sketches

5.8 Stakeholders

List of the Stakeholders of the system.

Purpose

It is essential to know all Stakeholders to respond to their concerns and to build a system that meets all their Requirements.

Description

A Stakeholder is a person or an organization who has concerns about the system that can be the source for Requirements of the system. The Stakeholder can have a direct link to the system like the future users or an indirect link like an authority that has published laws or rules that affect the system. The latter has only indirect concerns about the system. They must not have a direct link to the system or even know it.

System Objectives and Requirements have trace relationships to the Stakeholders who are the source of this information (pre-traceability).

Relationships

Responsibility	6.4 Requirements Engineer
Output of Methods	4.8 Identify Stakeholders
Input of Methods	4.10 Model Requirements
Example	8.5 Stakeholders

Representation

- SysML requirements diagram, tables, and matrices
- SYSMOD stereotype *«extendedStakeholder»* (section 9.6)

5.9 Risks

The Risks specify the potential inability to achieve the System Objectives.

Purpose

Requirements and architectures contain risks, and risks, in turn, have an impact on Requirements and architectures. It is essential to have the Risks and links to other elements in the model even if they are mainly managed by an external risk management tool.

Description

The Risks are linked to other model elements to ensure traceability and not to overlook the Risks. For lightweight risk management, the SYSMOD modeling of the Risks could be sufficient. If the Risks are managed in an external risk management tool, the Risks in the model are proxies to establish links and traceability to other model elements.

Relationships

Responsibility	6.4 Requirements Engineer
Output of Methods	4.9 Model Risks
Input of Methods	4.10 Model Requirements
Example	8.7 Example Risks

Representation

- SysML requirements diagrams, tables, and matrices
- SYSMOD stereotype *«risk»*

5.10 Requirements

The Requirements specify functions, non-functional properties, or constraints that must be satisfied by the system.

Purpose

The Requirements are the contract between the Stakeholders of the system and the Systems engineers who build the system.

Description

The Requirements are the list of functions, non-functional properties, and constraints that must be satisfied by the system of interest. Requirements are handled very differently by projects: from rough to very detailed requirement specifications.

Nowadays, typically, Requirements are text-based. Even in a SysML model, the core of the requirement model element is pure text. The *«extendedRequirement»* model element defined in the SYSMOD Profile enables that any model element can be a requirement. For example, a single state transition, a complete state machine, or an activity.

You can define textual and non-textual model-based Requirements.

Relationships

Responsibility	6.4 Requirements Engineer
Output of Methods	4.10 Model Requirements
Input of Methods	4.11 Identify the System Context, 4.12 Identify System Use Cases, 4.14 Model Use Case Activities, 4.16 Specify Test Cases, 4.18 Model the Logical Architecture
Example	8.8 Requirements

Representation

- SysML requirements diagrams, tables, and matrices
- SYSMOD stereotype *«extendedRequirement»* and specialized stereotypes to model requirement categories (for example *«functionalRequirement»*) (section 9.6)

5.11 System Context

The System Context lists the external entities that interact with the system and shows relevant structures between and inside the external entities.

Purpose

The System Context depicts how the system is embedded in its environment, i.e., the system actors, interfaces, and communication links between the actors and the system.

Description

A system is embedded in an environment and provides and requests functions. The system must handle events and effects from the outside. It is essential to know the full context of the system.

The System Context is a list of the external entities, and the relevant item flows between the system and the entities. The entities are also called system actors.

If relevant for the system of interest, the system context also describes structures of the system actors and links between the actors as well as interfaces.

The System Context should consider at least four categories of actors: human actors, external systems, environmental effects, and the environmental impact. If necessary, more categories can be defined as part of the tailoring of the methodology (section 4.1). See section 9.2 for more information about actor categories in SYSMOD.

Relationships

Responsibility	6.4 Requirements Engineer
Output of Methods	4.11 Identify the System Context
Input of Methods	4.12 Identify System Use Cases, 4.18 Model the Logical Architecture
Example	8.9 System Context

Representation

- SysML block definition diagram and internal block diagram
- SYSMOD stereotypes *«system»*, *«systemContext»* (section 9.3), and SYSMOD stereotypes for actors (section 9.2)

5.12 System Use Cases

The System Use Cases are a table of content of the services provided by the system to its system actors.

Purpose

The System Use Cases provide a view on the system functions from the perspective of the system actors and enable an optimized development of the requirements and the usability of the system. They represent the purposes of the system functions as well as supporting functions.

Description

A System Use Case is triggered by a system actor and returns a result that is of value for actors or Stakeholders of the system. The behavior is timely cohesive, that means, there is no timely interruption supported by the system like storing the state of the behavior to resume it later.

For example, the System Use Case *Buy a ticket* for a train ticket machine. When triggered by the system actor *Customer*, the *Customer* cannot interrupt the function after a ticket was selected and go away to drink a cup of coffee and proceed with the payment when coming back. The System Use Case *Buy a ticket* must be executed till the intended end or entirely canceled. The *Customer* receives the ticket, or the use case must be canceled and can be started again from the beginning if triggered again.

The use case *Report an alarm* of an alarm system is an example of a use case whose result is not of value for the actor (= the thief), but for the stakeholder (= the owner of the property). The actor *Thief* triggers the use case, and the stakeholder *Owner* of the property is interested in the result.

The properties of a System Use Case are:

- the associated system actors
- the trigger that starts the use case
- the result of the use case
- a brief textual description (2-5 sentences)
- pre- and postconditions
- the Use Case Activity.

The Continuous Use Case is a special System Use Case. It represents a continuous behavior of the system. The trigger can be an internal event like a system state switch instead of an external trigger initiated by an actor. The result is typically a continuous output, such as compliance with a condition.

The metaphor *Function Bucket* illustrates the two concepts of System Use Cases and Use Case Activities (figure 5.1). The bucket is filled with all functions that must be performed by the system.

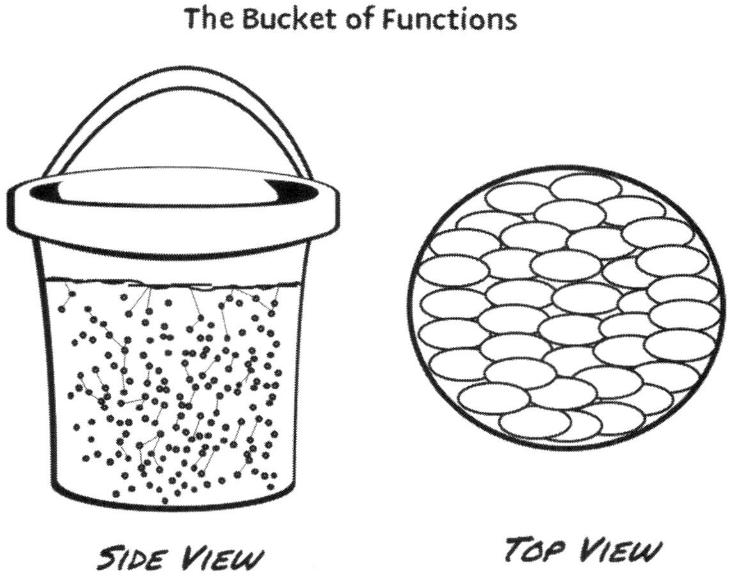

Figure 5.1: Function Bucket

The functions are linked if a function calls another one. The functions are
Use Case Activities. The System Use Cases swim on the surface and are the list of functions provided by the system to the system actors.

Relationships

Responsibility	6.4 Requirements Engineer
Output of Methods	4.12 Identify System Use Cases
Input of Methods	4.14 Model Use Case Activities, 4.13 Identify System Processes, 4.18 Model the Logical Architecture
Example	8.10 Use Cases

Representation

- The System Use Cases are depicted in SysML use case diagrams and tables or matrices.
- A single System Use Case is a SysML *UseCase* model element with SYSMOD stereotypes (section 9.8)
  - *«systemUseCase»* for the standard use case. The stereotype adds properties like trigger, result, and essentials.
  - *«continuousUseCase»* for a continuous use case. It is a specialization of the *«systemUseCase»* stereotype and adds the same properties to the model element.

5.13 System Processes

The System Processes specify the logical order of execution of the System Use Cases.

Purpose

The System Processes describe the uses of the system on a higher level than the System Use Cases.

Description

The System Process is a process description on a higher level than the System Use Cases. For example, the process starting with the installation and initial setup of the system via some operational functions to shutdown and deinstallation. Typically, a System Process is a flow-oriented behavior. That means it describes the logical order of the System Use Cases. Alternatively, a System Process can also describe event-oriented behavior in the form of a state machine.

A System Process is a special use case with a flow- or event-oriented behavior.

Relationships

Responsibility	6.4 Requirements Engineer
Output of Methods	4.13 Identify System Processes
Input of Methods	None
Example	8.11 System Processes

Representation

- SysML use case diagrams and use cases with SYSMOD stereotype *«systemProcess»* (section 9.8)
- SysML activity diagram or state machine diagram

5.14 Use Case Activities

The Use Case Activities are specifications of the system functions represented by the System Use Cases.

Purpose

The Use Case Activities are the functional decompositions of the System Use Cases and specify the system functionality from the Requirements perspective.

Description

A System Use Case is only the abstract of the depicted system behavior and represents the purpose. The behavior itself is specified by a Use Case Activity.

A Use Case Activity defines the single functions of a System Use Case, their order of execution, and the flow of objects between the functions.

The Use Case Activity that is directly owned by the System Use Case is also called the primary Use Case Activity. The further decomposed functions on the lower levels are called secondary Use Case Activities.

The activity tree provides a structural view of the Use Case Activities (figure 5.2). The tree shows the included functions of the System Use Case where the tree hierarchy depicts a call hierarchy, i.e., a function is a sub-function of another function if that function calls it. It is an ownership of executions, but not ownership of the specifications of the functions.

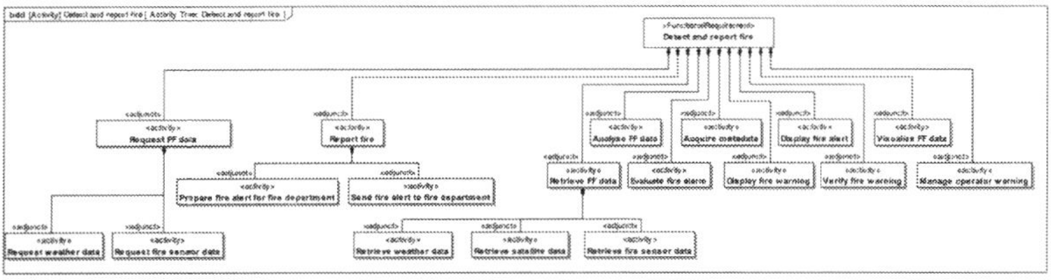

Figure 5.2: Activity Tree

Relationships

Responsibility	6.4 Requirements Engineer
Output of Methods	4.14 Model Use Case Activities
Input of Methods	4.15 Model the Domain Knowledge, 4.16 Specify Test Cases, 4.17 Model the Functional Architecture
Examples	8.12 Use Case Activities

Representation

- SysML activity diagrams
- SysML block definition diagrams for activity trees with SysML adjunct properties

5.15 Domain Knowledge

The Domain Knowledge is a specification of the domain objects used by the Use Case Activities, Requirements, and System Architectures.

Purpose

The Domain Knowledge specifies the data, physical entities, related value types, and units that are used ("known") by the system.

Description

The object flows of the Use Case Activities define the usage of domain objects by the system. The objects are data or physical entities. They are the inputs and outputs of system functions.

The domain objects are specified by domain blocks. The definition of a domain block requires, typically, value types and units. Both are also part of the Domain Knowledge.

Relationships

Responsibility	6.4 Requirements Engineer
Output of Methods	4.14 Model Domain Knowledge
Input of Methods	None
Example	8.13 Domain Knowledge

Representation

- SysML block definition diagrams with SYSMOD *«domainBlock»* (section 9.3)
- SysML ValueTypes and Units

5.16 Test Cases

The Test Cases specify procedures on how to test that the system satisfies the Requirements.

Purpose

The Test Cases close the loop, starting with the Requirements through the system analysis to the System Architectures and implementation, and assure that the modeled and implemented system satisfies the Requirements.

Description

The Test Cases are behavioral descriptions of how to test the system. It can be, for example, a step by step work description of a manual test for a System Tester, a specification for test scripts, or an executable behavior.

The Test Case behavior returns a verdict that represents the test result (pass, fail, and so forth).

A Model Test Case is a special Test Case that does not test the system, but the model of the system, that means, it tests the specification of the system.

Relationships

Responsibility	6.7 System Tester
Output of Methods	4.16 Specify Test Cases
Input of Methods	4.22 Model the Test Architecture
Example	8.14 Example Test Cases

Representation

- SysML requirements diagram with SYSMOD stereotype *«systemTestCase»*, or *«modelTestCase»* (section 9.7)
- SysML activity diagram
- SysML block definition diagram and matrices to depict the relationship between Test Cases and Requirements and other artifacts

5.17 System Architecture

The System Architecture is the generic term for all architecture kinds of the system.

Purpose

The System Architecture represents the common concepts of all architecture kinds of a system.

Description

The System Architecture is an abstract SYSMOD Product, i.e., it does not exist in reality, but only one of the specialized architecture kinds:

- Base Architecture
- Functional Architecture
- Physical Architecture
- Logical Architecture
- Product Architecture
- Test Architecture

Figure 5.3 depicts the domain model of the SYSMOD architecture kinds.

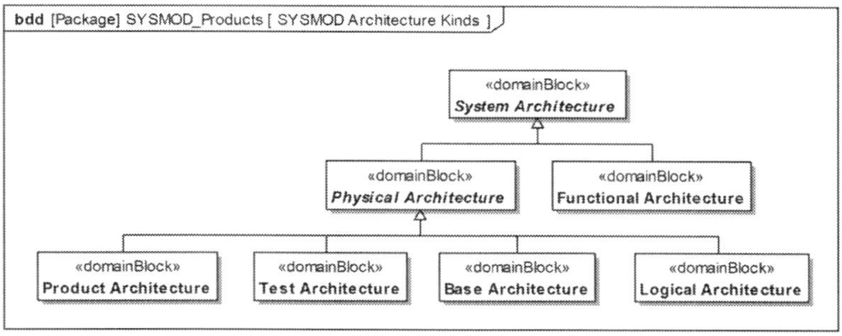

Figure 5.3: SYSMOD Architecture Kinds

Relationships

The System Architecture is an abstract concept and therefore has no relationships.

Representation

None

5.18 Functional Architecture

The Functional Architecture consists of functional elements, functional interfaces and flows, and architecture decisions.

Purpose

The Functional Architecture strengthens the functional aspect and is a technology-independent functional description of the system.

Description

The functional elements transform input flows into output flows. The functional interfaces are attached to the functional elements and specify the allowed input and output flows. Connectors between the functional elements specify the flow paths.

The Functional Architecture is derived from functional requirements, for example, from the Use Case Activities with the FAS method [We15]. The Functional Architecture is independent of the technical components of the Logical and Product Architecture. However, it depends on the technical components of the Base Architecture.

The Systems Engineering Body of Knowledge (SEBoK) defines the Functional Architecture as *"[...] a set of functions and their sub-functions that defines the transformations of input flows into output flows performed by the system to achieve its mission."* [SE16]. The definition is adapted from the ISO/IEC/IEEE 24748-4 standard. It conforms to the definition used here and by the FAS method.

The Functional Architecture is not a product of SYSMOD. It can be derived from SYSMOD Products, for example, by the FAS method. The Functional Architecture can be a valuable input to elaborate a Physical Architecture.

Relationships

Responsibility	6.5 System Architect
Output of Methods	4.17 Model the Functional Architecture
Input of Methods	4.18 Model the Logical Architecture

Example	11.2 Functional Architectures for Systems (FAS)

Representation

- SysML block definition and internal block diagrams
- FAS stereotypes from the FAS method (section 11.2)

5.19 Physical Architecture

The Physical Architecture is the general term for Logical Architecture, Product Architecture, Base Architecture, and Test Architecture.

Purpose

The Physical Architecture represents the common concepts of all System Architecture kinds for physical entities.

Description

Sometimes the term *Physical Architecture* is used for the architecture kind that I call the Product Architecture, for example, in ISO/IEC 2010. The SEBoK [SE16] defines a Physical Architecture based on ISO/IEC 2010:

"A physical architecture is an arrangement of physical elements (system elements and physical interfaces) which provides the design solution for a product, service, or enterprise, and is intended to satisfy logical architecture elements and system requirements. It is implementable through technologies."

The part *"and is intended to satisfy logical architecture"* fits my definition of a Logical Architecture, and the part *"design solution for a product" fits my definition of a Product Architecture.

I do not insist on my definitions. It is crucial that you have your own clear definition of the different architecture kinds that you use in your projects and methodologies, and it does not matter if they are identical with the SYSMOD definitions, or ISO definitions. If you understand the mean of the architecture kinds, you know how to use the appropriate SYSMOD Methods to create them.

Note that software is also a physical element and part of the Physical Architecture. A physical element represents a real-world element.

Relationships / Representation

The Physical Architecture is an abstract concept and therefore has no relationships with other SYSMOD elements and no representations.

5.20 Logical Architecture

The Logical Architecture specifies the architectural and technical concepts and principles of the system.

Purpose

The Logical Architecture covers the essential technical notion of the system and is reusable for similar systems like product families or generations.

Description

The Logical Architecture is more abstract than a Product Architecture. The elements specify general technical concepts like a motor or a control unit.

If strongly coupled with a Base Architecture, the root element and, if necessary other elements of the Logical Architecture specializes elements of the Base Architecture. That makes only sense if the Base Architecture is more abstract than the Logical Architecture. The core architecture elements of the Logical Architecture can also be loosely coupled with the Base Architecture elements.

If loosely coupled with a Base Architecture, elements of the Logical Architecture have allocate-relationships from elements of the Base Architecture (see section 11.7 about the coupling of System Architectures).

The standard ISO/IEC/IEEE 42010:2011 defines the Logical Architecture [ISO42010] as well as the SEBoK [SE16] with a slightly different definition:

"The logical architecture of a system is composed of a set of related technical concepts and principles that support the logical operation of the system. It includes a functional architecture, a behavioral architecture, and a temporal architecture."

In my terminology, the Functional Architecture is independent of the Logical Architecture and not a part of it. The functional blocks of the Functional Architecture are mapped to the blocks of the Logical Architecture. However, the Logical Architecture in my terminology also includes functional aspects, but not a Functional Architecture like it is used in this book or by the FAS method [We15].

Relationships

Responsibility	6.5 System Architect
Output of Methods	4.18 Model the Logical Architecture
Input of Methods	4.19 Model the Product Architecture, 4.20 Revise an Architecture with Scenarios
Example	8.15 Logical Architecture

Representation

- SysML block definition and internal block diagrams
- SYSMOD stereotypes for Discipline-specific Elements (mechanical, electrical, software) (section 9.4)

5.21 Product Architecture

The Product Architecture specifies the concrete Physical Architecture of the system of interest.

Purpose

The Product Architecture is the most detailed System Architecture specification of the system in the system model.

Description

The Product Architecture is a concretization of the Logical Architecture, i.e., of architectural and technical concepts and principles, and the lowest level of abstraction of an architecture described in the system model.

The next level of detail below the Product Architecture is part of specific engineering models, for example, a software model or a CAD model, and out of the scope of the system model.

The Product Architecture is as detailed and concrete as necessary for the system model. The Product Architecture can be strongly coupled to a Logical Architecture using the generalization relationship or loosely coupled using the allocate relationship. See section 11.7 about the coupling of System Architectures).

The discussion in section 5.18 clarifies the different usages of the terms Physical Architecture, Product Architecture, and Logical Architecture.

Relationships

Responsibility	6.5 System Architect
Output of Methods	4.19 Model Product Architecture
Input of Methods	4.20 Revise an Architecture with Scenarios
Example	8.16 Product Architecture

Representation

- SysML block definition and internal block diagrams
- SYSMOD stereotypes for Discipline-specific Elements (mechanical, electrical, software) (section 9.4)

5.22 Scenarios

A Scenario describes a concrete collaboration of actors and system parts to perform a system function.

Purpose

A Scenario checks whether all parts and connections exist for a specific system function.

Description

A Scenario describes how parts of the system collaborate to perform a single path through a Use Case Activity. When you specify a scenario, you must necessarily check if all necessary parts and connections are correctly defined in the model. The modeler does a virtual tour through the system and checks if everything is in place.

Relationships

Responsibility	6.5 System Architect
Output Methods	4.20 Revise an Architecture with Scenarios
Input Methods	None
Example	8.17 Scenarios

Representation

SysML Interaction depicted in a SysML sequence diagram

5.23 System States

The System States describe the relevant conditions of the system or parts of the system.

Purpose

The System States are pre- and postconditions of functions and control the behavior of the system and system parts when events are received.

Description

The System States described in this section are part of an architecture. In the context of System Use Cases, the modeling of states is part of a System Process.

The System States are used to specify the behavior of system parts, including the whole system. A state represents a condition and specifies the reaction when an event is received. A reaction could be the execution of a function or the transition to another state or both.

Relationships

Responsibility	6.5 System Architect
Output Methods	4.21 Define System States
Input Methods	None
Example	8.18 System States

Representation

SysML state machine diagram

5.24 Test Architecture

Purpose

The Test Architecture specifies the setup of the tests as well as the test systems itself.

Description

The Test Architecture specifies on the top-level how the system under test is integrated into the test environment. The test environment includes the test context, i.e., actors, including test systems that perform the Test Cases.

The test systems are systems on their own. Their specifications can be part of the Test Architecture or only be referenced by the Test Architecture and specified in separate system models created with SYSMOD or any other MBSE Methodology whereby the test system is the system of interest.

Relationships

Responsibility	6.7 System Tester
Output of Methods	4.22 Model the Test Architecture
Input of Methods	4.20 Revise an Architecture with Scenarios
Example	8.19 Example Test Architecture

Representation

- SysML block definition and internal block diagrams

- SYSMOD stereotypes for Discipline-specific Elements (mechanical, electrical, software) (section 9.4)

6. SYSMOD Roles

The SYSMOD Roles describe the competency profiles for the people who perform the SYSMOD Methods and are responsible for the SYSMOD Products.

Skills maps depict the skills of the roles. The scale 1-6 relates loosely to the Bloom taxonomy [Bl56]. The meaning of each grade is:

0	No skills.
1	Exhibits knowledge of the topic.
2	Demonstrates an understanding of the topic and applies basic concepts.
3	Solves new problems by applying the knowledge.
4	Analyses the topic, makes inferences, and could easily apply the knowledge.
5	Combines elements in new patterns and propose alternatives.
6	Makes judgments about the topic and validates the quality of work.

The objective of the skills maps is to get an idea of the required competencies. It is not worth to discuss the distinction between each grade in detail. Finally, the competency is specific to the requirements of each project or organization.

A role is not necessarily a full-time job description. It is a competencies profile that has to have an engineering team. The competency can be provided by several people, or by a single person.

Below is the list of SYSMOD Roles in alphabetical order:

- 6.1 SME Administrator
- 6.2 MBSE Methodologist
- 6.3 Project Manager
- 6.4 Requirements Engineer
- 6.5 System Architect
- 6.6 Systems Engineer
- 6.7 System Tester

6.1 SME Administrator

The SME Administrator sets up and maintains the SME.

Description

The SME Administrator sets up the SME of the systems engineering project. That includes the configuration of the modeling tools (e.g., customizing, installing profiles, add-ons, and libraries), the configuration management environment for the models and engineering artifacts (for example a repository server) as well as installation and configuration of adapters to other engineering tools like a requirements management tool, PLM, CAD, or a simulation tool.

Skills

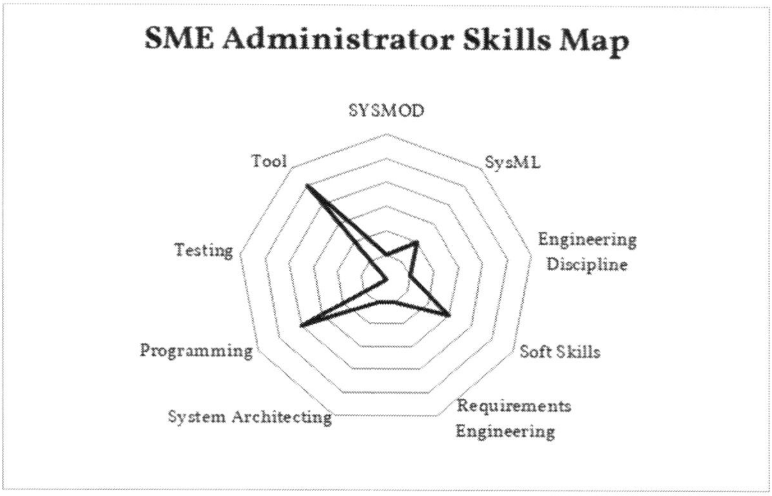

Figure 6.1: SME Administrator Skills Map

Methods

The SME Administrator is responsible for the following SYSMOD Methods:

- 4.2 Set up and maintain the SME

Products

The SME Administrator is responsible for the following SYSMOD Products:

- 5.2 SME

6.2 MBSE Methodologist

The MBSE Methodologist is responsible for the MBSE Methodology.

Description

The MBSE Methodologist defines the MBSE Methodology and tailors it for the specific project or organization. The Role is responsible for communicating the MBSE Methodology to all relevant Stakeholders. Also, the MBSE Methodologist provides the documentation, good practices, and tools that are necessary to apply the methodology.

The Role gets the feedback of the projects about their experiences with MBSE and incorporates it into the tailored MBSE Methodology and deploys updates.

The MBSE Methodologist has a close interface to the SME Administrator. For example, implementing and deploying a model query requires knowledge about the methodology and language architecture, but also programming and tool skills. Conversely, special features of a tool can make methodical steps possible in the first place and thus have an effect on the methodology.

Depending on the concrete competencies of the MBSE Methodologists and the SME Administrators, they allocate themselves the tasks that need to be done.

The MBSE Methodologists are a center of competence of the MBSE Methodology and provide MBSE Trainings and coaching for the organization. Partly external consultants can be used well to get fresh expertise and a critical view from the outside and to outsource the training tasks. The main part of the MBSE Methodologists capability should be inside the organization.

Skills

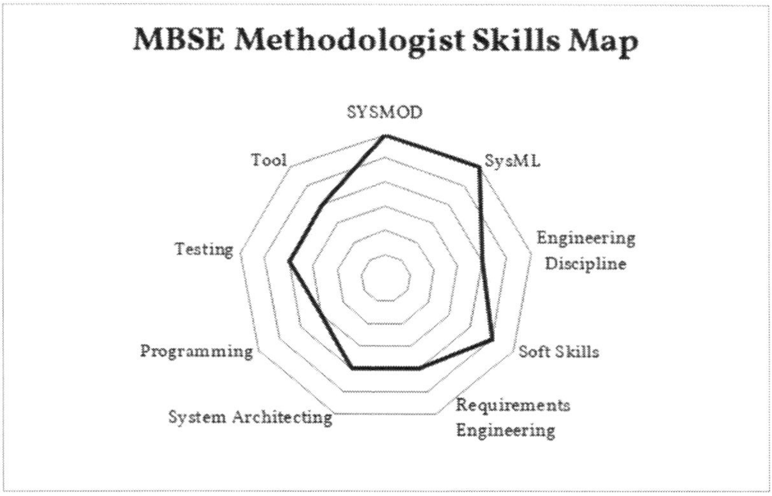

Figure 6.2: MBSE Methodologist Skills Map

Methods

The MBSE Methodologist is responsible for the following SYSMOD Methods:

- 4.1 Tailor the MBSE Methodology
- 4.3 Deploy the MBSE Methodology
- 4.4 Provide MBSE Training and Coaching

Products

The MBSE Methodologist is responsible for the following SYSMOD Products

- 5.1 MBSE Methodology
- 5.3 MBSE Training

6.3 Project Manager

The Project Manager is the manager of the systems development project.

Description

The Project Manager does the managing of the project and is partly directly involved in the SYSMOD Methods.

Skills

Naturally, the Project Manager must have excellent skills in project management. Since it is out of the scope of SYSMOD, the project management skill is not covered by the skills map.

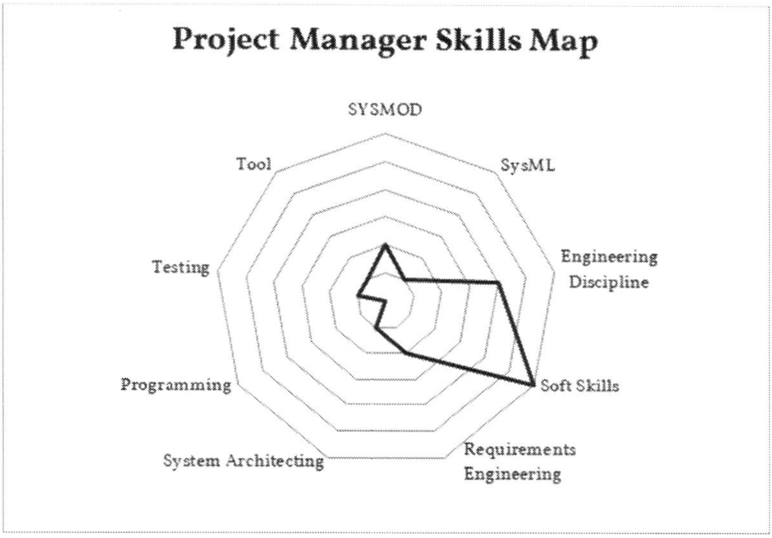

Figure 6.3: Project Manager Skills Map

Methods

The Project Manager is responsible for the following SYSMOD Methods:

- 4.5 Analyze the Problem
- 4.6 Describe System Idea and System Objectives

Products

The Project Manager is responsible for the following SYSMOD Products:

- 5.4 Problem Statement
- 5.5 System Idea
- 5.6 System Objectives

6.4 Requirements Engineer

The Requirements Engineer is responsible for identifying, describing, and managing the Requirements of the systems of interest.

Description

The Requirements Engineer identifies the requirements, i.e., retrieves the requirements from the principal or elaborates them together with the Stakeholders. The Requirements Engineer closely communicates with the System Architect.

In SYSMOD, the Systems Engineer is a collective term for Requirements Engineer, System Architect, and System Tester.

Skills

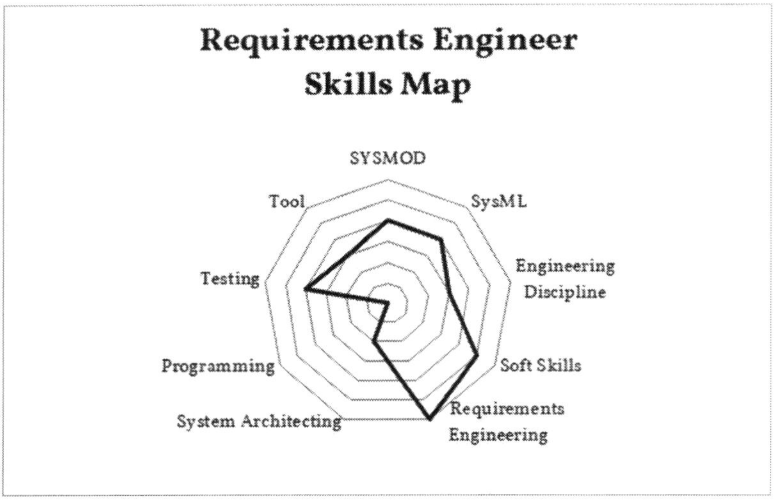

Figure 6.4: Requirements Engineer Skills Map

Methods

The Requirements Engineer is responsible for the following SYSMOD Methods:

- 4.8 Identify Stakeholders
- 4.9 Model Risks
- 4.10 Model Requirements
- 4.11 Identify the System Context
- 4.12 Identify System Use Cases
- 4.13 Identify System Processes
- 4.14 Model Use Case Activities
- 4.15 Model the Domain Knowledge

Products

The Requirements Engineer is responsible for the following SYSMOD Products:

- 5.8 Stakeholders
- 5.10 Requirements
- 5.11 System Context
- 5.12 System Use Cases
- 5.13 System Processes
- 5.14 Use Case Activities
- 5.15 Domain Knowledge

6.5 System Architect

The System Architect is responsible for the System Architecture.

Description

The System Architect derives the solution space from the problem space (requirements).

The role closely communicates with the Requirements Engineer.

In SYSMOD, the Systems Engineer is a collective term for Requirements Engineer, System Architect, and System Tester.

Skills

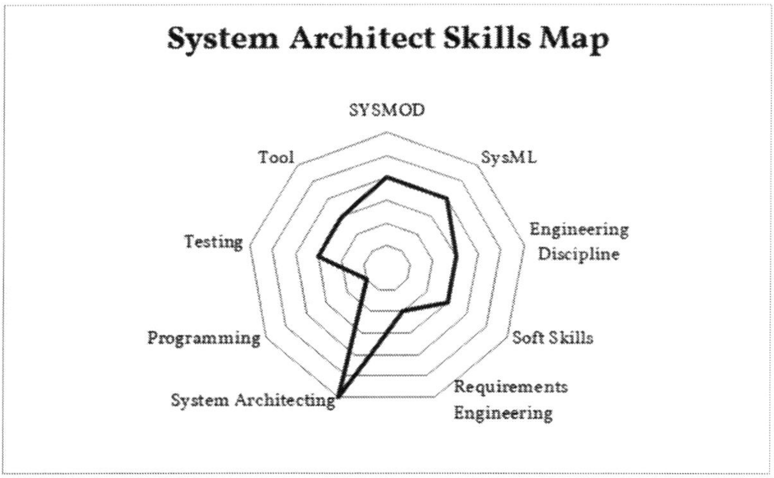

Figure 6.5: System Architect Skills Map

Methods

The System Architect is responsible for the following SYSMOD Methods:

- 4.7 Describe the Base Architecture

- 4.17 Model the Functional Architecture
- 4.18 Model the Logical Architecture
- 4.19 Model the Product Architecture
- 4.20 Revise an Architecture with Scenarios
- 4.21 Define System States

Products

The System Architect is responsible for the following SYSMOD Products:

- 5.7 Base Architecture
- 5.18 Functional Architecture
- 5.20 Logical Architecture
- 5.21 Product Architecture
- 5.22 Scenarios
- 5.23 System States

6.6 Systems Engineer

A systems engineer is "a person who practices systems engineering" and whose systems engineering capabilities and experience include sustained practice, specialization, leadership or authority over systems engineering activities. Systems engineering activities may be conducted by any competent person regardless of job title or professional affiliation. [SE16]

The Systems Engineer is the generalization of the SYSMOD Roles Requirements Engineer, System Architect, and System Tester (figure 6.6).

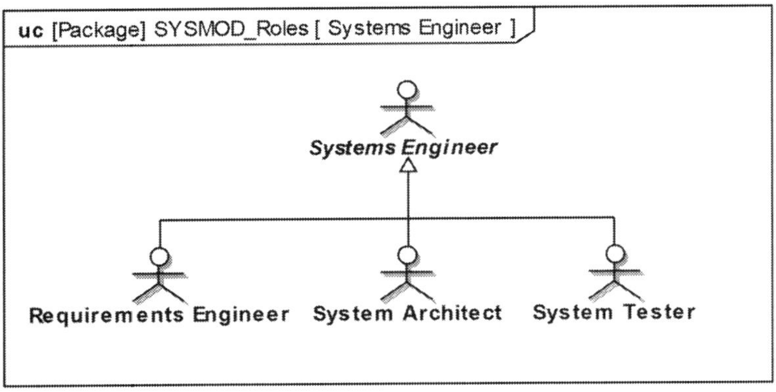

Figure 6.6: SYSMOD Role: Systems Engineer

See sections about the specialized SYSMOD Roles Requirements Engineer, System Architect, and System Tester for the linked Methods and Products.

6.7 System Tester

The System Tester is responsible for describing and performing the system Test Cases, and for specifying the Test Architecture.

Description

Ideally, the System Tester is part of the development team and not a member of a separate testing team. From early artifacts of the requirements analysis, the System Tester could derive test cases and add specific Requirements for testing purposes (build-in testability).

In SYSMOD, the Systems Engineer is a collective term for Requirements Engineer, System Architect, and System Tester.

Skills

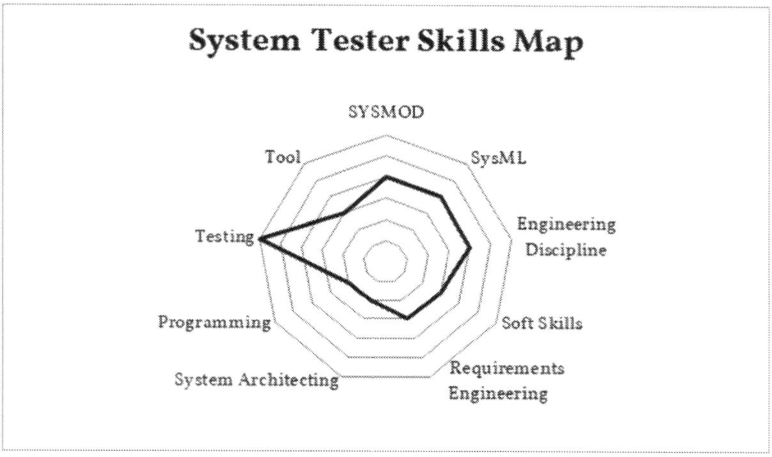

Figure 6.7: System Tester Skills Map

Methods

The System Tester is responsible for the following SYSMOD Methods:

- 4.16 Specify Test Cases
- 4.22 Model the Test Architecture

Products

The System Tester is responsible for the following SYSMOD Products:

- 5.16 Test Cases
- 5.24 Test Architecture

7. SYSMOD Modeling Guidances

The SYSMOD Modeling Guidances give a detailed description of how to do the modeling for the SYSMOD Methods. The guidances are based on SysML and SYSMOD and are independent of specific modeling tools. The SYSMOD Examples presented in chapter 8 were created with a real modeling tool, and include some tool-specific features.

There are many ways how to apply the SYSMOD Methods. I present one of those ways. It is not a general recommendation to perform them exactly like that. You must consider many aspects and customize the methods and guidances for your application (see section 10.2).

The guidances describe how to model the SYSMOD Methods and also how to map engineering information from a document-based on a model-based approach. Often, the information about the system Requirements is described in documents, for example, as input from Stakeholders or as a documentation of the outcome of a workshop. The documents are the structured input for the modeling. At the same time, these documents are also useful templates for views on the model to present the model data in a document-based way to Stakeholders.

Tables and matrices are sometimes more suitable than diagrams. They are also part of the SysML specification. Nevertheless, they are not supported by all modeling tools sufficiently. If you use such a tool, you must use a standard diagram if the Modeling Guidance describes a table or diagram.

The following list itemizes the SYSMOD Modeling Guidances in a logical order according to the SYSMOD Processes:

- 7.1 How to Set up an initial Package Structure
- 7.2 How to Analyze the Problem
- 7.3 How to Model the System Idea
- 7.4 How to Model the System Objectives
- 7.5 How to Model the Base Architecture
- 7.6 How to Model Stakeholders
- 7.7 How to Model Risks
- 7.8 How to Model Requirements
- 7.9 How to Model the System Context
- 7.10 How to Model System Use Cases
- 7.11 How to Model System Processes
- 7.12 How to Model Use Case Activities
- 7.13 How to Model the Domain Knowledge
- 7.14 How to Specify Test Cases
- 7.15 How to Model the Logical Architecture
- 7.16 How to Model the Product Architecture
- 7.17 How to Revise an Architecture with Scenarios
- 7.18 How to Model System States
- 7.19 How to Model the Test Architecture

7.1 How to Set up an initial Package Structure

Context

SYSMOD Methods
    4.2 Set up and maintain the SME
SYSMOD Products
    5.2 System Modeling Environment (SME)
SYSMOD Roles
    6.1 SME Administrator
Examples
    8.1 Example Model Structure

How to model

Figure 7.1 is a screenshot of a modeling tool that shows the system model packages structure. SysML does not provide such a tree view of the model structure. Note that the tree also contains some tool-specific elements that are not part of SysML.

You could create a tree-like view with a SysML package diagram by arranging the packages in the diagram in a tree structure. However, that requires much effort, must be kept manually in sync with the model, and needs much more diagram space.

In the first view, it seems to be simple to define the package structure of a SysML model. However, a model has many orthogonal aspects and abstraction layers that could be mapped into the package structure, for example, domain concepts, methods, or organizational aspects. You can easily mix up those aspects in the package structure and get finally lost.

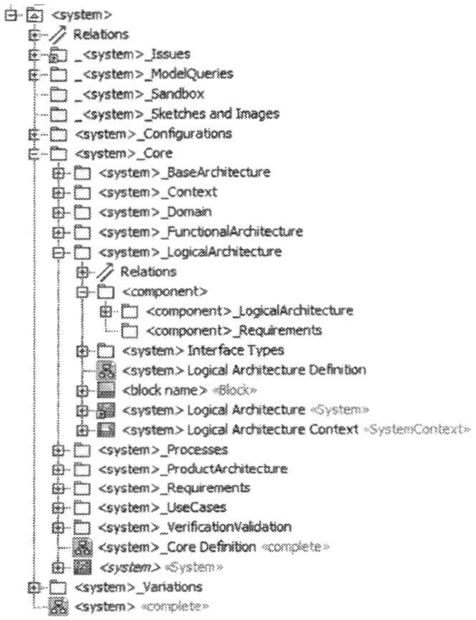

Figure 7.1: Package Structure of a System Model

The MBSE Challenge Team SE^2 for Telescope Modeling describes a best practice for the package structure in the MBSE Cookbook [MBSECook]. The proposed model package structure of SYSMOD is based on that concept.

The root package represents the complete system model. On the next level, we separate the different modeling aspects like system context, requirements, structure, and so on. The list in the figure is not a complete listing. There are many other possible aspects. You need a customized version for your projects. The prefix of each package is the enclosing namespace. Otherwise, you would have many packages of the same name in the model, for example, *Requirements*. The prefix shows the context of the specific package and supports orientation in the model.

The architecture packages contain the architectural elements of the system, in particular the structural elements. Each element with a detailed description has its own package on the next level. Again, you treat that package like the system root package and create the same package structure inside. For example, the package *<component>_Requirements* in figure 7.1 contains all Requirements that are directly related to the *<component>*. Again, it also includes architecture packages that contain further packages with the same structure.

Overall, the package structure is straightforward and scalable. It works for models of any size and gives the model builder and users a good orientation.

The following steps describe how to model the structure:

1. Make sure that the model is empty, and that there are no predefined package structures. Sometimes, modeling tools create an initial package structure for a new model.
2. Create a SysML model element *Model* with the name of your system.
3. Inside the model element, create the three top-level packages for the core, configurations, and variations as well as some auxiliary packages for issues, notes, or other things that are not a direct part of the system model. See Figure 7.1 for the naming conventions.
4. Inside the core package, create the top-level packages for the SYSMOD Products like context or requirements. See Figure 7.1 for the naming conventions.
5. Create a SYSMOD *«system»* element with name *<system> Base Architecture* in the package *<system>_BaseArchitecture.* Replace the term *<system>* with the name of your system of interest.

6. Create an abstract SYSMOD *«system»* element with the name of your system in the core package. If you would like to have a strong coupling to the Base Architecture, model a generalization relationship to the system element of the Base Architecture. See also section 11.7 about the coupling of architectures.

It is helpful to create a template for system models that already provides an initial package structure. You should also add some more things than shown in Figure 7.1, like special diagrams, tables, or model element structures that are commonly used in your projects. Most modeling tools provide the feature to define templates for models.

7.2 How to Analyze the Problem

Context

SYSMOD Methods
    4.5 Analyze the Problem
SYSMOD Products
    5.4 Problem Statement
SYSMOD Roles
    6.3 Project Manager
Examples
    8.2 Example Problem Statement

Document-based Information

The template in figure 7.2 is an example of how to present the Problem Statement in a document.

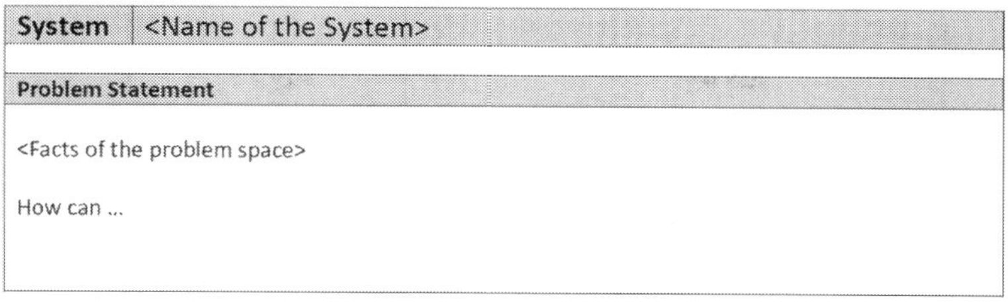

System	<Name of the System>
Problem Statement	
<Facts of the problem space> How can ...	

Figure 7.2: Document Template for Problem Statement

How to model

1. Select the system element in the root package of the core.
2. The SYSMOD stereotype *«system»* has a property *problemStatement* to store the Problem Statement.

Section 11.11 and section 11.12 describe the workshop tools 6M and 5-Why's that can be used to analyze the problem space for the system of interest. The Problem Statement summarizes the conclusion of this analysis.

Figure 7.3 depicts the Problem Statement in a block compartment notation in a block definition diagram.

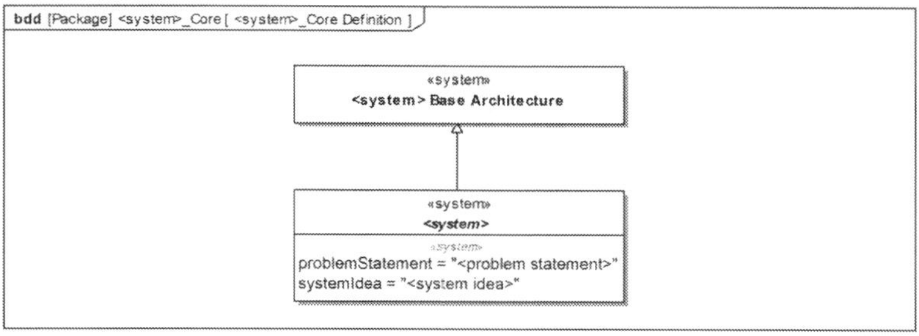

Figure 7.3: Model Template for the Problem Statement

7.3 How to Model the System Idea

Context

SYSMOD Methods
4.6 Describe the System Idea and the System Objectives
SYSMOD Products
5.5 System Idea
SYSMOD Roles
6.3 Project Manager
Examples
8.3 Example System Idea

Document-based Information

Helpful and effective tools to collect information about the System Idea are the product box (section 11.8), the product vision board (section 11.9), and the SAMS method (section 11.10).

The template in figure 7.4 is an example of how to present the System Idea in a document.

System	<Name of the system of interest> (<abbreviation>)
System Idea	
<elevator pitch> <main features> <story board>	

Figure 7.4: Document Template for System Idea

How to model

1. Select the system element in the root package of the core.
2. The SYSMOD stereotype *«system»* has a property *systemIdea* to store the System Idea. If the System Idea is more than text, for example, if it includes graphics, put a reference to the external source in the model.

Figure 7.3 depicts the System Idea in the model, and the strong-coupling approach to connect the Base Architecture by a generalization relationship. See also section 11.7 about the coupling of architectures.

7.4 How to Model the System Objectives

Context

SYSMOD Methods
    4.6 Describe the System Idea and the System Objectives
SYSMOD Products
    5.6 System Objectives
SYSMOD Roles
    6.3 Project Manager
Examples
    8.4 Example System Objectives

Document-based Information

Like for the System Idea, the workshop tools product box (section 11.8), the product vision board (section 11.9), and the

SAMS method (section 11.10) can be used to elaborate the System Objectives.

The template in figure 7.5 is an example of how to present the System Objectives in a document.

As mentioned in the method chapter 4, there are two kinds of System Objectives: system-related and organization related objectives. In figure 7.5, both types are indicated by the prefix of the ID *OBJ-S<x>*, respectively *OBJ-O<x>*.

System Objectives			
#ID	*Stakeholder*	*Name*	*Description*
<id>	<name of the stakeholder>	<name of the objective for the system>	<description of the objective>
<id>	<name of the stakeholder>	<name of the objective for the organization>	<description of the objective>
...	...	...	...
Relationship to Business Models / Processes			
<describe relationship>			

Figure 7.5: Document Template for System Objectives

How to model

1. Select the package *Objectives.*
2. Create a table named *System Objectives* and configure it to depict the objectives with id, name, text, and the related Stakeholder.
3. Create an SYSMOD *«objective»* as the root element for all System Objectives. The text value of the objective is "Objectives of the system <name of the system>".
4. Create one SYSMOD *«objective»* for each identified System Objective. The text value is the documentation of the objective. The identifier can be as proposed above.

5. Create a containment relationship from the root element to all other System Objectives.
6. If the Stakeholder of the System Objectives is not part of the model, create them as described in section 7.6. Create a trace relationship from each System Objective to the Stakeholder, who is the source of the objective.

Figure 7.6 depicts a template of a System Objective in a requirements diagram. The root element *Objectives of the system <system>* represents the whole set of System Objectives. The relationship between the root element and all the other objective elements is the namespace containment.

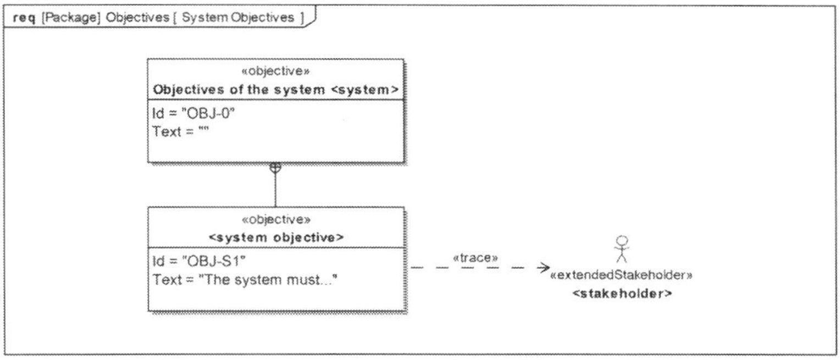

Figure 7.6: Model Diagram Template for System Objectives

As mentioned above in the guidance, you should use a table rather than a diagram to manage the System Objectives in the model. Figure 7.7 shows a table template depicting the same information as figure 7.6.

#	Id	Name	Text	Stakeholder
1	OBJ-0	Objectives of the system <system>		
2	OBJ-S1	<system objective>	The system must...	<stakeholder>

Figure 7.7: Model Table Template for System Objectives

Figure 7.8 shows the location of the System Objective in the system model package structure.

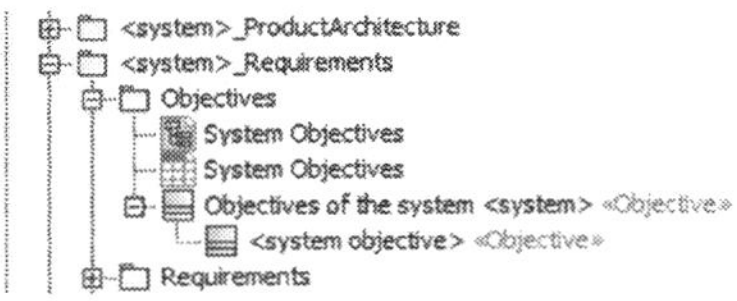

Figure 7.8: System Objectives in the model package structure

7.5 How to Model the Base Architecture

Context

SYSMOD Methods
    4.7 Describe Base Architecture
SYSMOD Products
    5.7 Base Architecture
SYSMOD Roles
    6.5 System Architect
Examples
    8.6 Example Base Architecture

Document-based information

Figure 7.9 shows a simple template of a table in a text document for the Base Architecture information.

Base Architecture of <name of the system>	
<sketch of the base architecture>	
Brief description	
<brief description of the base architecture>	
Architecture decisions	
<list of architecture decisions>	
Elements of the Base Architecture	
Name	*Description*
<name of element>	<brief description> Interfaces: • <interface 1> • <interface 2>
...	...

Figure 7.9: Document Template for the Base Architecture

How to model

1. Select the package *<system>_BaseArchitecture.*
2. Create a SysML block definition diagram named *<system> Base Architecture Definition.*
3. If you want to describe the Base Architecture textually instead of modeling the structure, you can use the property *systemIdea* of the SYSMOD stereotype *«system»* that is applied to the Base Architecture for the text or to reference external resources like a sketch of the Base Architecture. See section 7.3 about how to model the System Idea.
4. Create a SysML *Block* with appropriate features for every part of the Base Architecture. Use the documentation field of the model elements or a linked SysML *Comment* for a brief textual description of the element.

5. Create part properties and connect the parts in a SysML internal block diagram. See section 7.14 about more details on how to model an architecture.
6. Typically, the context of the system is also relevant to the Base Architecture. In that case, create an SYSMOD *«systemContext»* with name *<system> Base Architecture Context.* The Base Architecture system element is part of the context as well as the actors. See also section 7.8: How to model the System Context.
7. The Base Architecture can also be a kind of a constraint requirement (see section 7.8: How to Model Requirements).

Figure 7.10 depicts the model elements of a Base Architecture in a block definition diagram, figure 7.11 depicts the Base Architecture, including the context on an internal block diagram, and figure 7.12 shows the Base Architecture elements in the model package structure.

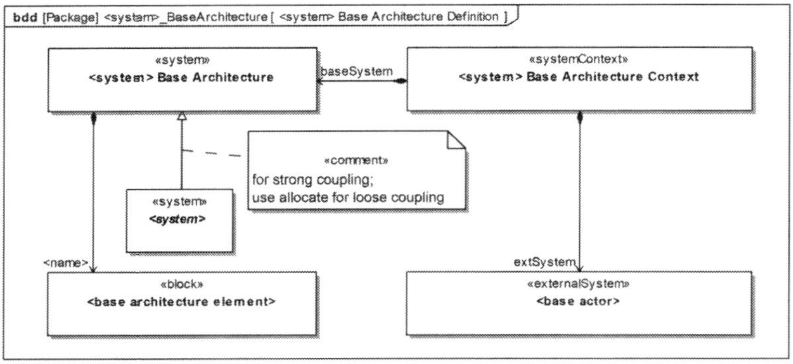

Figure 7.10: Model Template for Base Architecture Definition

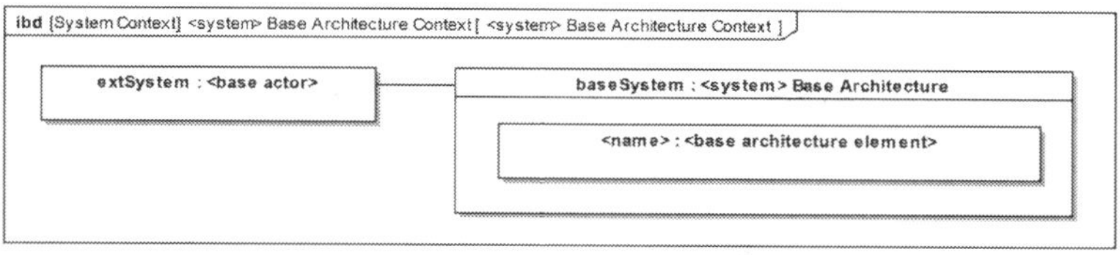

Figure 7.11: Model Template for Base Architecture context and internal structure

Figure 7.12: Base Architecture in the Model Package Structure

7.6 How to Model Stakeholders

Context

SYSMOD Methods
    4.8 Identify Stakeholders
SYSMOD Products
    5.8 Stakeholders
SYSMOD Roles
    6.4 Requirements Engineer
Examples
    8.5 Example Stakeholder

Document-based information

Figure 7.13 shows a template of a table for Stakeholders in a text document.

Stakeholder					
Name	*Categories*	*Effort*	*Priority*	*Concern*	*Contact*
<Name of the Stakeholder>	<Requirement owner | Expert | User>	<low | medium | high>	<critical | high | medium | low>	<Concerns of the stakeholder>	<Contact information, e.g. email>
...					

Figure 7.13: Document Template for Stakeholders

How to model

1. Select the package *Stakeholders* below the package *<sys-tem>_Requirements.*
2. Create a table named *Stakeholders.*
3. Create an SYSMOD *«extendedStakeholder»* for each identified Stakeholder and fill out the properties.

Typically, there are no relationships between the Stakeholders. You could think of abstract Stakeholders and generalization relationships from concrete Stakeholders to create a taxonomy of Stakeholders. However, you should consider that the properties of stereotypes are not inherited in SysML.

Therefore, depicting Stakeholders in a diagram is not very useful. Instead, Figure 7.14 shows a template of a table of the list of SYSMOD *«extendedStakeholder»*.

#	Name	Documentation	Concern	Priority	Effort	Categories	Contact
1	<stakeholder name>	The <stakeholder> is...	<stakeholders concern>	Critical	Medium	Expert	

Figure 7.14: Model Template for Stakeholders

Figure 7.15 depicts the Stakeholders in the model package structure.

Figure 7.15: Stakeholders in the Model Package Structure

7.7 How to Model Risks

Context

SYSMOD Methods
  4.9 Model Risks
SYSMOD Products
  5.9 Risks
SYSMOD Roles
  6.4 Requirements Engineer
Examples
  8.7 Example Risks

Document-based Information

Figure 7.16 shows the template for a single Risk in a text document. Each Risk is documented in a table to store the information in a uniform structured format.

Risk <ID>	<Risk name>	<kind>
Text	<description>	
Severity	<1-10>	
Occurrence	<1-10>	
Stability	Stable/unstable	

Figure 7.16: Document Template of a System Risk

How to model

1. Select the package *<system>Risks.*
2. Create a table to depict the Risks.
3. For each identified Risk, create an appropriate SYSMOD risk element, and fill out the properties of the Risk.

Figure 7.17 shows a risk table view.

#	Id	Name	Text	kind	severity	occurrence
1	<risk ID1>	<risk name 1>	<risk description>	technical	3	5
2	<risk ID2>	<risk name 2>	<risk description>	cost	7	2

Figure 7.17: Model Template of a Risk - Table

Figure 7.18 shows the Risk in the model package structure.

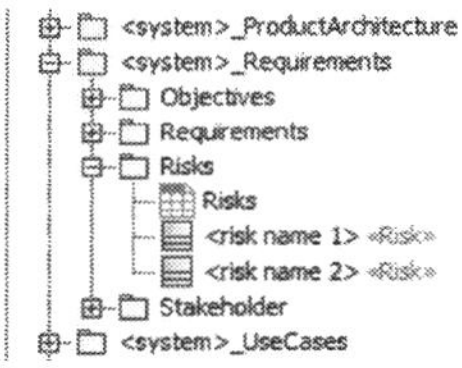

Figure 7.18: Model Template of a Risk - Structure

7.8 How to Model Requirements

Context

SYSMOD Methods
    4.10 Model Requirements
SYSMOD Products
    5.10 Requirements
SYSMOD Roles
    6.4 Requirements Engineer

Examples

8.5 Example Stakeholder

Document-based Information

Figure 7.19 shows the template for a single Requirement in a text document. Each Requirement is documented in a table to store the information in a uniform structured format.

<table>
<tr><th><requirement ID></th><th><requirement name></th><th><functional|performance|...></th></tr>
<tr><td>Text</td><td colspan="2"><requirement text, e.g. „The system must...“></td></tr>
<tr><td>Motivation</td><td colspan="2"><Why do we need this requirement?></td></tr>
<tr><td>Stakeholder</td><td colspan="2"><Who is the stakeholder of the requirement?></td></tr>
<tr><td>Stability</td><td colspan="2"><instable, stable></td></tr>
<tr><td>Obligation</td><td colspan="2"><nonobligatory, obligatory></td></tr>
<tr><td>Priority</td><td colspan="2"><critical, high, medium, low></td></tr>
<tr><td>Risks</td><td colspan="2"><risks></td></tr>
<tr><td>Details</td><td colspan="2"><More detailed description of the requirement></td></tr>
</table>

Figure 7.19: Document Template of a System Requirement

How to model

1. Select the package *<system>_Requirements.*
2. Create a table to depict the Requirements.
3. For each identified Requirement, create an appropriate SYSMOD requirement element, for example, *«performanceRequirement»*, and fill out the properties of the Requirement. A Use Case Activity can also be a *«functionalRequirement»*. See section 7.12 about how to model Use Case Activities and how to define one as a *«functionalRequirement»*.
4. Typically, you have so many Requirements that you need more structure in the model. Create packages and requirements containment hierarchies as necessary.

5. If you want to cover the Base Architecture with a Requirement, create a constraint requirement of name *Base Architecture* and model a refine relationship from the Base Architecture element to the constraint Requirement. Alternatively, you can also assign the stereotype *«performanceRequirement»* directly to the block of the base architecture. In this case, however, you must not forget this requirement in queries, since it is located in a different area in the model.

Figure 7.20 depicts a Requirement in a requirements diagram and figure 7.21 the same Requirement in a table view. The table represents only some of the requirement properties that fit on one typical page when printing.

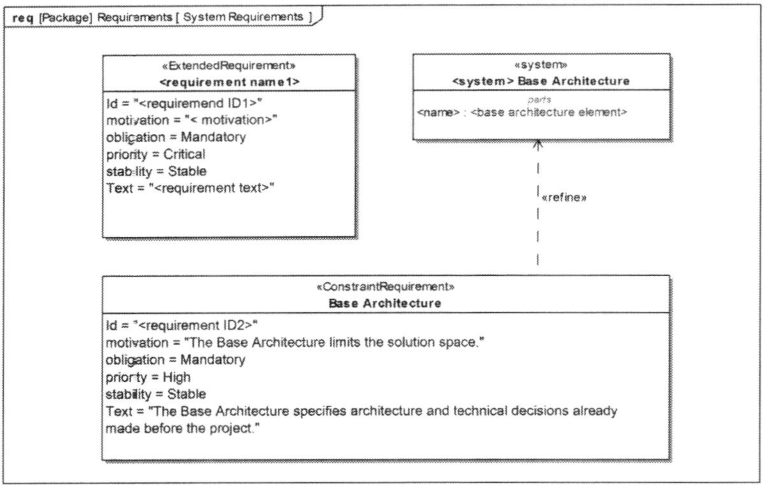

Figure 7.20: Model Template of a System Requirement - Diagram

#	Id	Name	Text	Motivation	Priority	Obligation	Stability	Risks
1	<requiremend ID1>	<requirement name1>	<requirement text>	< motivation>	Critical	Mandatory	Stable	<risk name 1>
2	<requirement ID2>	Base Architecture	The Base Architecture specifies architecture and technical decisions already made before the project.	The Base Architecture limits the solution space.	High	Mandatory	Stable	<risk name 1> <risk name 2>
3	<requirement ID3>	<continuous use case name>	see activity diagram	<motivation>	High	Mandatory	Stable	
4	<requirement ID4>	<system use case name1>	see activity diagram	<motivation>	High	Mandatory	Stable	
5	<requirement ID5>	<system use case name2>	see activity diagram	<motivation>	High	Optional	Stable	<risk name 2>
6	<requirement ID6>	<requirement name2>	<requirement text>	<motivation>	Medium	Mandatory	Stable	

Figure 7.21: Model Template of a System Requirement - Table

Figure 7.22 shows the Requirements in the model package structure.

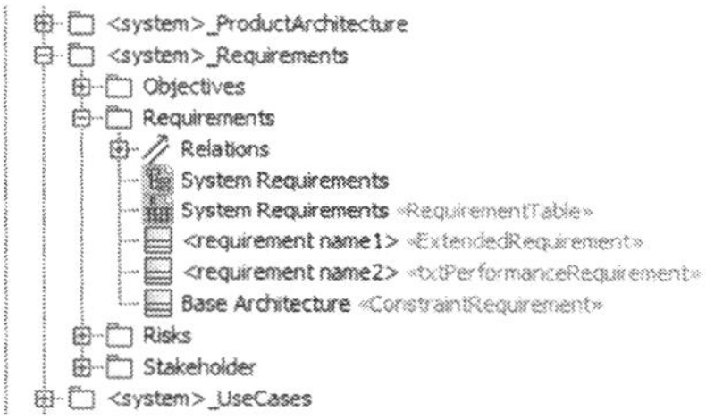

Figure 7.22: Model Template of a System Requirement - Structure

7.9 How to Model the System Context

Context

SYSMOD Methods

4.11 Identify the System Context

SYSMOD Products

5.11 System Context

SYSMOD Roles

6.4 Requirements Engineer

Examples

8.9 Example System Context

Document-based Information

Figure 7.23 shows a template for the list of system actors of the System Context in a text document.

System Context – Actors of the System				
Type	*Name*	*Description*	*Item flows to the system*	*Item flows from the system*
<human|external system|environmental effect|...>	<name of the actor>	<brief description of the actor>	<list of items>	<list of items>
...				
...				

Figure 7.23: Document Template for the System Context

How to model

1. Select the package *<system>_Context.*
2. Create a SysML block definition diagram with name *<system> System Context Definition.*
3. Create an SYSMOD *«systemContext»* with name *<system> System Context.* If you have chosen a strong coupling to the Base Architecture, model a generalization relationship from the *<system> System Context* to the *<system> Base Architecture System Context* element (see section 7.5 and section 11.7).
4. For each identified system actor, create an SYSMOD actor, for example, *«externalSystem».*
5. Typically, a human actor is also a Stakeholder of the system. You can apply both stereotypes to the model element: *«extendedStakeholder»* and *«user».* Actors of the other actor categories are themselves, typically, no Stakeholders, but the responsible person or organization behind the actor. You can model this relationship with a trace relationship from the actor to the Stakeholder.
6. Add the special actor *Planet Environment* from the SYSMOD Library *Engineering4Planet* as an additional

mandatory actor. Every system has an impact on the planet.

7. Place the system element from the core package on the diagram.
8. Model directed composition relationships from the system context to each system actor, and the system model element. Alternatively, since SysML 1.6, you can model the part properties directly without the composite relationships (= associations).
9. If you have modeled a generalization relationship to the Base Architecture context element, check if inherited properties must be redefined. For example, very likely, this is the case for the part property representing the system (see figure 7.24).
10. Create a SysML internal block diagram for the system context. This diagram is called the *System Context Diagram*. Note that SysML does not have a system context diagram. The diagram only exists in MBSE methodologies like SYSMOD.
11. Place all parts on the internal block diagram and connect the actor parts with the system part.
12. If the information is important, model an item flow between the actor parts and the system part. The item type is a domain block (see section 7.13: How to model the Domain Knowledge).
13. Place an item flow on the connector between the system and the actor *Planet Environment*. The item that flows is of type *Planet Impact* from the SYSMOD library *Engineering4Planet* or a user-defined specialization of it.

Figure 7.24 depicts the definition of the System Context elements, and figure 7.25 the System Context.

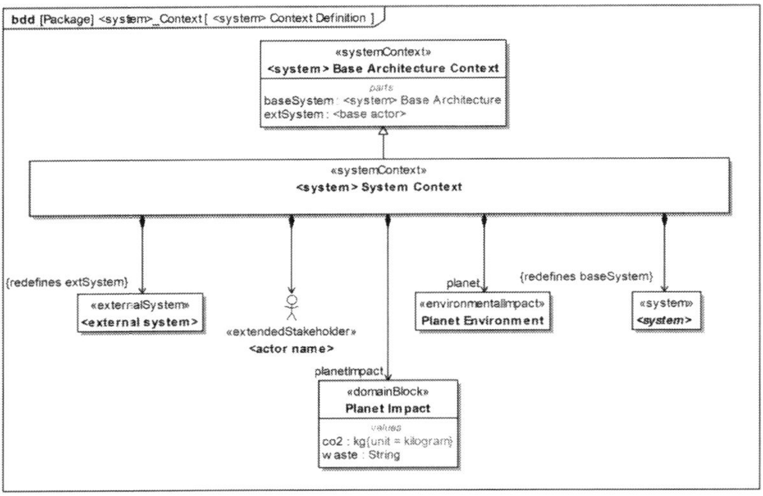

Figure 7.24: Model Template of a System Context Definition

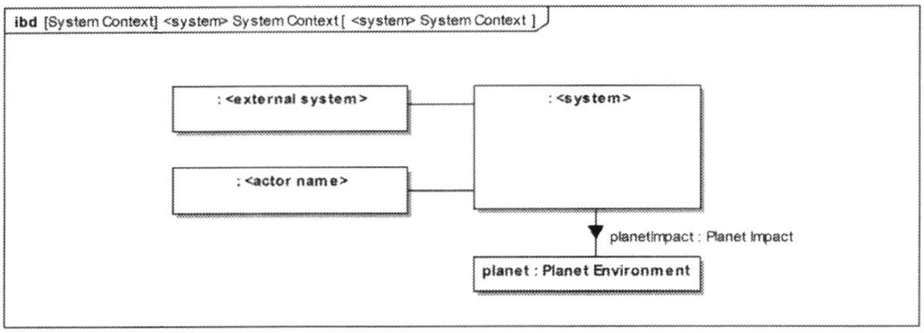

Figure 7.25: Model Template of a System Context

Figure 7.26 shows the System Context elements in the model package structure.

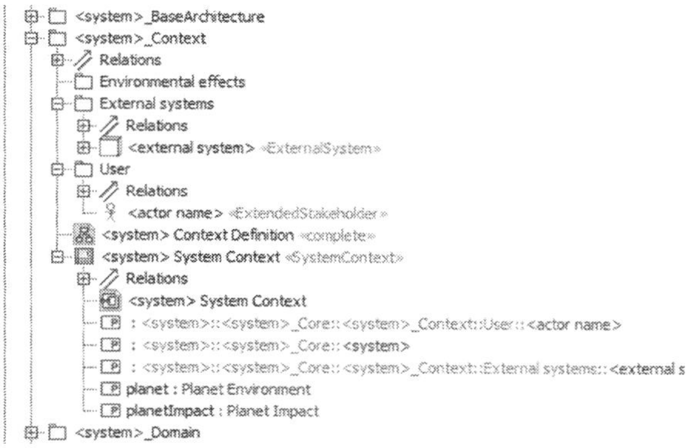

Figure 7.26: System Context in the model package structure

7.10 How to Model System Use Cases

Context

SYSMOD Methods
  4.12 Identify System Use Cases
SYSMOD Products
  5.11 SystemUse Cases
SYSMOD Roles
  6.4 Requirements Engineer
Examples
  8.10 Example System Use Cases

Document-based Information

Figure 7.27 shows a table template for a System Use Case description in a text document.

<table>
<tr><th colspan="3"><name of the use case></th><th><system | continuous></th></tr>
<tr><td colspan="2">Description</td><td colspan="2"><description of the use case></td></tr>
<tr><td colspan="2">Actorsr</td><td colspan="2"><list of the actors who are involved in the use case></td></tr>
<tr><td colspan="2">Trigger</td><td colspan="2"><what triggers the use case></td></tr>
<tr><td colspan="2">Result</td><td colspan="2"><output of the use case observable by the actors or stakeholders></td></tr>
<tr><td colspan="2">Precondition</td><td colspan="2"><internal condition that must be always true to execute the use case></td></tr>
<tr><td colspan="2">Postcondition</td><td colspan="2"><internal condition that is always true after the execution of the use case></td></tr>
<tr><td colspan="2"></td><td colspan="2"></td></tr>
<tr><th colspan="4">Use Case Activity</th></tr>
<tr><td>Step No.</td><td>Step name</td><td colspan="2">Step description</td></tr>
<tr><td rowspan="3"><no.></td><td rowspan="3"><name></td><td>Input:</td><td><list of input objects></td></tr>
<tr><td colspan="2"><description of the step></td></tr>
<tr><td>Output:</td><td><list of output objects></td></tr>
<tr><td rowspan="3"><no.></td><td rowspan="3"><name></td><td>Input:</td><td><list of input objects></td></tr>
<tr><td colspan="2"><description of the step></td></tr>
<tr><td>Output:</td><td><list of output objects></td></tr>
<tr><td rowspan="3">...</td><td rowspan="3"></td><td></td><td></td></tr>
<tr><td colspan="2"></td></tr>
<tr><td></td><td></td></tr>
<tr><td colspan="2"><guard condition></td><td colspan="2"><description of guard condition></td></tr>
<tr><td colspan="2">...</td><td colspan="2"></td></tr>
</table>

Figure 7.27: Document Template for a System Use Case

How to model

1. Select the package *<system>_UseCases.*
2. For each primary system actor, create a SysML use case diagram with name *<actor name> Use Cases.*
3. For each identified use case of the primary actor, create an SYSMOD *«systemUseCase»* or *«continuousUseCase»* and fill out the properties *name, trigger,* and *result.* Use the documentation field of your modeling tool or create a linked comment for the brief textual description of the use case.
4. Place the actors of the System Use Case on the diagram and model associations between the System Use Cases and their primary and secondary actors.
5. Optionally, you can create a SysML *Signal* with the name *Sig<use case name>* that represents the trigger of the use case and place it in the package *Use Case Triggers.* This naming is the default if you do not know a more appropriate name for it. The signal can be used as triggers in state machines (see, for example, section

7.18). Assign the signal to the property *signalTrigger* of the System Use Cases.

Figure 7.28 depicts templates for System Use Cases in a use case diagram, and figure 7.29 in a table view.

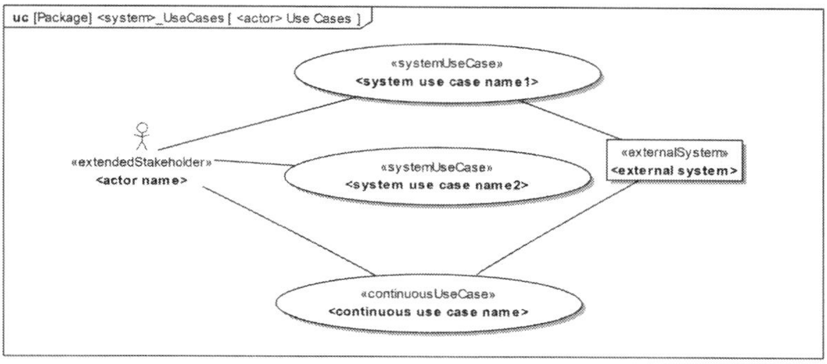

Figure 7.28: Model Diagram Template for System Use Cases

#	Name	Documentation	trigger	triggerSignal	result
1	<system use case name1>	<brief description of the use case>	<textual description of the trigger>	Sig<use case trigger1>	<textual description of the result>
2	<system use case name2>	<brief description of the use case>	<textual description of the trigger>	Sig<use case trigger2>	<textual description of the result>
3	<continuous use case name>	<brief description of the use case>	<textual description of the trigger>	Sig<use case trigger3>	<textual description of the result>

Figure 7.29: Model Table Template for System Use Cases

Figure 7.30 shows System Use Cases in the model package structure.

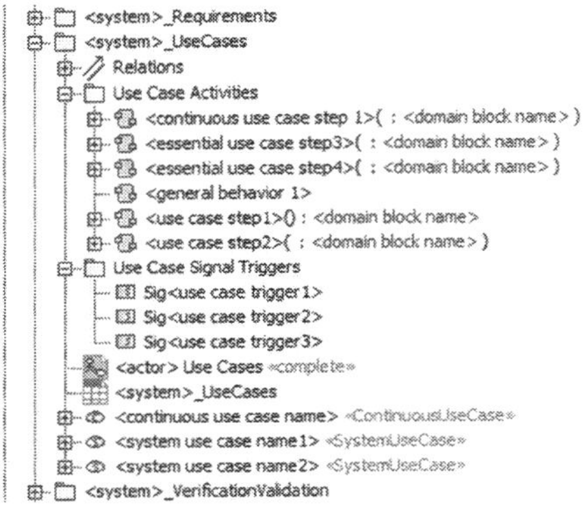

Figure 7.30: System Use Cases in the model package structure

7.11 How to Model System Processes

Context

SYSMOD Methods
  4.13 Identify System Processes
SYSMOD Products
  5.13 System Processes
SYSMOD Roles
  6.4 Requirements Engineer
Examples
  8.11 Example System Process

Document-based Information

Figure 7.31 shows a table template for a System Process description in a text document.

Description of the Domain Blocks of the Domain Knowledge		
Context objects		
<name of domain block>	<description of the domain block>	
	<property name and type>	<description of the property>
	...	...
System objects		
<name of domain block>	<description of the domain block>	
	<property name and type>	<description of the property>
	...	...

Figure 7.31: Document Template for a System Process

How to model

1. Select the package *<system>_Processes.*
2. Create a SysML use case diagram with name *<system> Processes.*
3. For each identified system process, create an SYSMOD *«systemProcess»*. Use the documentation field of the *«systemProcess»* model element or a linked SysML *Comment* to add a brief textual description of the System Process.
4. For each System Process define a SysML *Activity* with *CallBehaviorActions* that call the appropriate Use Case Activities of the included System Use Cases. Define the control and object flows as needed.

Figure 7.32 depicts a template for a System Process in a use case diagram, and figure 7.33 in a table view.

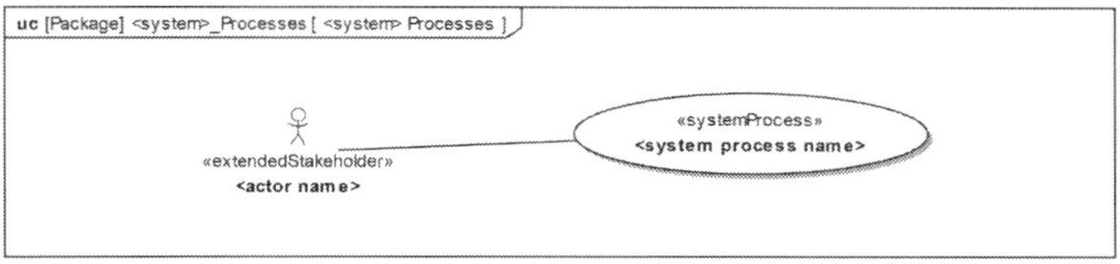

Figure 7.32: Model Diagram Template for a System Process

#	Name	Documentation	Actors	Included Use Case Activities
1	<system process name>	<brief description of the system process>	<actor name>	<system use case name1> <system use case name2>

Figure 7.33: Model Table Template for a System Process

Figure 7.34 depicts the activity of a System Process. The actions show the stereotype *«functionalRequirement»*, which is applied to the respective called activity.

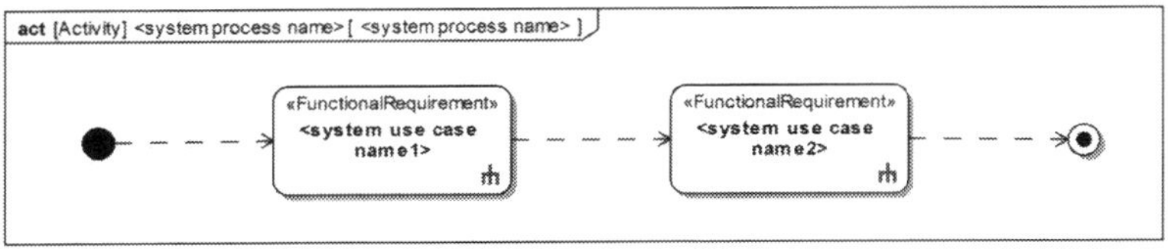

Figure 7.34: Model Activity Diagram Template for a System Process

Figure 7.35 shows System Process in the model package structure.

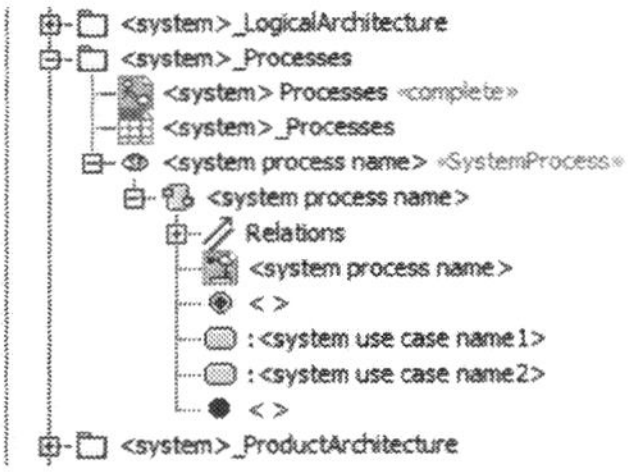

Figure 7.35: System Process in the model package structure

7.12 How to Model Use Case Activities

Context

SYSMOD Methods

4.14 Model Use Case Activities

SYSMOD Products
    5.14 Use Case Activities
SYSMOD Roles
    6.4 Requirements Engineer
Examples
    8.12 Example Use Case Activities

Document-based information

Figure 7.36 shows a template for a Use Case Activity description in a text document. It is the bottom of the table for a System Use Case description, as shown in figure 7.27.

Use Case Activity				
Step No.	*Step name*	*Step description*		*Partition*
<no.>	<name>	*Input:*	<list of input objects>	<I/O, core, ...>
		<description of the step>		
		Output:	<list of output objects>	
<no.>	<name>	*Input:*	<list of input objects>	<I/O, core, ...>
		<description of the step>		
		Output:	<list of output objects>	
...				
<guard condition>		<description of guard condition>		<I/O, core, ...>
...				

Figure 7.36: Document Template for a Use Case Activity

The use case step numbers are just identifiers without any further semantics. You could use them to describe an execution order of the use case steps. In that case, the ordering scheme of the use case step numbers is 1, 2, 3, etc. Alternatives are depicted with 1a, 1b, 1c, etc. Complex flow behaviors are not very well presented in a table structure and require a graphical presentation like an activity diagram.

How to model

For each System Use Case:

1. Select a System Use Case.
2. Create a SysML *Activity* with an activity diagram that is owned by the System Use Case.
3. If the System Use Case description defines pre- and postconditions (see section 7.9), define appropriate conditions for the activity.
4. Model the steps of the Use Case Activity with *CallBehaviorActions*. That means you create an activity for each action if the activity does not already exist in the model or a model library. If not called by other activities, the activities of the steps are owned by the activity that is owned by the System Use Case.
5. It is a good practice to separate steps responsible for input and output functionality from the other steps. The I/O steps are often less dependent on the core functionality of the use case and strongly dependent on technologies. Use SysML activity partitions to separate I/O related steps.
6. Model the control flows between the use case steps, including decision, fork, merge, join, and other control nodes.
7. Model the object flow. The type of input and output pins are domain blocks from the Domain Knowledge (see section 7.12). The SYSMOD Methods Model Use Case Activities and Model Domain Knowledge cannot be performed in a strict order. They are mutually dependent.
8. Use the documentation field of the model elements or a linked SysML *Comment* to add brief textual descriptions for each called activity and non-obvious guards of the decision nodes.

Figure 7.37 depicts a Use Case Activity template in the model.

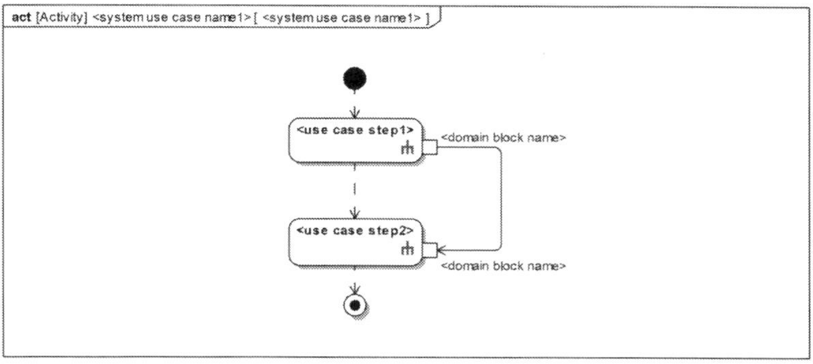

Figure 7.37: Model Template for a Use Case Activity

Figure 7.38 shows the Use Case Activity elements in the model package structure.

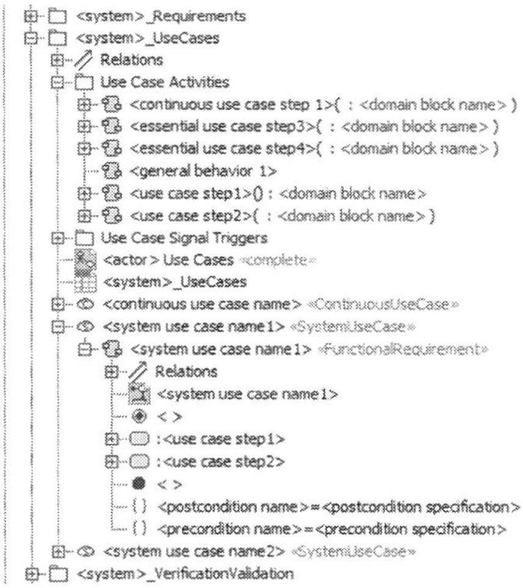

Figure 7.38: Use Case Activities in the model package structure

7.13 How to Model the Domain Knowledge

Context

SYSMOD Methods
  4.14 Model Domain Knowledge
SYSMOD Products
  5.13 Domain Knowledge
SYSMOD Roles
  6.4 Requirements Engineer
Examples
  8.13 Example Domain Knowledge

Document-based information

Figure 7.39 shows a template for the Domain Knowledge in a text document.

Description of the Domain Knowledge		
Context objects		
<name of domain block>	<description of the domain block>	
	<property name and type>	<description of the property>
System objects		
<name of domain block>	<description of the domain block>	
	<property name and type>	<description of the property>

Figure 7.39: Document Template for the Domain Knowledge

How to model

1. Select the package *<system>_Context Domain.*

2. Create a SysML block definition diagram with name *<system> Context Domain Knowledge.*
3. For each identified context domain block, create an SYSMOD *«domainBlock»*. Specify the properties of the block and associations to other domain blocks.
4. Use the documentation field of the domain block and its properties or linked SysML *Comments* to add brief textual descriptions.
5. Repeat steps 1-4 for the system domain blocks.

Figure 7.40 depicts a template of a Domain Knowledge in the model.

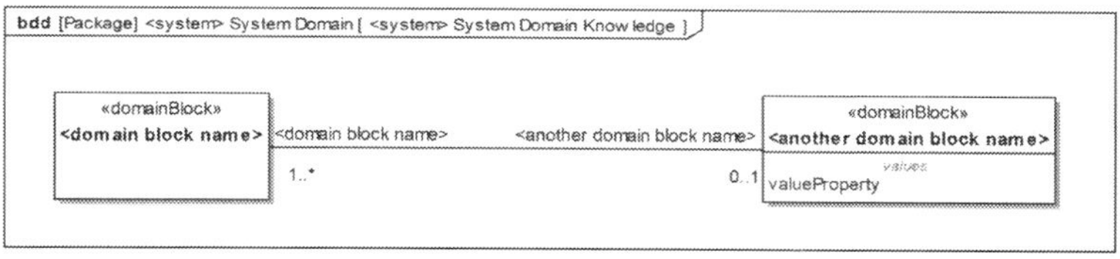

Figure 7.40: Model Template for the Domain Knowledge

Figure 7.41 depicts the domain knowledge in the model package structure.

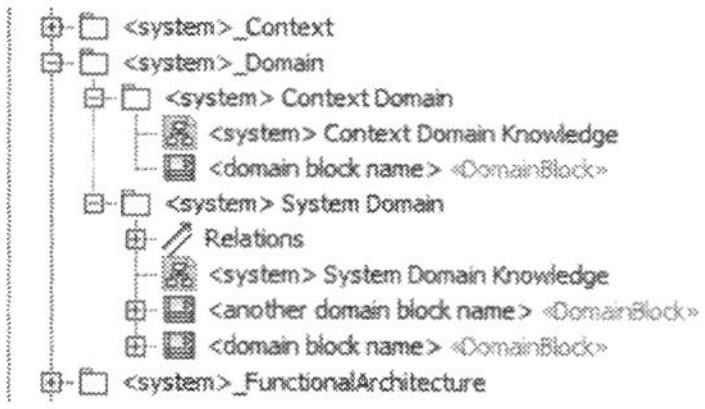

Figure 7.41: Domain Knowledge in the model package structure

7.14 How to Specify Test Cases

Context

SYSMOD Methods
 4.16 Specify Test Cases
SYSMOD Products
 5.16 Test Cases
SYSMOD Roles
 6.7 System Tester
Examples
 8.14 Example Test Cases

Document-based information

Figure 7.42 shows a template for a Test Case description in a text document. It is similar to the template for System Use Cases.

<name of the test case>			**<testType>**
Description	<description of the test case>		
Precondition	<internal condition that must be always true to execute the test case>		
Postcondition	<internal condition that is always true after the execution of the test case>		
Priority	<test case priority>		
Test data	<test data>		
Component under Test	<component(s) under test>		
Verifies	<verified requirements>		
Dependant test cases	<list of test cases>		
Test Case Steps			
Step No.	*Step name*	*Step description*	
<no.>	<name>	*Input:*	<list of input objects>
		<description of the step>	
		Output:	<list of output objects>
<no.>	<name>	*Input:*	<list of input objects>
		<description of the step>	
		Output:	<list of output objects>
...			
<guard condition>		<description of guard condition>	
...			

Figure 7.42: Document Template for a Test Case

How to model

1. Select the package *<system>_VerificationValidation.*
2. Create a table *<system>_TestCases* that depicts all Test Cases in the package with the related information (see figure 7.44).
3. For each identified Test Case, create a SysML block definition diagram with the name *<test case>_Definition (see figure 7.43).
4. Create the Test Case element in the diagram.
5. Place all dependent Test Cases on the diagram and model the dependency relationships
6. Place the Requirements that are verified by the Test Case on the diagram and model the verify relationships from the Test Case to the Requirements.
7. Place all test data instance specifications used by the Test Case on the diagram and model the usage relationships from the Test Case to the instance specifications.
8. Select the Test Case.
9. Create a SysML *Activity* with an activity diagram that is owned by the Test Case.
10. Define pre- and postconditions for the activity if appropriate.
11. Model the steps of the Test Case, including control and object flow if necessary.
12. Use the documentation field of the model elements or a linked SysML *Comment* to add brief textual descriptions for each action and non-obvious guards of the decision nodes.

Figure 7.43 depicts a template of a test case in the model, and figure 7.44 shows a template of a table view for test cases.

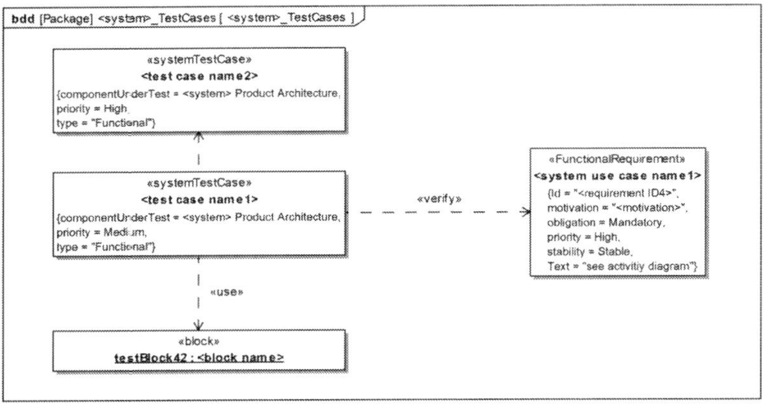

Figure 7.43: Model Template for a Test Case

#	Type	Name	Priority	Component Under Test	Documentation	Verifies	Test data	Dependent Test Cases
1	Functional	<test case name1>	Medium	<system> Product Architecture	<description of the test case>	<system use case name1>		<test case name2>
2	Functional	<test case name2>	High	<system> Product Architecture	<description of the test case>	<requirement name1>	testBlock42 : <block name>	

Figure 7.44: Model Template for a Test Cases table

Figure 7.45 depicts the Test Cases in the model package structure.

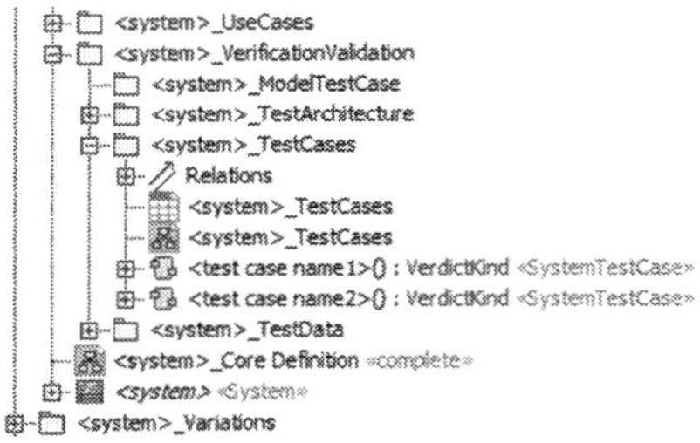

Figure 7.45: Test Cases

7.15 How to Model the Logical Architecture

Context

SYSMOD Methods
- 4.17 Model Logical Architecture

SYSMOD Products
- 5.20 Logical Architecture

SYSMOD Roles
- 6.5 System Architect

Examples
- 8.15 Example Logical Architecture

Document-based information

Logical Architecture of <name of the system>	
<sketch of the logical architecture>	
Brief description	
<brief description of the logical architecture>	
Architecture decisions	
<list of architecture decisions>	
Elements of the Logical Architecture	
Name	*Description*
<name of element>	<brief description> Interfaces: • <interface 1> • <interface 2>
...	...

Figure 7.46: Document Template for the Logical Architecture

Figure 7.46 shows a simple template for a Logical Architecture in a text document.

How to model

1. Select the package *<system>_LogicalArchitecture.*
2. Create a SysML block definition diagram with name *<system> Logical Architecture Definition.*
3. Create an SYSMOD *«system»* with name *<system> Logical Architecture* and model a SysML *Generalization* relationship to the system element in the package *<system>_Core.*
4. For each identified part type of the Logical Architecture, create a SysML *Block* with appropriate properties, proxy ports (see also Proxy versus Full Ports), constraints, and operations. Use the documentation field or a linked SysML *Comment* to add a brief textual description to the block and its features.
5. Create a package *<system>_Interface Types* for the types of the ports. Create the appropriate SysML *InterfaceBlocks* for the proxy port types in this package, if not already defined somewhere else, for example, in a model library.
6. Model the logical hierarchy of the system breakdown structure by creating appropriate part properties in the blocks.
7. Create a SysML internal block diagram for the root element *<system> Logical Architecture* and populate it with the part properties. Repeat this step for each block that owns part properties.
8. Model the connections between the part properties and ports. A connector represents any kind of interaction.

If appropriate, apply one of the SYSMOD discipline specific stereotypes to the connector (see section 9.4).

9. Create a SYSMOD *«systemContext»* with name *<system> Logical Architecture Context.* The element is a specialization of the *<system> System Context* (see section 7.8) and owns a property that redefines the system property by setting the type to the *<system> Logical Architecture.*
10. Create a SysML internal block diagram for the *<system> Logical Architecture Context* to model connections from the system actor parts that are specific for the *<system> Logical Architecture.*

If a part type of the Logical Architecture is further detailed with its Requirements, architecture, etc., create a package for the part type with a package structure similar to the system package structure (see section 7.1).

Figure 7.47 depicts a template of the Logical Architecture definition. The part properties are defined by directed composition association relationships. They can also be defined directly as part properties of a block without the association. In that case, fewer model elements are required, but you cannot depict a tree structure in the block definition diagram.

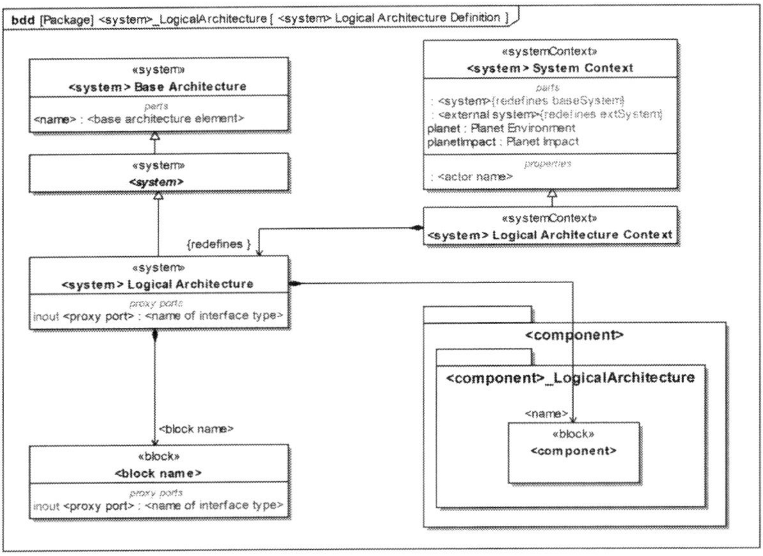

Figure 7.47: Model Template for the Logical Architecture Definition

Figure 7.48 depicts the internal structure of the Logical Architecture.

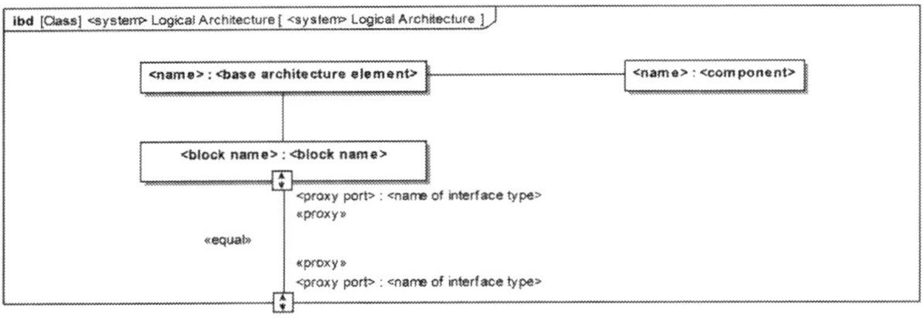

Figure 7.48: Model Template for the Logical Architecture

Figure 7.49 shows the Logical Architecture in the model package structure.

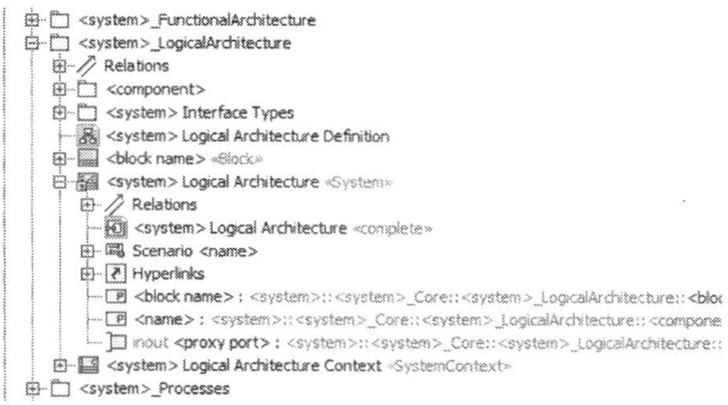

Figure 7.49: Logical Architecture in the model package structure

7.16 How to Model the Product Architecture

Context

SYSMOD Methods
    4.19 Model Product Architecture
SYSMOD Products
    4.20 Product Architecture
SYSMOD Roles
    6.5 System Architect
Examples
    8.16 Example Product Architecture

Document-based information

Figure 7.50 shows a template for a Product Architecture in a text document.

Product Architecture of <name of the system>	
<sketch of the product architecture>	
Brief description	
<brief description of the product architecture>	
Architecture decisions	
<list of architecture decisions>	
Elements of the Product Architecture	
Name	*Description*
<name of element>	<brief description> Interfaces: • <interface 1> • <interface 2>
...	...

Figure 7.50: Document Template for the Product Architecture

How to model

The modeling of the Product Architecture is similar to the Logical Architecture. If the Product Architecture should be strongly coupled with the Logical Architecture, the root element of the Product Architecture is a specialization of the Logical Architecture root element, as depicted in figure 7.51. See section 11.7 about the coupling of architectures.

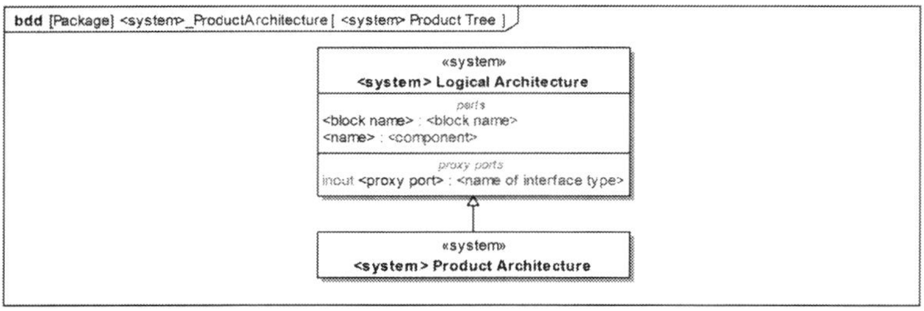

Figure 7.51: Model Template for the Product Architecture Definition

Note that it is not mandatory to strictly separate the concepts of the Logical Architecture and the Product Architecture in the system model. Only spend the effort if you benefit from the value. Suppose you do not separate the architectures in the model, model only one architecture, and call it Physical or Product Architecture.

7.17 How to Revise an Architecture with Scenarios

Context

SYSMOD Methods
  4.20 Revise an Architecture with Scenarios
SYSMOD Products
  5.18 Scenarios
SYSMOD Roles
  6.5 System Architect
Examples
  8.17 Example Scenarios

Document-based information

Figure 7.52 depicts a document template for a Scenario.

<name of the scenario>		
Defined by use case:	<name of system use case>	
Scenario steps		
From	*Message: Description*	*To*
<name of part>	<message with parameters>: <description>	<name of part>
...	...	...

Figure 7.52: Document Template for a scenario

How to model

1. Select the context element of the scenario. Typically, it is either the System Context or the root element of an architecture. However, it can be any block of the system.
2. Create a SysML *Interaction* and a SysML sequence diagram with the name of the scenario.
3. Model a SysML *Trace* relationship from the interaction model element to the Use Case Activity that specifies the behavior of the scenario.
4. Place the part and reference properties that are the interaction partners of the scenario as lifelines on the sequence diagram.
5. Model the messages between the lifelines based on a single path in the related Use Case Activity.

Figure 7.53 depicts a template for a Scenario in the model.

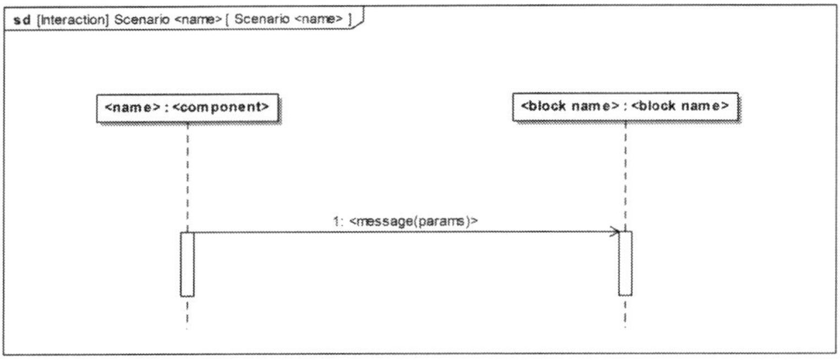

Figure 7.53: Model Template for a Scenario

Figure 7.54 depicts the model structure of a scenario.

Figure 7.54: Scenario in the model package structure

7.18 How to Model the System States

Context

SYSMOD Methods

4.21 Define System States SYSMOD Products

5.23 System States

SYSMOD Roles

6.5 System Architect

Examples

8.18 Example System States

Document-based information

Figure 7.51 depicts a document template for the System States.

<name of the state machine>		
Owner:	<name of the owning block>	
States and Transitions		
State	*Description*	
<name of state>	<description of the state>	
	Transition	*Target state*
	<trigger, guard, and effect of outgoing transition>	*<name of target state>*
...	...	
	Transition	*Target state*
	...	...

Figure 7.51: Document Template for a state machine

How to model

1. Select the context element (owner) of the state machine, for example, the root element of an architecture. However, it could be any block of the system.
2. Create a SysML *StateMachine* and a SysML state machine diagram with the name of the state machine.
3. Model the states and transitions as needed.

Figure 7.52 depicts a state machine template for the System States in the model. The transition between *<state 1>* and *<state 2>* is a template for a transition that is triggered by a System Use Case trigger and with the appropriate use case as an effect of the transition. The effect is an activity that calls the Use Case Activity. The effect can not be directly the Use Case Activity itself, because the transition must be the owner of the effect behavior.

<state 1> fullfills the precondition of the System Use Case. *<state 2>* is a postcondition of the System Use Case.

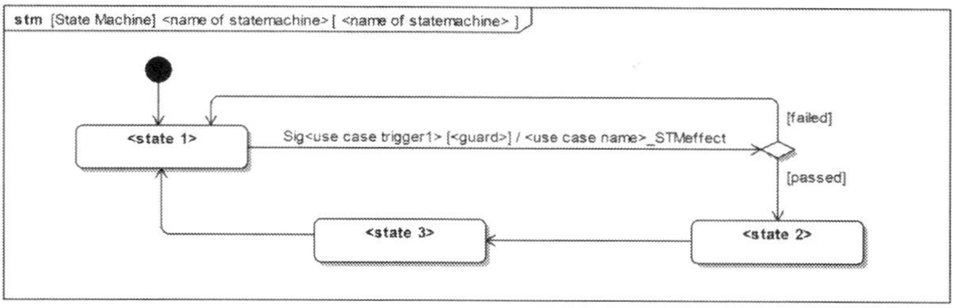

Figure 7.52: Model Template for a state machine

Figure 7.53 depicts the activity that is defined as the effect at a state machine transition, and is owned by the transition (see figure 7.54). The SysML specification requires that the transition model element owns the effect. Therefore, it cannot be the Use Case Activity itself. The effect activity includes a SysML CallBehaviorAction to call the Use Case Activity.

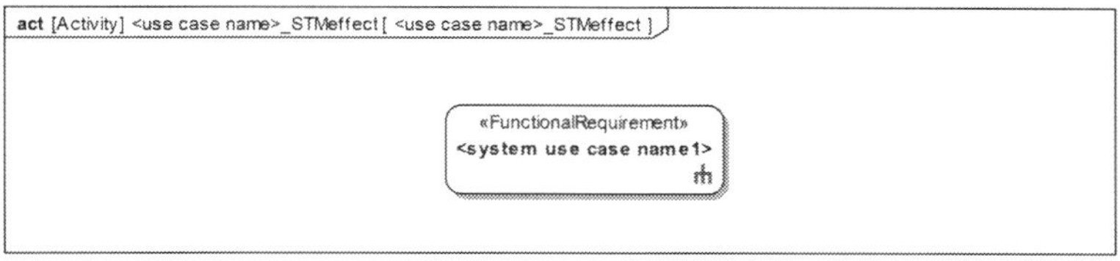

Figure 7.53: Model Template for an activity at a state machine transition

Figure 7.54 shows the state machine and its elements in the model package structure.

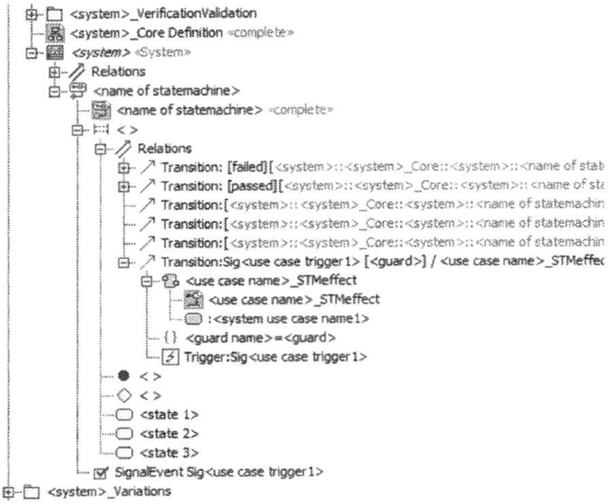

Figure 7.54: State machine in the model package structure

7.19 How to Model the Test Architecture

Context

SYSMOD Methods
    4.22 Model the Test Architecture
SYSMOD Products
    5.24 Test Architecture
SYSMOD Roles
    6.7 System Tester
Examples
    8.19 Example Test Architecture

Document-based information

Figure 7.55 shows a simple template for a Test Architecture in a text document.

Test Architecture of the FFDS	
<sketch of the test architecture>	
Brief description	
<brief description of the test architecture>	
Architecture decisions	
<list of architecture decisions>	
Elements of the Test Architecture	
Name	*Description*
<name of element>	<brief description> Interfaces: • <interface 1> • <interface 2>
...	...

Figure 7.55: Document Template for the Test Architecture

How to model

1. Select the package *<system>_TestArchitecture.*
2. Create a SysML block definition diagram with name *<system> Test Architecture Definition.*
3. Create an SYSMOD *«system»* with name *<system> Test Architecture.*
4. For each identified part type of the Test Architecture, create a SysML *Block* with appropriate properties, proxy ports (see also section 11.4), constraints, and operations. Use the documentation field or a linked SysML *Comment* to add a brief textual description to the block and its features.

5. Create a package *<system>_Interface Types* for the types of the ports. Create the appropriate SysML *Interface-Blocks* for the proxy port types in this package, if not already defined somewhere else, for example, in a model library.
6. Model the logical hierarchy of the test system breakdown structure by creating appropriate part properties in the blocks.
7. Create a SysML internal block diagram for the root element *<system> Test Architecture* and populate it with the part properties. Repeat this step for each block that owns part properties.
8. Model the connections between the part properties and ports. A connector represents any kind of interaction. If appropriate, apply one of the SYSMOD discipline specific stereotypes to the connector (see section 9.4).
9. Create a SYSMOD *«systemContext»* with name *<system> Test Architecture Context.*
10. Create a SysML internal block diagram for the *<system> Test Architecture Context* and model the connectors to the actors.

Figure 7.56 shows the definition of the test architecture element, including the test context.

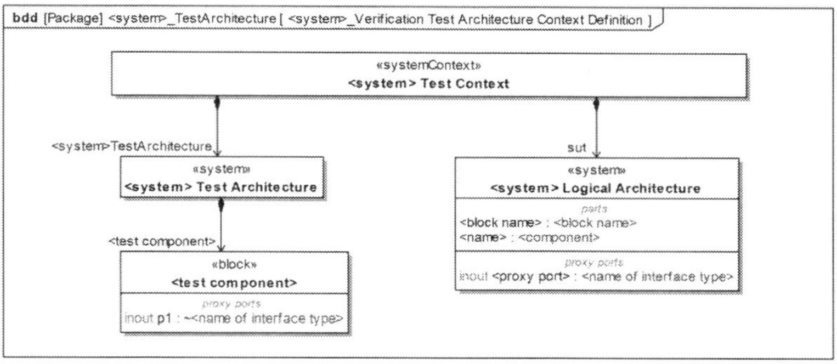

Figure 7.56: Model Template for the Test Architecture Definition

Figure 7.57 depicts the internal structure of the Test Architecture.

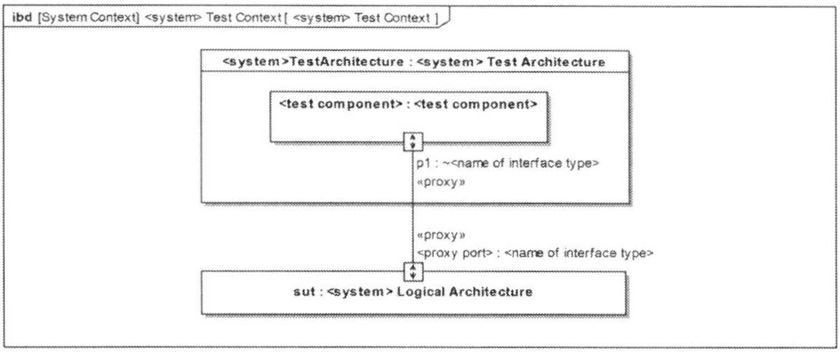

Figure 7.57: Model Template for the Test Architecture

Figure 7.58 shows the Test Architecture in the model package structure.

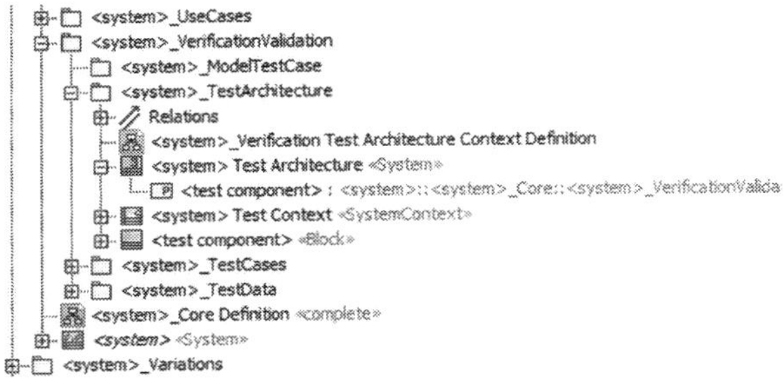

Figure 7.58: Test Architecture in the model package structure

8. SYSMOD Examples

The SYSMOD Examples in this chapter were created with a SysML modeling tool. I used the *Cameo Systems Modeler* from *Dassault*[1]. This is not a general tool recommendation. The best modeling tool depends on your specific requirements. I selected the Cameo System Modeler because it mostly conform to the SysML standard.

All examples are about the same system. It is a fictional example of a forest fire detection system (FFDS). The FFDS is a multifaceted system, sophisticated enough for a valuable demonstration, and easy to understand without specific domain knowledge (at least on the level of detail I cover it in this book). I must admit that I am not an expert in forest fire detection systems. So, please be patient if something seems to be weird. And of course, the examples are incomplete and do not cover a complete specification of a FFDS.

This is a book and not a model. The examples can only cover some aspects of the model. Their purpose is to get a better understanding of the SYSMOD Methods, Products, and the Guidances.

The example model uses the FAS plugin. You can download the latest version of the FAS plugin from the Sourceforge project site[2], and you find more information about FAS (Functional Architectures for Systems) in section 11.2.

---

[1]www.nomagic.com
[2]sourceforge.net/projects/fas4md/.

The model of the sample system is part of the SYSMOD plugin for the Cameo Systems modeler and can be downloaded from www.mbse4u.com.

The SYSMOD Examples provide a document and a model representation of the SYSMOD Products as presented in the chapter SYSMOD Modeling Guidances.

The following list summarises the SYSMOD Examples in a logical order according to the SYSMOD Processes:

- 8.1 Example Model Package Structure
- 8.2 Example Problem Statement
- 8.3 Example System Idea
- 8.4 Example System Objectives
- 8.5 Example Stakeholders
- 8.6 Example Base Architecture
- 8.7 Example Risks
- 8.8 Example Requirements
- 8.9 Example System Context
- 8.10 Example Use Cases
- 8.11 Example System Processes
- 8.12 Example Use Case Activities
- 8.13 Example Domain Knowledge
- 8.14 Example Test Cases
- 8.15 Example Logical Architecture
- 8.16 Example Product Architecture
- 8.17 Example Scenarios
- 8.18 Example System States
- 8.19 Example Test Architecture

8.1 Example Model Package Structure

Context

SYSMOD Methods

4.2 Set up and maintain the SME

SYSMOD Products

5.2 System Modeling Environment (SME)

SYSMOD Roles

6.1 SME Administrator

Modeling Guidance

7.1 How to Set up an initial Package Structure

Document

Typically, there is no information about the model structure in a document.

Model

The model structure of the FFDS closely follows the template given in
section 7.1. Figure 8.1 depicts the top-level packages of the FFDS model. It is not a SysML package diagram but a screen-shot of the containment tree of the modeling tool. Therefore, it contains some non-SysML graphical elements.

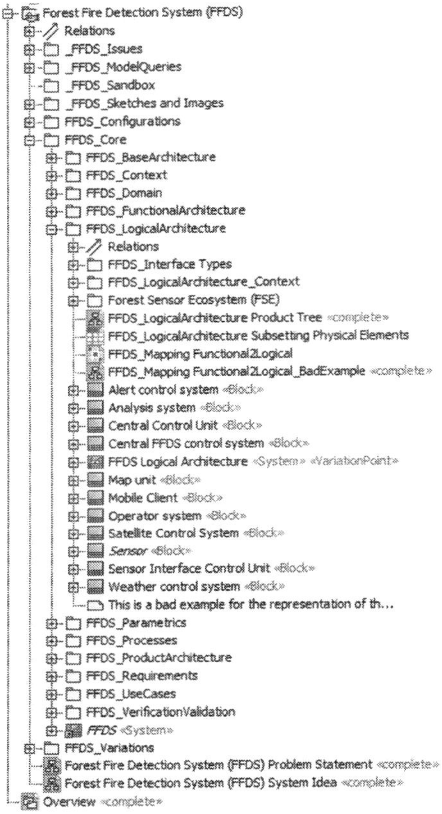

Figure 8.1: Model Structure

8.2 Example Problem Statement

Context

SYSMOD Methods

4.5 Analyze the Problem

SYSMOD Products

5.4 Problem Statement

SYSMOD Roles

6.3 Project Manager

Modeling Guidance

7.2 How to Analyze the Problem

Document

Figure 8.2 shows an extract of a document that covers the Problem Statement.

System	Forest Fire Detection System (FFDS)
Problem Statement	
How can we provide a forest fire detection system for forest authorities that can be scaled to any forest size, is affordable, highly reliable and accurate in detecting forest fires.	

Figure 8.2: Problem Statement in a text document

Model

Figure 8.3 depicts the abstract system element with the Problem Statement shown in a separate compartment.

The system element is located in the package *FFDS_Core* as depicted in the header of the diagram. Here, it is tightly coupled with the Base Architecture by using the generalization relationship. If the Base Architecture also has a Problem Statement, it is not inherited by the system element. The *problemStatement* is a property of the stereotype *«system»*, and the generalization relationship does not cover stereotypes and stereotype properties.

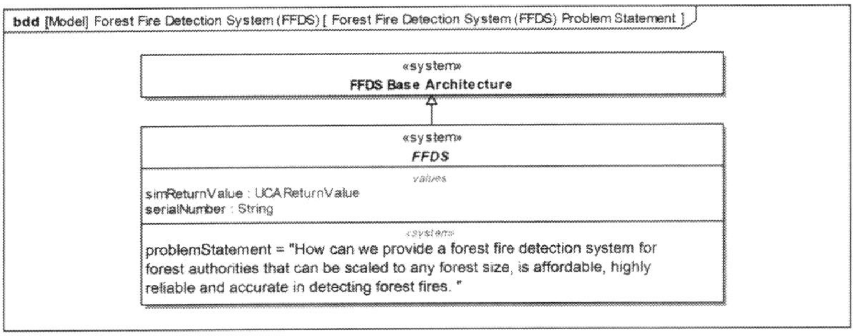

Figure 8.3: Problem Statement in the model

8.3 Example System Idea

Context

SYSMOD Methods
    4.6 Describe the System Idea and the System Objectives
SYSMOD Products
    5.5 System Idea
SYSMOD Roles
    6.3 Project Manager
Modeling Guidance
    7.3 How to describe the System Idea

Document

Figure 8.4 shows an extract of a document that covers the System Idea. It is a free text that describes the notion and main features of the system.

System	Forest Fire Detection System (FFDS)

System Idea

The FFDS is a satellite-based system to detect forest fires in very large areas. The system is also equipped with stationary sensors and animal sensors. Using different sources for the fire detection increases the reliability of the system and enables different system configurations for different environmental contexts and price segments.

Main features of the FFDS are

- Detecting and reporting forest fires on time
- Monitoring forest and fires
- Uses the behavior of forest animals to detect fires

Figure 8.4: System Idea in a text document

Model

Figure 8.5 depicts the abstract system element with the System Idea shown in a separate compartment.

The modeling is similar to the modeling of the Problem Statement described in the previous section 8.2.

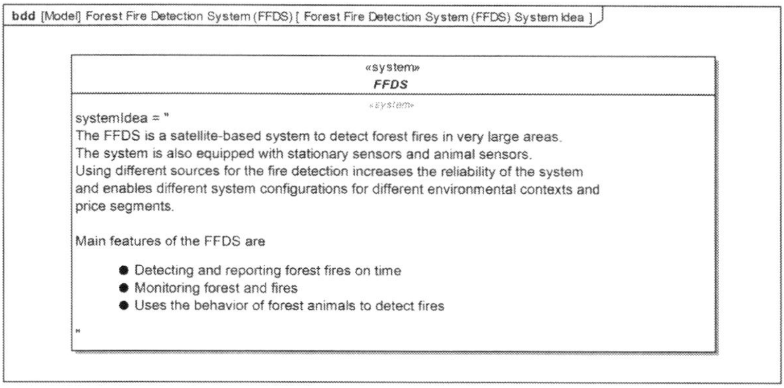

Figure 8.5: System Idea in the model

8.4 Example System Objectives

Context

SYSMOD Methods
4.6 Describe the System Idea and the System Objectives
SYSMOD Products
5.6 System Objectives
SYSMOD Roles
6.3 Project Manager
Modeling Guidance
7.4 How to describe the System Objectives

Document

Figure 8.6 shows a table in a document that lists the System Objectives. The columns are the properties and related elements of a System Objective: ID, stakeholder, name, and description.

The System Objectives are derived from the Problem Statement.

System Objectives			
#ID	*Stakeholder*	*Name*	*Description*
OBJ-S1	CEO FFDS Vendor	Reliable detection	Any forest fire is detected by the system on time to start effective counteractions.
OBJ-S2	CEO FFDS Vendor	Affordability	The system is affordable for any forest authority.
OBJ-B1	CEO FFDS Vendor	Market Leader	The system will make the vendor the market leader for forest fire detection systems.

Figure 8.6: System Objectives in a text document

Model

Figure 8.7 depicts the System Objectives in a requirements diagram.

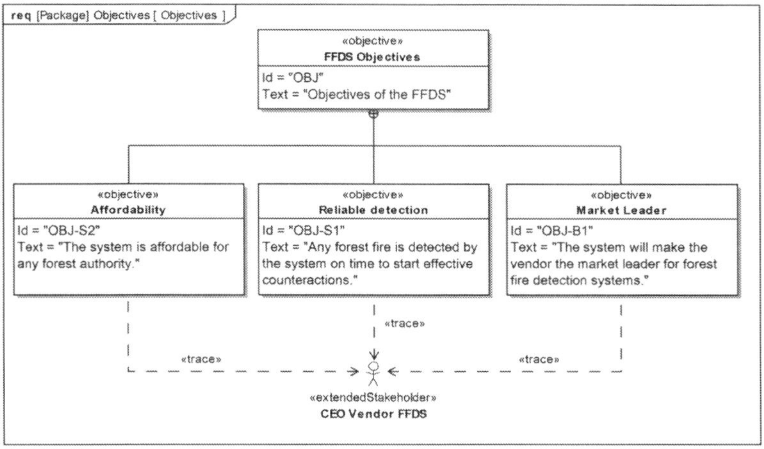

Figure 8.7: System Objectives in the model - Diagram

The properties of the objectives are shown in a compartment. The relationship to the Stakeholder is a SysML *Trace* relationship.

Figure 8.8 shows the same information in a table. Typically, the table view is more convenient to depict the System Objectives than the diagram view.

#	Id	Name	Text	Stakeholder
1	OBJ	FFDS Objectives	Objectives of the FFDS	
2	OBJ-B1	Market Leader	The system will make the vendor the market leader for forest fire detection systems.	CEO Vendor FFDS
3	OBJ-S1	Reliable detection	Any forest fire is detected by the system on time to start effective counteractions.	CEO Vendor FFDS
4	OBJ-S2	Affordability	The system is affordable for any forest authority.	CEO Vendor FFDS

Figure 8.8: System Objectives in the model - Table

Figure 8.9 depicts the location of the System Objectives in the model package structure.

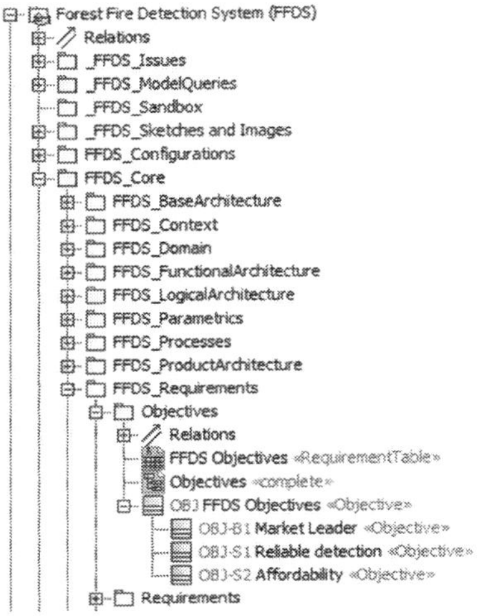

Figure 8.9: System Objectives in the model package structure

8.5 Example Stakeholders

Context

SYSMOD Methods

4.8 Identify Stakeholders

SYSMOD Products

5.8 Stakeholders

SYSMOD Roles

6.4 Requirements Engineer

Modeling Guidance

7.6 How to model Stakeholders

Document

Figure 8.10 shows a table in a document that lists some of the Stakeholders of the system. The columns are the properties of a Stakeholder: name, category, effort, priority, concern, and contact information.

Stakeholder					
Name	Categories	Effort	Priority	Concern	Contact
CEO Vendor FFDS	Requirement owner	Low	Critical	The CEO wants to build the best FFDS of the world to be the market leader for FFDS.	Phone ...
Forest Authority Expert	Expert	Medium	Critical	The expert has the domain knowledge about forest fires.	Email ...
Fire Department Expert	Expert	Medium	Critical	The expert has the domain knowledge about how to fight forest fires.	Email ...

Figure 8.10: Stakeholders in the document

Model

Figure 8.11 depicts a table view of modeled Stakeholders. Typically, this is the preferred view.

#	Name	Categories	Documentation	Concern	Priority	Effort	Contact
1	Administrator	User	Worker of the IT department who administrates the FFDS software	The Administrator needs	Medium	Low	Email ..., Office ...
2	CEO Vendor FFDS	Requirement owner	The CEO of the company that develops the FFDS.	The CEO wants to build t	Critical	Low	Phone ...
3	Fire Department Expert	Expert	A expert from a fire department who is familiar with fighting forest fires.	The expert has the dom	Critical	Medium	Email ...
4	Forest Authority Expert	Expert	An expert from the forest authority who is familiar with managing forest fires.	The expert has the dom	High	Medium	Email ...
5	Maintenance	User	Technician of the service department of the operator of the FFDS.	The Maintenance wants	Medium	Low	Email ..., Office ...
6	Operator	User	User of the FFDS in the monitoring and central center.	The Operator is the mair	Critical	Low	Email ..., Office ...

Figure 8.11: Stakeholder in the model - Table

However, you can also depict Stakeholders in a diagram. Figure 8.12 shows a notation with compartments and an alternative notation with an icon. The diagram kind is a SysML requirements diagram.

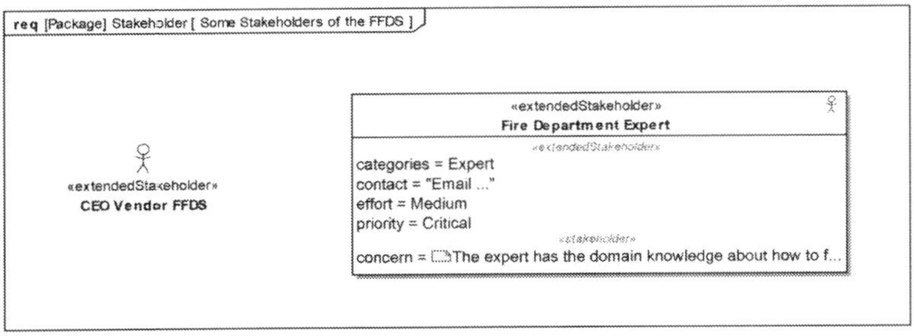

Figure 8.12: Stakeholder in the model - Diagram

The property *concern* has its own headline in the rectangle notation. It is part of the SysML model element *Stakeholder* while the other properties are part of the SYSMOD stereotype *«extendedStakeholder»*. The *concern* is a SysML *Comment* element.

Figure 8.13 depicts the Stakeholders in the model package structure. The Stakeholders in the category *user* are also actors of the system and located below the context package.

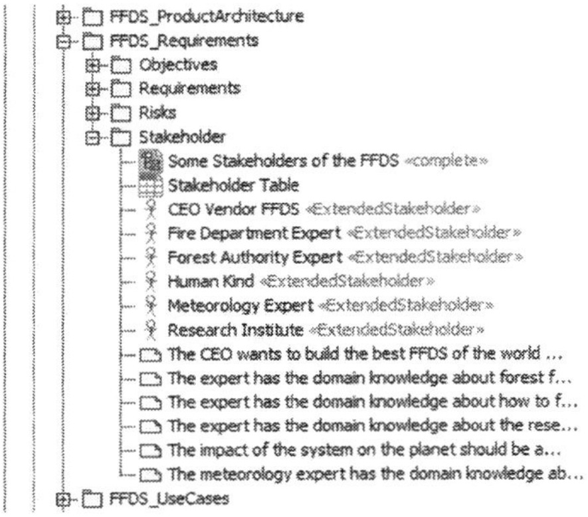

Figure 8.13: Stakeholder in the model package structure

8.6 Example Base Architecture

Context

SYSMOD Methods
    4.7 Describe Base Architecture
SYSMOD Products
    5.7 Base Architecture
SYSMOD Roles
    6.5 System Architect
Modeling Guidance
    7.5 How to describe the Base Architecture

Document

You need a graphical visualization for the Base Architecture in addition to the short descriptions of the architectural elements and concepts. Sometimes, I call the Base Architecture also the beermat or napkin architecture, because at least you need a sketch of the architecture that fits on a beermat or napkin (figure 8.14).

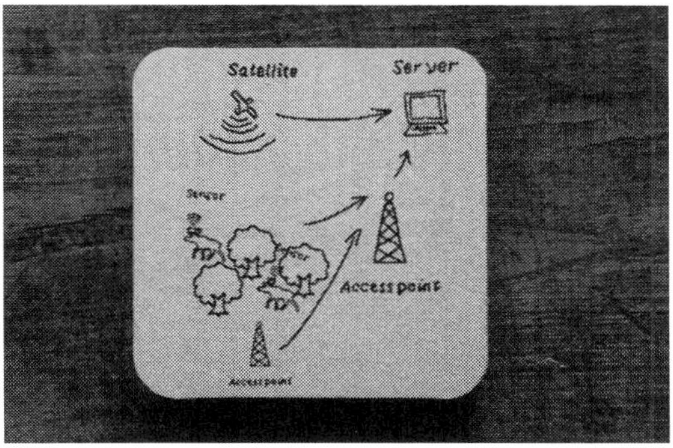

Figure 8.14: FFDS Base Architecture on a beermat

Additionally, a short description of the architecture in general and of each element should be given (figure 8.15).

Base Architecture of the FFDS

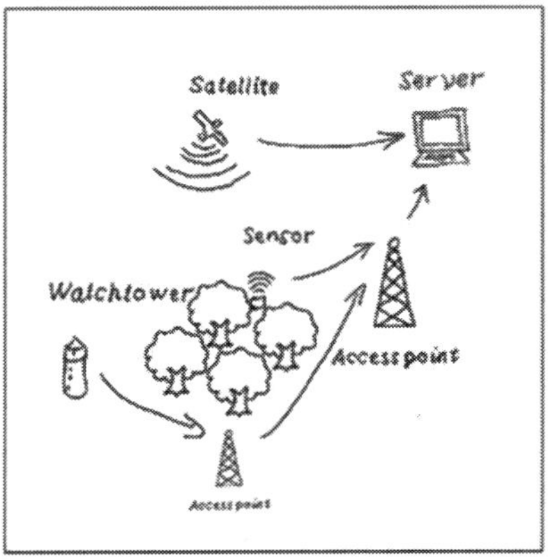

Brief description

The FFDS will have satellite observations, human-based and camera-based watchtowers, and local sensors. Everything will be controlled by a single central server.

Architecture decisions

- The satellite is an external system.
- The sensor and watchtower network is based on WiMAX.

Elements of the Base Architecture

Name	*Description*
Access point	Node of the network of sensors and watchtowers to be connected with the server.
Satellite	Forest fire observation from the orbit.
Sensor	Local sensor in the area of interest, for instance heat or smoke sensors.
Server	Central FFDS server that collect all the data.
Watchtower	Human-based and camera-based observation from a tower installed in the area of interest.
Animal	Forrest animal as a carrier for sensors
Animal Sensor	Special sensor attached at a animal in the forest.

Figure 8.15: FFDS Base Architecture in the Document

The architecture decisions that are not depicted in the architecture block diagram or sketch are also listed in the architecture description. And of course, feel free to add any further information needed to document your Base Architecture.

Model

The SysML block definition diagram in figure 8.16 shows the definition of the elements of the Base Architecture, including context elements.

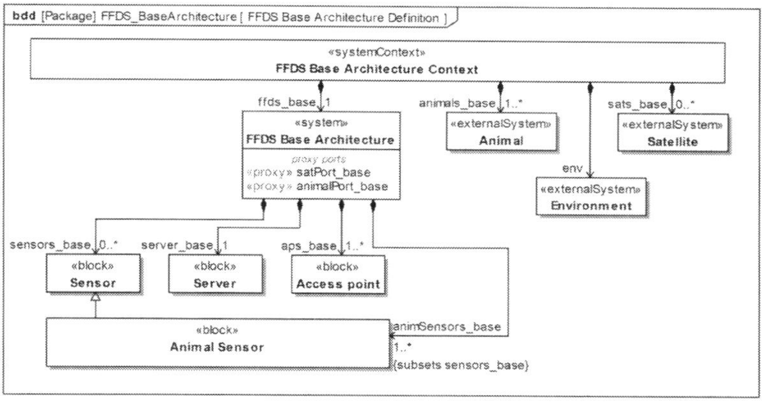

Figure 8.16: Example of the FFDS Base Architecture - Definiton

The internal block diagram in figure 8.17 shows the elements and the connections of the Base Architecture and the context.

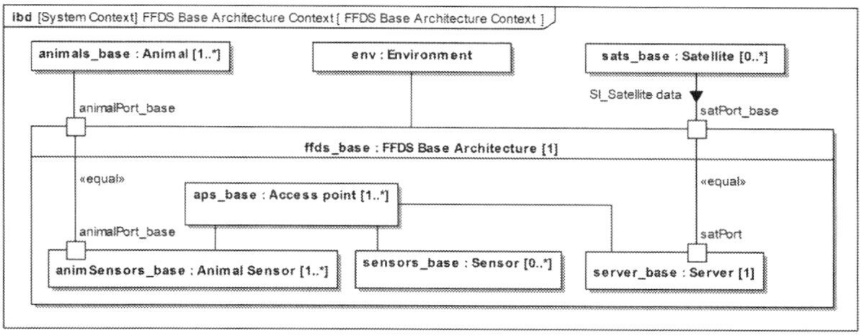

Figure 8.17: Example of the FFDS Base Architecture - Structure

Figure 8.18 depicts the Base Architecture in the model package structure.

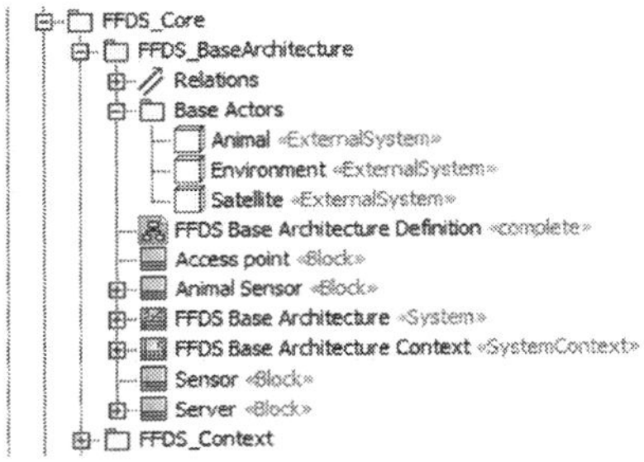

Figure 8.18: Stakeholder in the model package structure

8.7 Example Risks

Context

SYSMOD Methods
    4.9 Model Risks
SYSMOD Products
    5.9 Risks
SYSMOD Roles
    6.4 Requirements Engineer
Modeling Guidance
    7.7 How to Model Risks

Document

Figure 8.19 shows one Risk in a text document. Each Risk is depicted in a single table.

Risk #2	Late Detection	technical
Text	The fire is detected too late	
Severity	4	
Occurrence	2	
Stability	Stable	

Figure 8.19: FFDS Risk in a document

Model

Figure 8.20 shows a table view of Risks in the model.

#	Name	Text	Severity	Occurrence	Kind
1	Late Detection	The fire is detected too late.	4	2	technical
2	No Detection	The fire - in particular a small fire - is not detected.	3	2	technical
3	Data Loss	The data got lost.	2	2	technical
4	Market	The FFDS does not fit the target market.	3	3	cost

Figure 8.20: Example of FFDS Risks

Figure 8.21 depicts Risks in the model package structure.

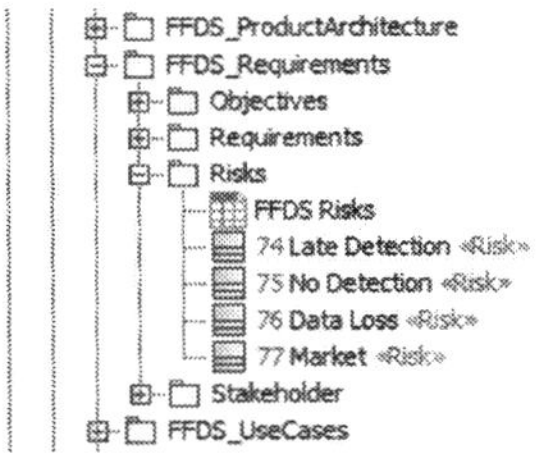

Figure 8.21: FFDS Risks in the model package structure

8.8 Example Requirements

Context

SYSMOD Methods

4.10 Model Requirements

SYSMOD Products

5.10 Requirements

SYSMOD Roles

6.4 Requirements Engineer

Modeling Guidance

7.8 How to Model Requirements

Document

Figure 8.22 and Figure 8.23 show Requirements in a text document. Each Requirement is depicted in a single table.

2	Fire Detection	functional
Text	The system must detect a small forest fire.	
Motivation	This is the main function of the system.	
Stakeholder	CEO FFDS Vendor	
Stability	Stable	
Obligation	Mandatory	
Priority	Critical	
Risks	• The fire is detected too late. • Small fires are not detected.	
Details	See use case analysis.	

Figure 8.22: FFDS Functional Requirement in a document

29	Operator User Interface	usability
Text	The user interface for the operator must be similar to the user interface of Android, iOS, or Windows operating systems.	
Motivation	Well knows user interfaces reduces the effort for the initial training.	
Stakeholder	CEO FFDS Vendor	
Stability	Stable	
Obligation	Optional	
Priority	Medium	
Risks	-	
Details	-	

Figure 8.23: FFDS Usability Requirement in a document

Model

Typically, it does not make sense to depict the SysML requirements in a diagram. It is easier to read them in a table, and it is easier to see the relationships in a matrix. The topology of a requirements diagram does not carry much information.

Figure 8.24 and figure 8.25[3] depict the Requirements in a requirements table view. Since there are many properties of a Requirement, it makes sense to provide different table views to reduce the number of columns of each table.

The tables also include the functional requirements that are modeled by Use Case Activities and performance requirements modeled by constraint blocks (*Alert Fire Timing*).

#	Id	Name	Text
1	2	Fire Detection	The system shall detect a small forest fire.
2	3	Size of fire	A small forest fire has a perimeter of at least 50 sqm.
3	10	Data Reporting	The system shall report the collected data in near real-time.
4	11	Continuous service	The system shall be available 24/7.
5	12	False Alarms	The probability of false alarms must be lower 5 %.
6	13	Geolocation	The system shall locate fires with an accuracy of 100m.
7	14	Data Collection	The system shall store the collected data older than 3 years on an archive system separated from the high-available data.
8	14.1	High-availability data colection	The system shall store the collected data not older than 3 years on a high-available medium.
9	14.2	Archived data	The system shall store the collected data.
10	15	Data History	The system shall have the capability to store the collected data for at least 5 years.
11	17	Forest Monitoring	The system shall continuously monitor the condition of the region of interest.
12	18	Fire Monitoring	The system shall continuously monitor the condition of a fire.
13	29	Operator User Interface	The user interface for the operator shall be similar to the user interface of Android, iOS, or Windows operating systems.
14	31	Alert Fire Timing	The system shall report a verified fire within 5 seconds.
15	38	Size of forest	The system shall be scalable for forest up to the size of 500 million hectare.
16	41	FFDS Market	The system shall be used worldwide.
17	42	Alert Fire Timing	The system shall report a verified fire within 5 seconds.
18	58	Ping a sensor	The system shall provide the capability to select and contact a sensor to check if it is alive.
19	59	Configure fire department connection	The system shall provide the capability to set up and configure a network connection from the FFDS to a fire department syster
20	60	Configure meteorology server connection	The system shall provide the capability to set up and configure a network connection from the FFDS to a meteorology system.
21	61	Configure satellite connection	The system shall provide the capability to set up and configure the connection from the FFDS to a satellite network.
22	62	Create user account	The system shall provide the capability to create user accounts for the human users of the FFDS.
23	63	Delete user account	The system shall provide the capability to delete an existing user account of the FFDS.
24	64	Detect and report fire	The system shall provide an observation loop and report any potential occurences of fire to the operator and fire department.
25	65	Install a sensor	The system shall provide the capability to install additional sensors.
26	66	Remove a sensor	The system shall provide the capability to remove installed sensors from the FFDS.
27	67	Run observation test	The system shall provide the capability to run a test of the observation loop to test components with simulated forest fires.
28	68	Start the system	The system shall provide a start function for the operator.
29	69	Stop the system	The system shall provide a stop function for the operator .
30	70	Switch to Maintenance mode	The system shall provide a maintenance mode.
31	71	Switch to Test mode	The system shall provide a test model.
32	72	Update user account	The system shall provide the capability to update user accounts.

Figure 8.24: FFDS System Requirements in the model (ID, name, text)

The table in figure 8.25 also lists the Risks that are linked to

[3]: A larger version of the diagram is available at www.mbse4u.com/sysmod-figures.

the Requirements.

#	Id	Name	Motivation	Obligation	Priority	Risks	Stability
1	2	Fire Detection	This is the main function of the system.	Mandatory	Critical	The fire - in particular a small fire - is not detected. The fire is detected too late.	Stable
2	3	Size of fire	The system shall detect fires as small as possible to be able to initiate reactive actions to cope the fire	Mandatory	Critical		Instable
3	10	Data Reporting	In particular during grave situations it is important to work with live data.	Mandatory	High		Stable
4	11	Continuous service	A forest fire could occur anytime.	Mandatory	Critical		Stable
5	12	False Alarms	A forest fire alarm triggers a lot of expensive actions.	Mandatory	High		Stable
6	13	Geolocation	The fire must be located to be easily found be air or ground troops.	Mandatory	Critical		Stable
7	14	Data Collection	The data should be used for further analysis.	Mandatory	High	The data got lost.	Stable
8	15	Data History	The system should provide historical data for research and legal purposes.	Mandatory	High		Stable
9	17	Forest Monitoring	In case of a forest fire or any other relevant condition it must be possible to monitor a specific region of interest.	Mandatory	High		Stable
10	18	Fire Monitoring	A detected fire must be monitored continuously to observe its development.	Mandatory	High		Stable
11	29	Operator User Interface	Well knows user interfaces reduces the effort for the initial training.	Optional	Medium		Stable
12	31	Alert Fire Timing	Every second counts when fighting a forest fire.	Mandatory	High		Stable
13	38	Size of forest	The system must be usable for different forest sizes in order to be of interest to as many customers as possible.	Mandatory	Medium	The FFDS does not fit the target market	Instable
14	14.1	High-availability data collection	The data shall be available for further analysis without delays.	Mandatory	High	The data got lost.	Stable
15	14.2	Archived data	The data shall be accessible for further analysis.	Mandatory	High	The data got lost.	Stable
16	41	FFDS Market	The system must be of interest to as many customers as possible.	Mandatory	High	The FFDS does not fit the target market	Stable
17	42	Alert Fire Timing	A late detection is not acceptable.	Mandatory	Critical	The fire is detected too late.	Stable
18	58	Ping a sensor	It is helpful for testing to know if a sensor is alive and avoide on-site checks	Mandatory	Medium		Stable
19	59	Configure fire department connection	The connection settings can change	Mandatory	High		Stable
20	60	Configure meteorology server connection	The connection settings can change.	Mandatory	High		Stable
21	61	Configure satellite connection	The connection settings can change.	Mandatory	High		Stable
22	62	Create user account	The users of the FFDS need their own password-protected account for personalized settings and to enable logging of user actions.	Mandatory	High		Stable
23	63	Delete user account	It must be possible to prevent access to the system, for example, if a user left the organization.	Mandatory	Medium		Stable
24	64	Detect and report fire	Derived from other requirements	Mandatory	Critical		Stable
25	65	Install a sensor	It must be possible to change the sensor configuration.	Mandatory	High		Stable
26	66	Remove a sensor	It must be possible to change the sensor configuration.	Mandatory	High		Stable
27	67	Run observation test	The observation capabilities are critical for the system and must be tested regularly.	Mandatory	Medium		Instable
28	68	Start the system	The operator must be able to start the system.	Mandatory	High		Stable
29	69	Stop the system	The operator must be able to stop the system.	Mandatory	High		Stable
30	70	Switch to Maintenance mode	The special maintenance mode prevents side-effects when maintaining the system.	Mandatory	Medium		Stable
31	71	Switch to Test mode	The test mode prevents side-effects when testing the system.	Mandatory	Medium		Stable
32	72	Update user account	User-specific settings may change.	Mandatory	Low		Stable

Figure 8.25: FFDS System Requirements in the model (additional properties)

As mentioned above, another useful model element to model a requirement is the constraint block. Figure 8.26 shows the performance constraint requirement (section 9.6) *Alert Fire Timing* in a parametric diagram. The following figure 8.27 depicts the definition of the appropriate elements in a block definition diagram.

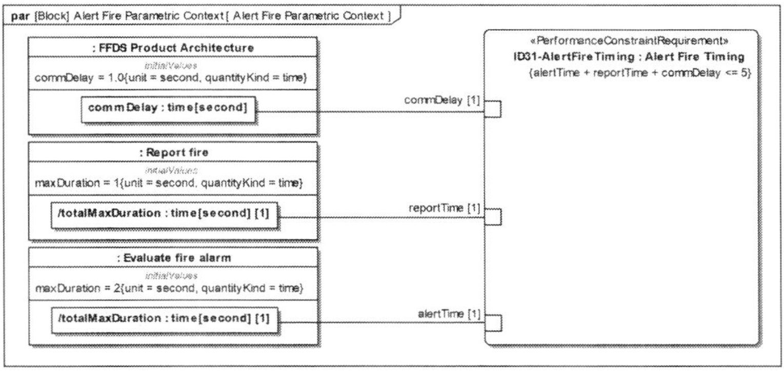

Figure 8.26: Example Performance Constraint Requirement in a Parametric Diagram

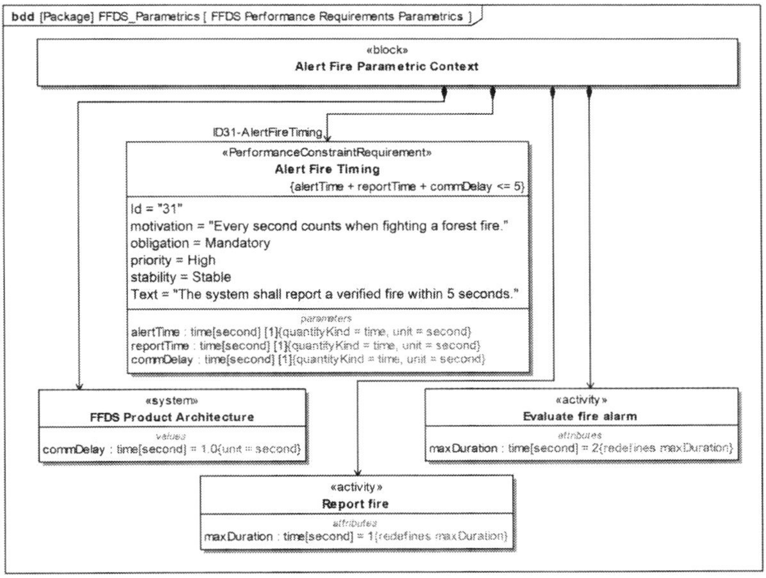

Figure 8.27: Definition of a Performance Constraint Requirement by a Constraint Block

Figure 8.28 depicts Requirements in the model package structure.

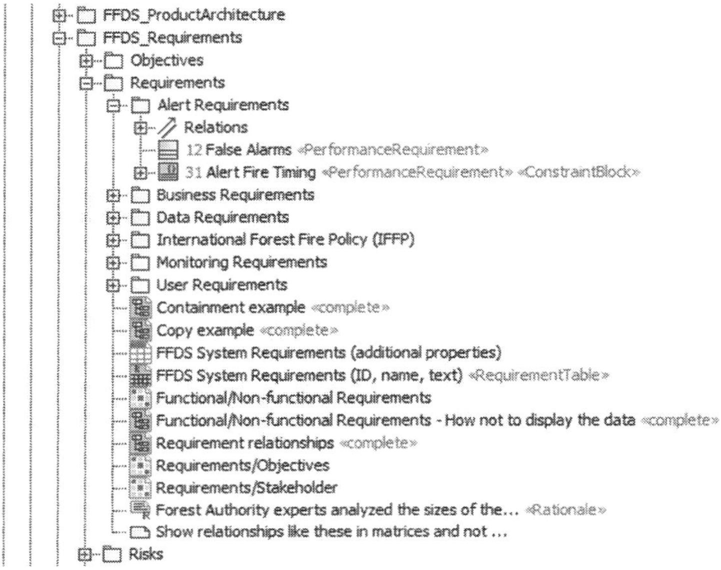

Figure 8.28: FFDS Requirements in the model package structure

8.9 Example System Context

Context

SYSMOD Methods
  4.11 Identify the System Context
SYSMOD Products
  5.11 System Context
SYSMOD Roles
  6.4 Requirements Engineer
Modeling Guidance
  7.8 How to Model System Context

Document

Figure 8.29 depicts a list of some system actors in a text document. The described item flows from and to the system are not intended to be a complete list. The item flows support only the understanding of the system context, whereas the list of system actors must be complete. Every missing actor can lead to serious problems during integration or system operation.

System Context – Actors of the System				
Type	*Name*	*Description*	*Item flows to the system*	*Item flows from the system*
human	Maintenance	Technician of the service department of the operator of the FFDS.	see use cases	
human	Operator	User of the FFDS in the monitoring and central center.	see use cases	
human	Administrator	Worker of the IT department who administrates the FFDS software	see use cases	
external system	Satellite	Inherited from base architecture	satellite images	
external system	Meteorology data system	Provides meterology data for the region of interest.	SI_Weather_data	
external system	Research analysis system	Requests FFDS data for research work.		
external system	Fire department	Alert system of the fire department responsible for the region of interest.		SI_Fire_Alert
environmental effect	Fire	The fire to be captured by the FFDS. Local sensors could be affected by the fire.	SI_Fire	
environmental effect	Climate	Represents climate conditions like temperature, humidity, and atmospheric pressure.		
environmental impact	Planet Environment	Represents the environment that is relevant to sustainability and influenced by the system.		Planet Impact

Figure 8.29: FFDS list of system actors in a document

Model

Figure 8.30 shows a system context diagram. It is a SysML internal block diagram. The satellite, the animals, and the environment actors are inherited from the Base Architecture context as depicted by the ^ symbol. The System Context element is tightly coupled with the Base Architecture context by a generalization relationship.

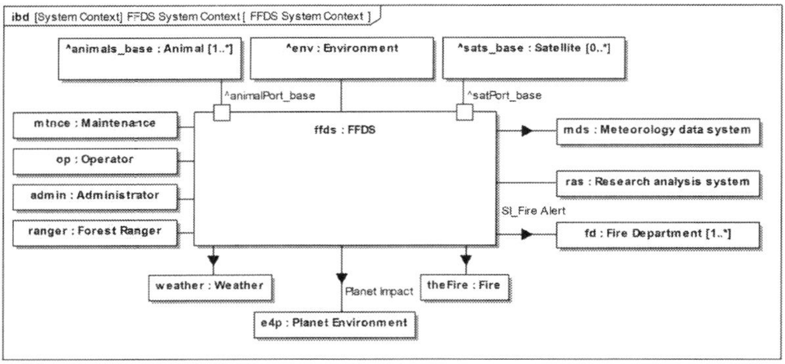

Figure 8.30: FFDS system context

Figure 8.31 depicts the definition of the System Context in a SysML block definition diagram, including the generalization relationship from the System Context to the system context element of the Base Architecture.

The item flow types like *SI_Fire_Alert* are domain blocks and defined in the Domain Knowledge model.

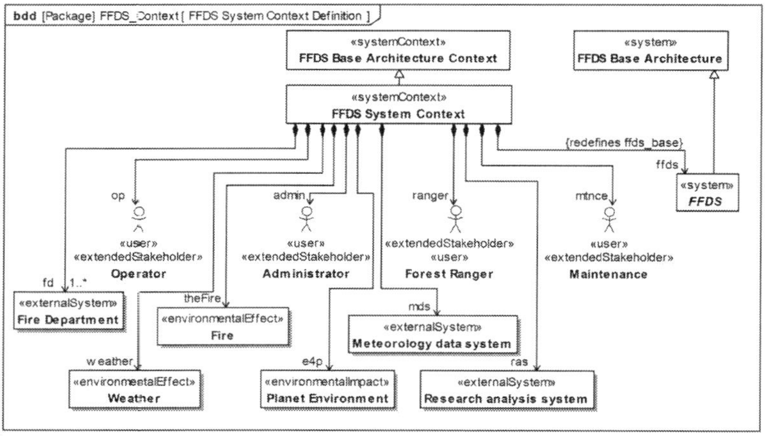

Figure 8.31: FFDS system context definition

Figure 8.32 shows the System Context elements in the model package structure.

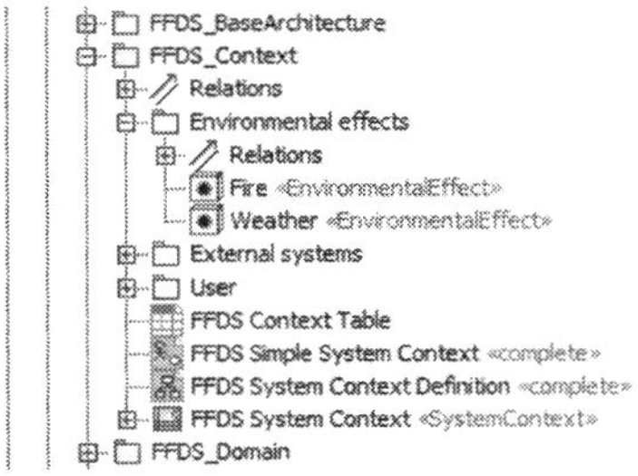

Figure 8.32: FFDS system context in the model package structure

8.10 Example System Use Cases

Context

SYSMOD Methods
    4.12 Identify System Use Cases
SYSMOD Products
    5.12 System Use Cases
SYSMOD Roles
    6.4 Requirements Engineer
Modeling Guidance
    7.10 How to Model System Use Cases

Document

Figure 8.33 depicts a System Use Case description in a document.

Detect and report fire	continuous
Description	Continuously observe the region of interest and check for indications of a forest fire. Report the potential fire to the operator and to the responsible fire departments.
Actorsr	Operator, Fire, Fire Department
Trigger	Operator activates observation mode.
Continuous Result	Potential forest fires are reported.
Precondition	FFDS is in ready mode.
Postcondition	None

Figure 8.33: A FFDS system use case in a document

Model

Figure 8.34 depicts System Use Cases of the actor *Operator* in a SysML use case diagram.

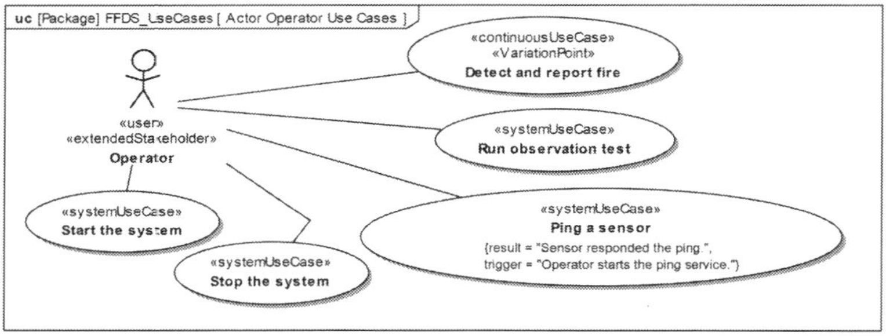

Figure 8.34: Actor Operator Use Cases

Figure 8.35 highlights the operator Use Case *Detect and report fire*. The comment symbol shows the properties of the Use Case. The diagram also shows the refine relationships from the Use Case to some functional requirements. The Use Case Activity owned by the Use Case is also a functional requirement derived from these high-level functional Requirements. Since the information represented by the refine relationships between the Use Case and the Requirements is redundant, the relationships could be skipped. They are only shortcuts and illustrate the relationships on the use case level.

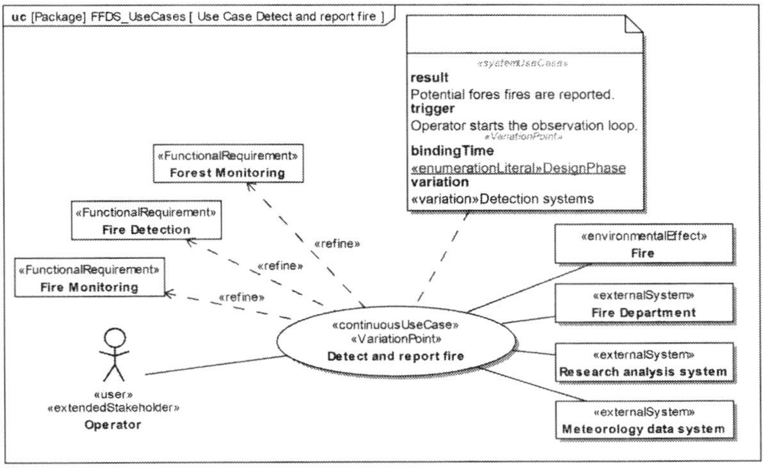

Figure 8.35: Use Case Detect and report fire

Figure 8.36 depicts some System Use Cases of the actor *Maintenance*, who is a specialization of the actor *Operator*. That means the actor can perform the same use cases. However, it does not necessarily mean that the actor *Maintenance* has the same access rights. This is a different aspect of the system.

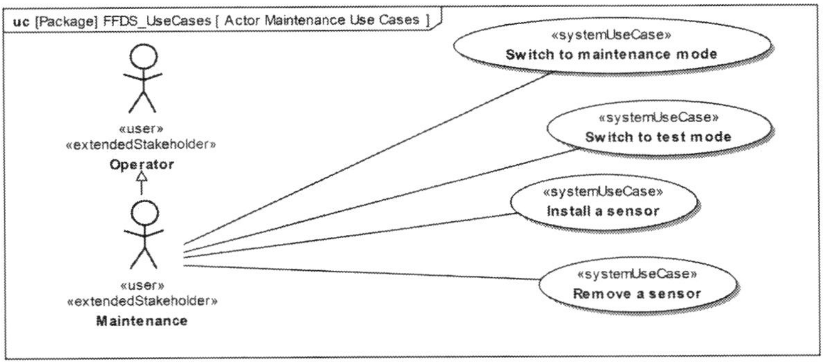

Figure 8.36: Actor Maintenance Use Cases

Figure 8.37 depicts the System Use Cases in the system model package structure.

Figure 8.37: FFDS System Use Cases in the model package structure

8.11 Example System Processes

Context

SYSMOD Methods
4.13 Identify System Processes
SYSMOD Products
5.13 System Processes
SYSMOD Roles
6.4 Requirements Engineer
Modeling Guidance
7.11 How to Model System Processes

Document

Figure 8.38 shows a System Process description in a text document. The System Process *System startup* describes the set of System Use Cases that must be performed in a specified order to switch the system from the *Off* mode to the *Operate* mode.

System Process: System startup	
Description	The startup of the system includes the technical startup of the system components, a test to verify the health status of the system, and finally the start of the forest fire detection loop.
Actors	Maintenance
Included system use cases:	1. Start the system 2. Run observation test 3. Detect and report fire
Behavior	Execute the included System Use Cases in the order as given above.

Figure 8.38: FFDS System Process in a document

Model

Figure 8.39 depicts the definition of the System Process *System startup* in a SysML use case diagram.

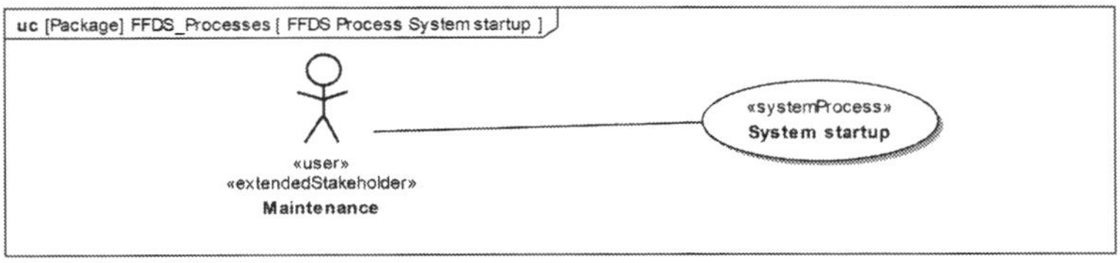

Figure 8.39: FFDS System Process *System startup* definition

Figure 8.40 depicts the definition of the behavior in a SysML activity diagram. The System Process activity calls the appropriate Use Case Activities. The call behavior actions in the figure depict the stereotype *«functionalRequirement»*. They are applied to the activities called by the actions and not the actions itself (see the following section about Use Case Activities).

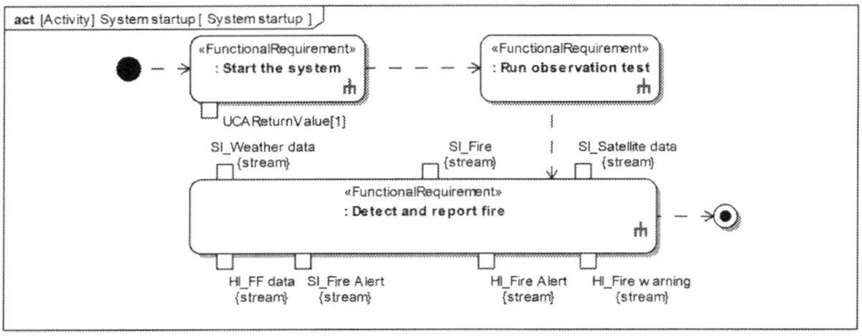

Figure 8.40: FFDS System Process *System startup* activity

Figure 8.41 shows the System Process in a table view. A table can easily show all properties of a set of System Processes in a single view.

#	Name	Documentation	Actors	Included Use Case Activities
1	System startup	The startup of the system includes the technical startup of the system components, a test to verify the health status of the system, and finally the start of the forest fire detection loop.	Maintenance	68 Start the system(context FFDS) 67 Run observation test(context FFDS) 64 Detect and report fire(context FFDS)

Figure 8.41: FFDS System Process in a table view

Figure 8.42 depicts the System Processes in the model package structure.

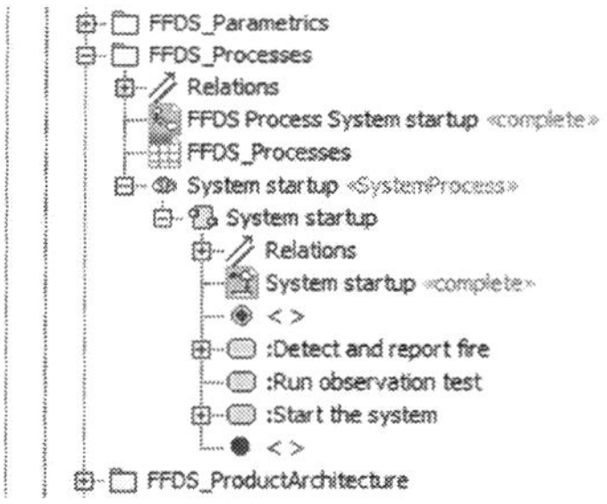

Figure 8.42: FFDS System Processes in the model package structure

8.12 Example Use Case Activities

Context

SYSMOD Methods
 4.14 Model Use Case Activities
SYSMOD Products
 5.14 Use Case Activities
SYSMOD Roles
 6.4 Requirements Engineer
Modeling Guidance
 7.12 How to Model Use Case Activities

Document

Figure 8.43 depicts the Use Case Activity *Detect and report fire* description in a document.

Here, the step numbers are only identifiers and do not indicate an execution order. You can use them to depict an ordering scheme. In that case, you need some conventions for optional and parallel steps.

Use Case Activity			
Step No.	*Step name*	*Step description*	
1	Request FF data	*Input:*	Region of Interest
		Request fire, weather, and satellite data (forest fire data) for the region of interest.	
		Output:	Fire sensors, weather server, satellites
2	Retrieve FF data	*Input:*	Fire sensors, weather server, satellites, Context representation of fire sensor data, weather data, and satellite data
		Retrieve fire sensor, weather, and satellite data from the given sources for the region of interest.	
		Output:	System representation of fire sensor data, weather data, satellite data
3	Acquire metadata	*Input:*	Weather data
		Collect supplemental data like map, weather and prepare it to be combined with the primary data	

Figure 8.43: FFDS Use Case Activity Detect and report fire (excerpt)

Model

Figure 8.44[4] shows the Use Case Activity *Detect and report fire* in a SysML activity diagram with control and object flows. Unfortunately, it is hard to show a complex activity diagram on a page with a book format. However, MBSE4U provides the original image on its website (see footnote). The primary intent here is to show an example of the overall structure of an activity.

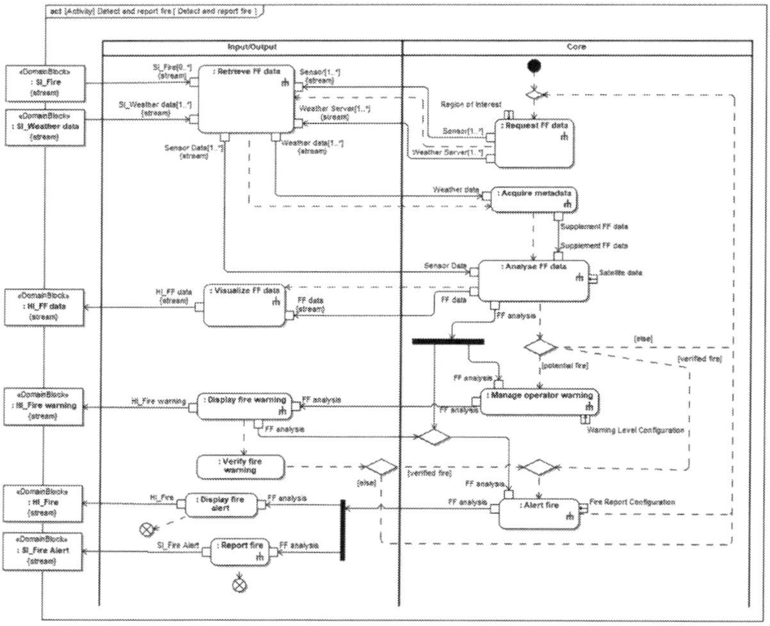

Figure 8.44: FFDS Use Case Activity Detect and report fire

Figure 8.45 depicts the Use Case Activities in the model package structure.

[4] A larger version of the diagram is available at www.mbse4u.com/sysmod-figures.

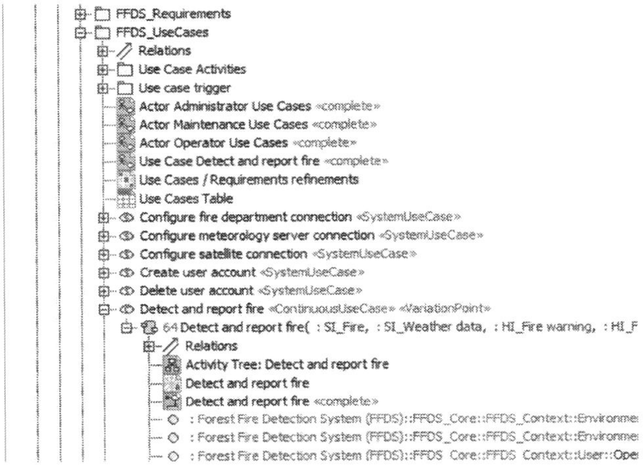

Figure 8.45: FFDS Use Case Activities in the model package structure

8.13 Example Domain Knowledge

Context

SYSMOD Methods
    4.14 Model Domain Knowledge
SYSMOD Products
    5.15 Domain Knowledge
SYSMOD Roles
    6.4 Requirements Engineer
Modeling Guidance
    7.12 How to Model Domain Knowledge

Document

Figure 8.46 depicts some of the domain block descriptions of the FFDS in a text document. The embedded table in the second column of the row *Fire sensor data* describes the properties of the domain block.

Description of the Domain Blocks of the Domain Knowledge			
System objects			
FF analysis	Analysis of the probability of forest fires in the region of interest.		
Fire sensor data	A single data unit from a fire sensor at a specific time.		
	timestamp	Date and time of the data measurement	
	data	Measured data. Details depend on the kind of the sensor.	
FF data	Comprehensive data about the forest fire observation of the region of interest including map, weather, etc.		

Figure 8.46: FFDS Domain Knowledge in a document

Model

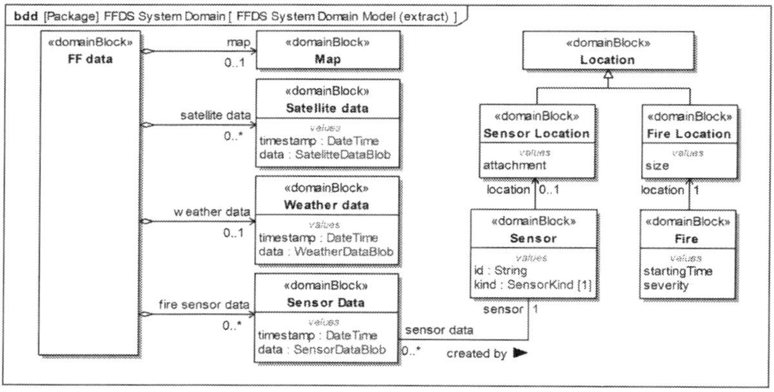

Figure 8.47: FFDS System Domain Knowledge

Figure 8.48 depicts some of the domain blocks of the context, and Figure 8.47 depicts some of the domain blocks of the system. Together they are part of the Domain Knowledge of the FFDS.

The context domain blocks are the types of the item flows in the System Context.

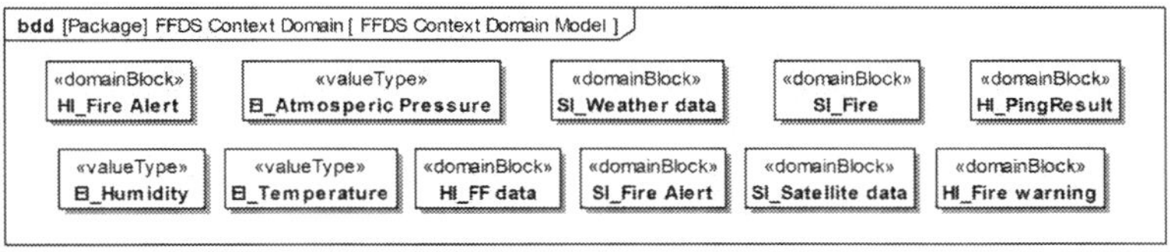

Figure 8.48: FFDS Context Domain Knowledge

Figure 8.49 depicts some of the value types of the FFDS domain. They are also part of the domain knowledge and good candidates for a model library.

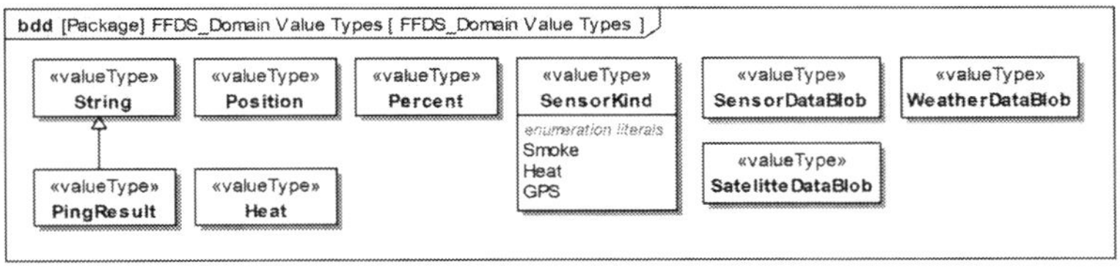

Figure 8.49: FFDS Value Types

Figure 8.50 depicts the Domain Knowledge in the model package structure.

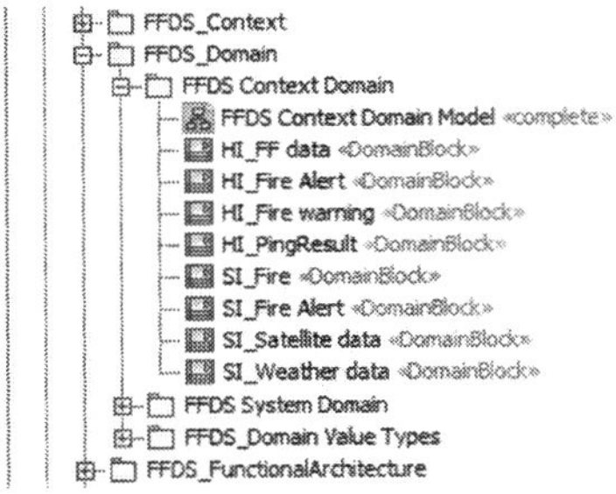

Figure 8.50: FFDS Domain Knowledge in the model package structure

8.14 Example Test Cases

Context

SYSMOD Methods
    4.16 Specify Test Cases
SYSMOD Products
    5.14 Test Cases
SYSMOD Roles
    6.7 System Tester
Modeling Guidance
    7.14 How to Specify Test Cases

Document

Figure 8.51 depicts a Test Case description in a document.

Verify Start the system			**functional**
Description	Start the system. check if all sensors are available, and the system is in the operational model.		
Precondition	System is off		
Postcondition	System is operational		
Priority	5		
Test data	None		
System under Test	TS42		
Verifies	68 - Start the system		
Dependant test cases	Verify Ping a sensor		
Test Case Steps			
Step No.	*Step name*	*Step description*	
1	Trigger system start	*Input:*	None
		Send start signal to system	
		Output:	None
2	Wait for 5 minutes	*Input:*	None
		Wait for 5 minutes to finish system start up phase	
		Output:	None
3	Check system mode	*Input:*	None
		Check if system mode is operational	
		Outptut:	None
...			

Figure 8.51: FFDS Test Case in a document

Model

Figure 8.52 shows a System Test Case and a Model Test Case and their relationships in a diagram. Typically, Test Cases are depicted in tables, but here the use case diagram illustrates the relationships.

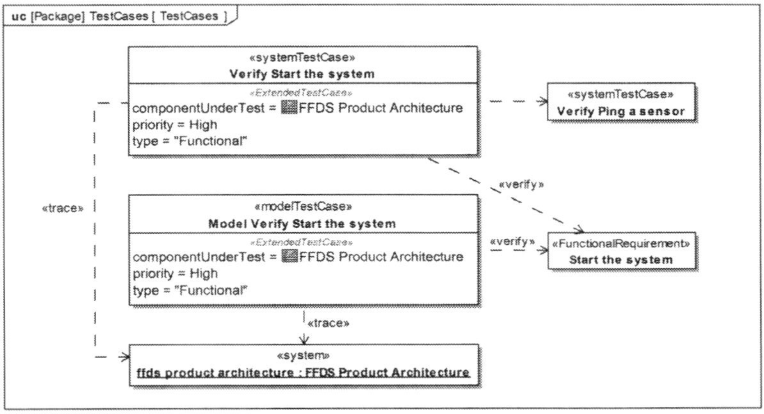

Figure 8.52: FFDS Test Case in the model

Figure 8.53 depicts Test Cases in a table view.

#	Type	Name	Priority	Documentation	Component Under Test	Test Data	Dependant Test Cases
1	Functional	ModelVerify Start the system	High	see activity diagram	FFDS Product Architecture	ffds product architecture :	
2	Functional	Verify Ping a sensor	Medium	see activity diagram	FFDS Product Architecture	ffds product architecture :	
3	Functional	Verify Start the system	High	see activity diagram	FFDS Product Architecture	ffds product architecture :	Verify Ping a sensor

Figure 8.53: FFDS Test Case table view

Figure 8.54 shows the activity diagram of the Model Test Case *Model Verify Start the system.* The Model Test Case verifies the specification in the model and not the real system.

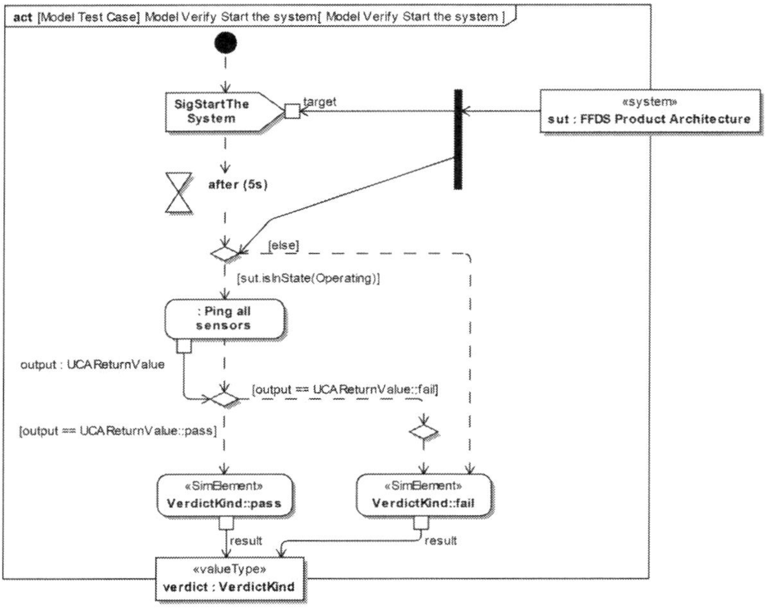

Figure 8.54: FFDS Model Test Case in the model

Figure 8.55 depicts the Test Cases in the model package structure.

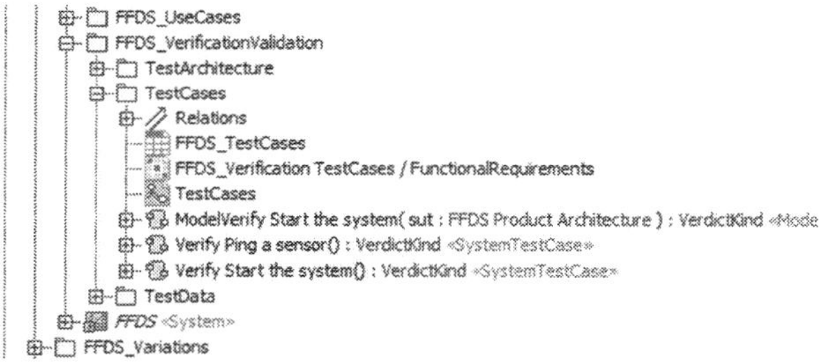

Figure 8.55: FFDS Test Cases in the model package structure

8.15 Example Logical Architecture

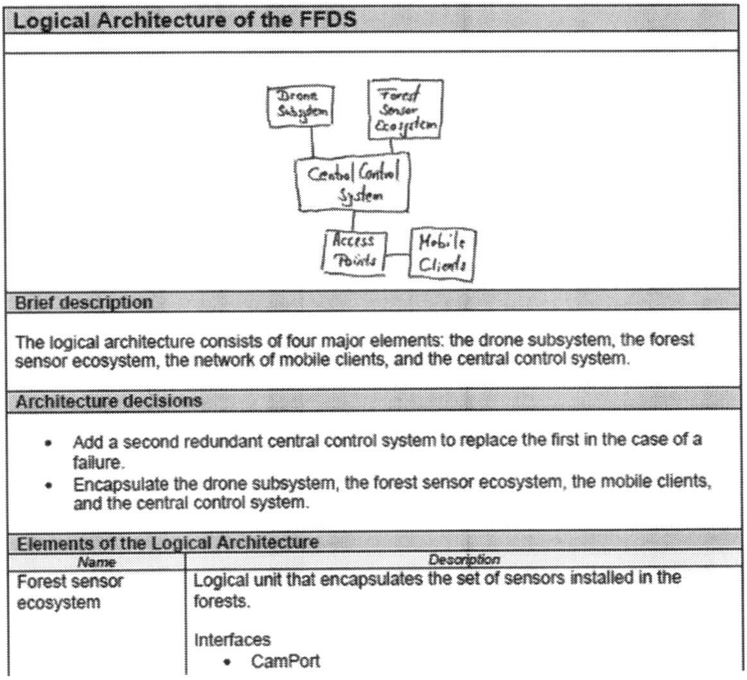

Logical Architecture of the FFDS

Brief description

The logical architecture consists of four major elements: the drone subsystem, the forest sensor ecosystem, the network of mobile clients, and the central control system.

Architecture decisions

- Add a second redundant central control system to replace the first in the case of a failure.
- Encapsulate the drone subsystem, the forest sensor ecosystem, the mobile clients, and the central control system.

Elements of the Logical Architecture

Name	Description
Forest sensor ecosystem	Logical unit that encapsulates the set of sensors installed in the forests. Interfaces • CamPort

Figure 8.56: FFDS Logical Architecture in the Document

Context

SYSMOD Methods

4.17 Model Logical Architecture

SYSMOD Products

5.20 Logical Architecture

SYSMOD Roles

6.5 System Architect

Modeling Guidance

7.14 How to Model Logical Architecture

Document

Figure 8.56 depicts a description of the Logical Architecture in a text document.

Model

Figure 8.57 depicts the definition of the Logical Architecture elements in a SysML block definition diagram (system breakdown, product tree). Check carefully if the value of the diagram view exceeds the effort in creating the visualization. Alternatively, you can display the block definitions in a table.

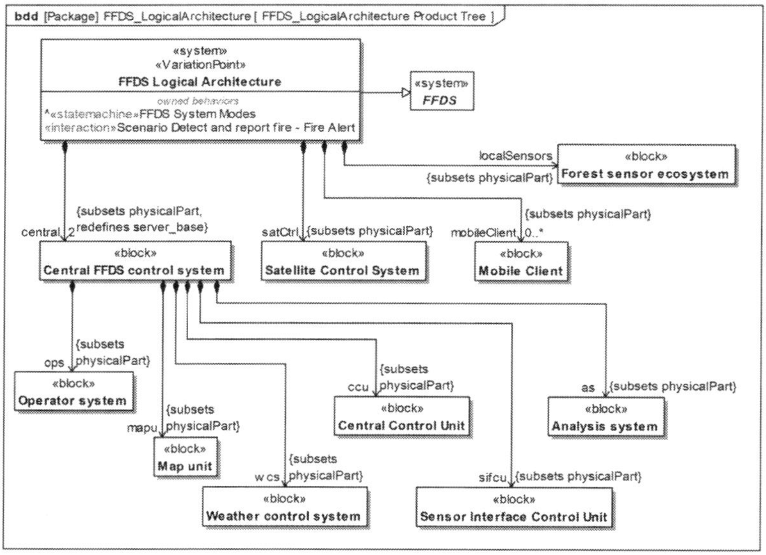

Figure 8.57: FFDS Logical Architecture Product Tree

Figure 8.58[5] depicts the information aspect of the structure of the Logical Architecture in a SysML internal block diagram. This is the main view of an architecture. Typically, it is not valuable to show all different aspects like information, mechanical, electrical, and others in a single diagram. Instead, each aspect is shown in a separate internal block diagram. The diagram name indicates the aspect. However, finally, the stakeholders decide about the view and the format and content of the diagrams.

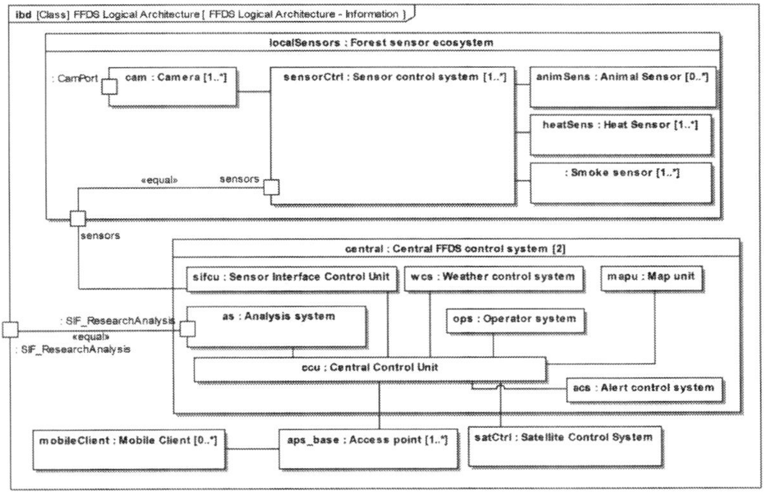

Figure 8.58: FFDS Logical Architecture

Figure 8.59 depicts the Logical Architecture in the model package structure.

---

[5]The figure should show the basic structure. The book format is too narrow to show this diagram in a readable size.

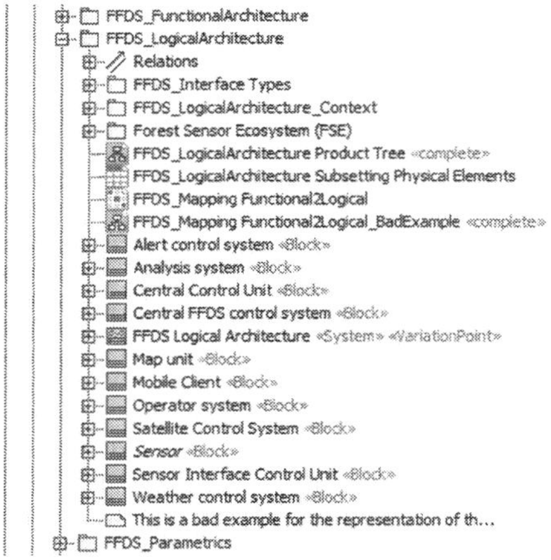

Figure 8.59: FFDS Logical Architecture in the model package structure

8.16 Example Product Architecture

Context

SYSMOD Methods
4.19 Model Product Architecture
SYSMOD Products
5.21 Product Architecture
SYSMOD Roles
6.5 System Architect
Modeling Guidance
7.15 How to Model Product Architecture

Since I am not an expert in forest fire detection systems, I will omit the Product Architecture of the FFDS. The Product Architecture requires detailed technical knowledge of the system. From the modeling perspective, the Product Architecture is the same as the Logical Architecture, but much more concrete and detailed.

8.17 Example Scenarios

Context

SYSMOD Methods
: 4.20 Revise an Architecture with Scenarios

SYSMOD Products
: 5.22 Scenarios

SYSMOD Roles
: 6.5 System Architect

Modeling Guidance
: 7.16 How to Verify Architecture with Scenarios

Document

Figure 8.60 depicts the scenario *Get data from sensors* in a document.

Scenario: Get data from the sensors		
Defined by use case:	Detect and report fire	
Scenario steps		
From	*Message*	*To*
ccu:Central Control Unit	Request data: Query the data from a selected sensor unit through the sensor interface unit.	sifcu:Sensor Interface Control Unit
sifcu:Sensor Interface Control Unit	Request data: Forward data request to the selected sensor control unit	:Sensor control system
ccu:Central Control Unit	Request data: Query weather data for the region of interest	wcs:Weather control system

Figure 8.60: FFDS Scenario in the document

Model

Figure 8.61[6] depicts the Scenario *Get data from sensors* in a SysML sequence diagram.

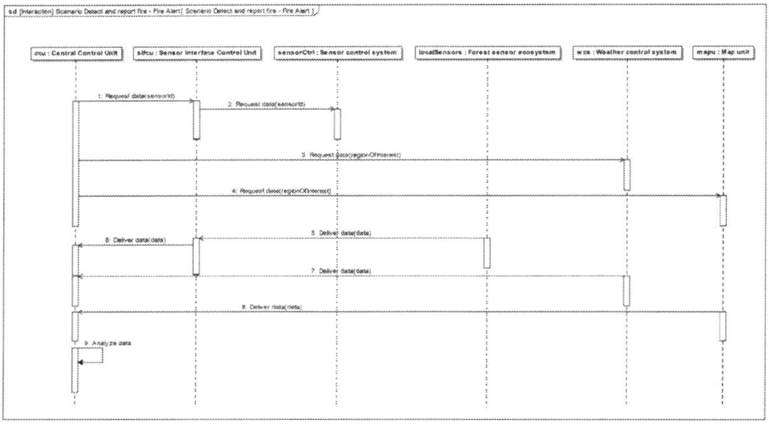

Figure 8.61: FFDS scenario

Figure 8.62 depicts the Scenario in the model package structure.

Figure 8.62: FFDS scenario

[6] A larger version of the diagram is available at www.mbse4u.com/sysmod-figures.

8.18 Example System States

Context

SYSMOD Methods
 4.21 Define System States
SYSMOD Products
 5.23 System States
SYSMOD Roles
 6.5 System Architect
Modeling Guidance
 7.18 How to Model the System States

FFDS System Modes

Owner:	FFDS Logical Architecture	
States and Transitions		
State	*Description*	
Off	The system is switched off.	
	Transition	*Target state*
	Start the system	*Testing*
Operating	The system observes the region of interest and detects and reports forest firest.	
	Transition	*Target state*
	Stop the system	*Off*
	Switch to Test mode	*Testing*
	Switch to Maintenance mode	*Maintenance*
	Detect and report fire	*<internal>*
Testing	The system test mode allows testing of the system components and functions without triggering a real fire alarm. Test data could be injected into the system, for instance sensor data of a real forest fire.	
	Transition	*Target state*
	Switch to Maintenance mode	*Maintenance*
	Run observation test	*Operating*
Maintenance	The system could be maintained. Parts of the system could be switched off. No real forest fire alarms are triggered.	
	Transition	*Target state*
	Switch to Test mode	*Testing*
	Stop the system	*Off*

Figure 8.63: FFDS System modes in a document

Document

Figure 8.63 depicts a state machine in a document.

Model

Figure 8.64 depicts a state machine that specifies the system modes of the FFDS, and the System Use Cases that can be executed in a mode, or that leads to another mode.

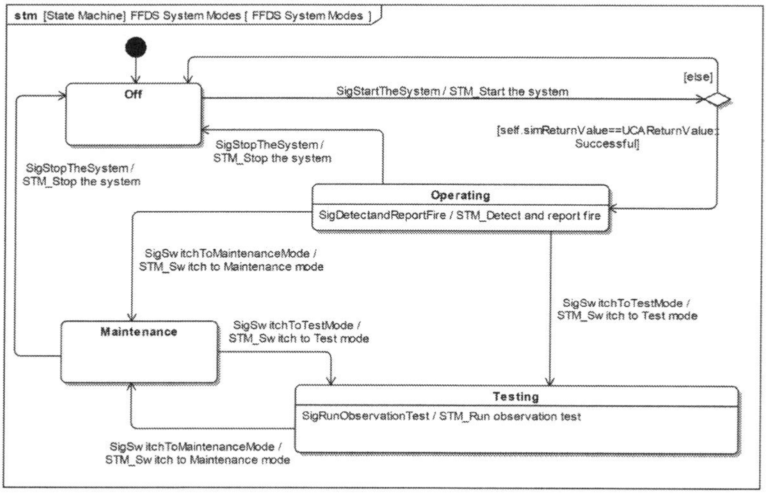

Figure 8.64: FFDS System modes specified by a state machine

Figure 8.65 depicts the state machine in the model package structure. At the top, you see the *FFDS Logical Architecture* system element. It is the context of the state machine.

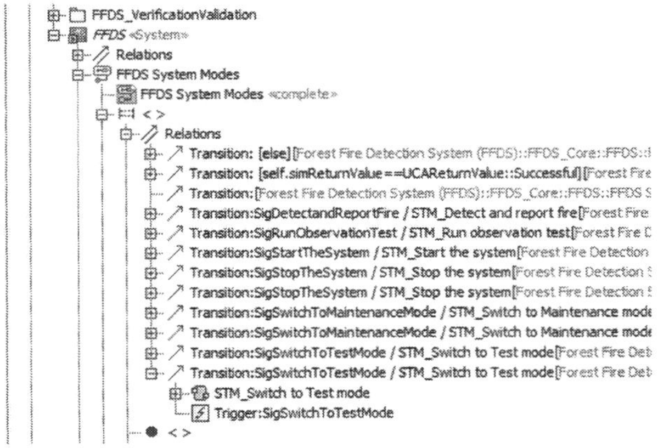

Figure 8.65: FFDS System modes state machine in the model package structure

Below the architecture element, you see all of its properties followed by the state machine model element *FFDS System Modes* and, in the next level, the state machine diagram with the same name.

The second transition owns the activity *STM_Detect and report fire*. It is the effect of the transition. The activity contains only one call behavior action to call the appropriate Use Case Activity *Detect and report fire* (see section 8.12).

8.19 Example Test Architecture

Index: test architecture

Context

SYSMOD Methods
4.22 Model the Test Architecture

SYSMOD Products

5.24 Test Architecture

SYSMOD Roles

6.7 System Tester

Modeling Guidance

7.19 How to Model the Test Architecture

Document

Figure 8.66 depicts a test architecture description of the FFDS in a document.

Test Architecture of the FFDS

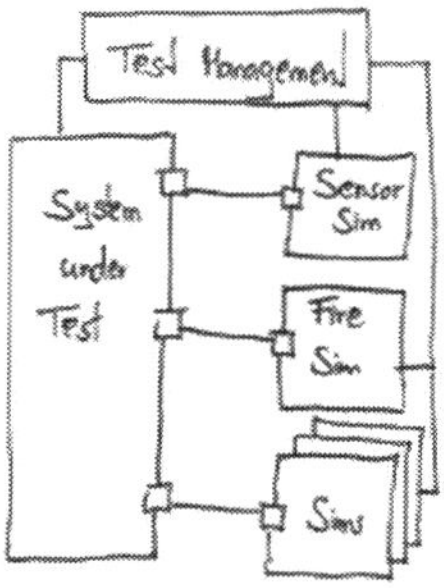

Brief description

The test architecture consists of three main pillars: the system under test, the test management component, and the simulators for external entities.

Architecture decisions

- For each external entity, we provide a simulator.
- It is possible to fully simulate the environment, or only partly together with real external entities.

Elements of the Test Architecture

Name	Description
System under Test	The FFDS system to be tested.
Test Management	Component to manage the test cases
Sims	Simulator components for the external entities

Figure 8.66: FFDS Test Architecture description in a document

Model

Figure 8.67 shows a simple test architecture in the model. It is an internal block diagram of the context, including the system under test, the test system, and the test management component.

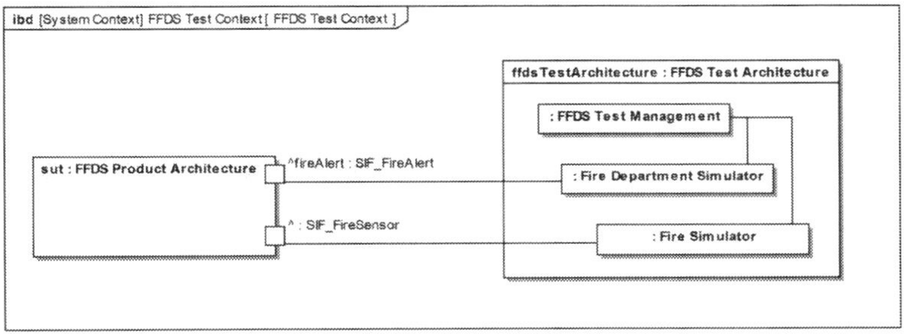

Figure 8.67: FFDS Test Architecture

Figure 8.68 shows the appropriate definitions of the test architecture blocks.

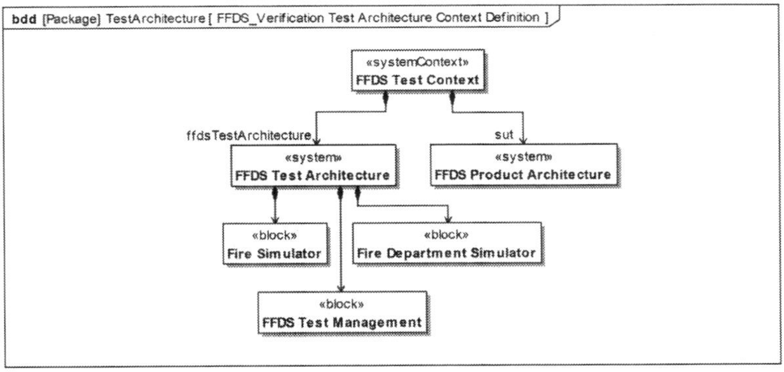

Figure 8.68: FFDS Test Architecture definitions

Figure 8.69 depicts the test architecture in the model package structure.

Figure 8.69: FFDS Test Architecture in the model

9. SYSMOD Profile and Model Libraries

The SYSMOD Profile is a set of stereotypes adding some SYSMOD-specific elements to the SysML vocabulary. SysML is too general to be used out-of-the-box without any extensions. For example, SysML does not provide elements for system hierarchies like system or subsystem or different requirement kinds and additional requirement properties. See section 12.11 for more details about profiles.

The following sections describe each SYSMOD stereotype and its formal definition to easily define yourself an SYSMOD Profile in your modeling tool. You can also download the SYSMOD Profile for some modeling tools from the website www.mbse4u.com.

Alphabetical list of SYSMOD stereotypes:

- 9.2 *«actuator»*
- 9.2 *«boundarySystem»*
- 9.6 *«businessRequirement»*
- 9.5 *«conjugated»*
- 9.6 *«constraintRequirement»*
- 9.1 *«continuousActivity»*
- 9.8 *«continuousUseCase»*
- 9.3 *«documentBlock»*
- 9.3 *«domainBlock»*
- 9.4 *«electrical»*

- 9.2 *«environmentalEffect»*
- 9.2 *«environmentalImpact»*
- 9.5 *«exDeriveReqt»*
- 9.6 *«extendedRequirement»*
- 9.6 *«extendedStakeholder»*
- 9.7 *«extendedTestCase»*
- 9.2 *«externalSystem»*
- 9.6 *«functionalRequirement»*
- 9.6 *«legalRequirement»*
- 9.4 *«mechanical»*
- 9.2 *«mechanicalSystem»*
- 9.7 *«modelTestCase»*
- 9.6 *«non-functionalRequirement»*
- 9.6 *«objective»*
- 9.3 *«parametricContext»*
- 9.6 *«performanceRequirement»*
- 9.6 *«performanceConstraintRequirement»*
- 9.6 *«physicalRequirement»*
- 9.6 *«reliabilityRequirement»*
- 9.9 *«requires»*
- 9.6 *«risk»*
- 9.2 *«sensor»*
- 9.4 *«software»*
- 9.3 *«subsystem»*
- 9.6 *«supportabilityRequirement»*
- 9.3 *«system»*
- 9.3 *«systemContext»*
- 9.8 *«systemProcess»*
- 9.7 *«systemTestCase»*
- 9.8 *«systemUseCase»*
- 9.6 *«usabilityRequirement»*
- 9.2 *«user»*

- 9.3 *«userInterface»*
- 9.2 *«userSystem»*
- 9.9 *«variant»*
- 9.9 *«variantConfiguration»*
- 9.9 *«variation»*
- 9.5 *«weightedAllocate»*
- 9.5 *«weightedSatisfy»*
- 9.5 *«weightedVerify»*
- 9.9 *«xor»*

Alphabetical list of SYSMOD Enumerations elements:

- 9.10 EffortKind
- 9.10 ObligationKind
- 9.10 Planet Environment
- 9.10 PriorityKind
- 9.10 StabilityKind
- 9.10 StakeholderCategoryKind

SYSMOD provides some additional model libraries. They offer some useful elements and serve as an example of what a model library can look like.

Section 9.11 describes the PartsCatalogue, section 9.12 describes a library for simulation elements, and section 9.13 describes the Engineering4Planet library for modeling of sustainability aspects.

9.1 Activities

The continuous activity is a marker for a Use Case Activity of a continuous System Use Case. A constraint of the continuous use case stereotype assures that its activity is a *«continuous-Activity»* (see section 9.8).

Figure 9.1 depicts the definition of the SYSMOD stereotype *«continuousActivity»* for Activities.

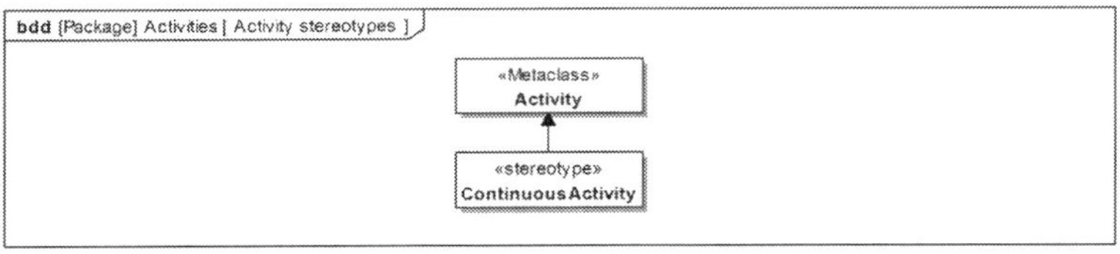

Figure 9.1: SYSMOD stereotype for SysML *Activities*

9.2 Actors

SysML has only a single general model element to model the concept of an actor, i.e., an external entity that interacts with the system of interest. Specific actor kinds like human or external systems are not part of the standard. That is a task for profiles. The SYSMOD Profile provides a set of some specific actor kinds. Figure 9.2 depicts the definition of the stereotypes: *«user»*, *«externalSystem»*, *«environmental-Effect»*, *«mechanicalSystem»*, *«sensor»*, *«actuator»*, *«boundary-System»*, *«userSystem»*.

All stereotypes are specializations of the SysML *Block*. See section 11.1: Death of the Actor for more details. If you still want to use the SysML *Actor* model element, you must change the definition of the SYSMOD actor stereotypes. Remove the generalization relationships to the SysML *Block* and change the extended metaclass from *Class* to *Actor*.

For backward compatibility with older SYSMOD versions, the SYSMOD User stereotype can also still be applied to the

SysML Actor element.

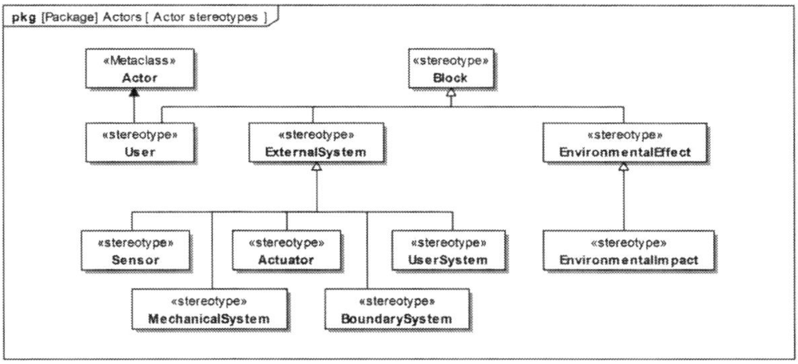

Figure 9.2: SYSMOD stereotypes for SysML *Actors*

There are three top-level actor kinds:

User
: Represents a human actor. The stereotype can be used in combination with the stereotype 9.6 *«extendedStakeholder»*.

Environmental effect
: Represents a relevant effect from the environment on the system, e.g., temperature or humidity.

External system
: Represents a non-human actor.

Further actor kinds are specializations of the external system actor:

Mechanical system
: External system that has only mechanical interfaces to the system of interest, for example, the floor.

Sensor
: External system that provides data from the environment to the system of interest.

Actuator
: External system that has an effect on the environment and is controlled by the system of interest.

User system
: External system that is an interface between a human and a system of interest.

Boundary system
: External system that is an interface between another external system and the system of interest.

Environmental impact
: Impact of the system on the environment in the sense of sustainability (see chapter 2).

The actor kinds *Sensor*, *Actuator*, *User system*, and *Boundary system* are, in particular, useful for embedded systems. In more holistic system development, these entities are typically part of the system of interest and are not actors.

The stereotypes also define their own notation by icons that depict the kind of system actor. Figure 9.3 shows the icons of the SYSMOD stereotypes for actors.

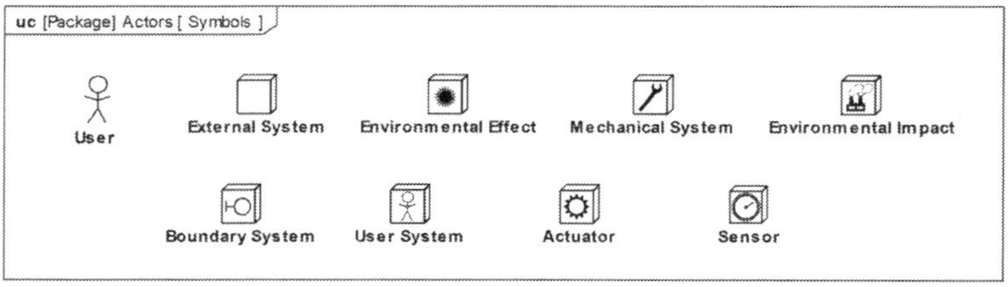

Figure 9.3: Icons for SYSMOD actor stereotypes

9.3 Blocks

SYSMOD defines several stereotypes for SysML *Block* and *InterfaceBlock*.

The stereotype *«userInterface»* marks an interface block that specifies an interaction point between the system and a human. These interfaces are different from technical interfaces like an API, or a mechanical connection. For example, a user interface defines operations that represent the usage of a lever or button.

The stereotype *«system»* marks a block that represents a system. A model can have more than one system element. For example, a system element for the Base Architecture (see section 8.6: Example Base Architecture), and another one for the Logical Architecture (see section 8.15: Example Logical Architecture). Typically, all system elements are specializations of the abstract system element. The system stereotype defines properties for the System Idea and the Problem Statement.

To define another level of a system breakdown structure, the stereotype *«subsystem»* is applied to blocks that represent system-like parts of the system.

The stereotype *«systemContext»* is a block that specifies the communication links between the system and the system actors. Internal block diagrams of the system context element depict the System Context.

The stereotype *«documentBlock»* represents a document and can be used as a proxy for the information of the document in the model. For example, a document block that represents an interface specification document and is used as the type of a port. The property *reference* stores the source of the document, for example, a URL or a link to the document in a file system.

The stereotype *«domainBlock»* is an element of the Domain Knowledge (section 5.15). It represents a concept of the domain that is "known" by the system.

Figure 9.4 depicts the definitions of the SYSMOD stereotypes for SysML *Blocks*.

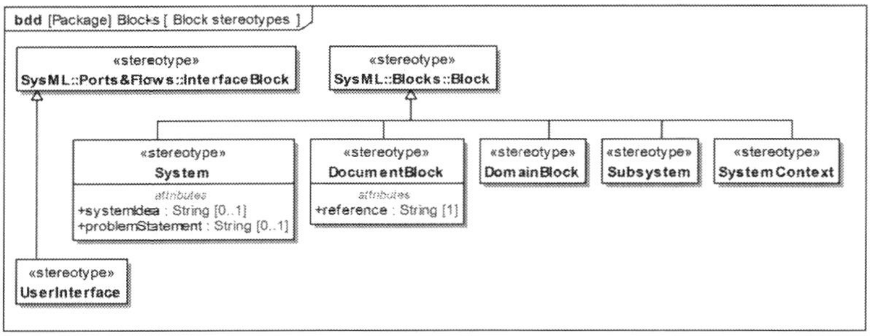

Figure 9.4: SYSMOD stereotypes for SysML *Blocks*

9.4 Discipline-specific Elements

As a rule of thumb, the model elements at the lowest level of the system breakdown structure can be fully allocated to a specific engineering discipline. For example, a block that represents a pure software, mechanical, or electrical artifact.

The SYSMOD stereotypes for discipline-specific elements are markers for those elements. The base class is *NamedElement*, i.e., the stereotypes can be applied to any model element that has a name. Typically, it is used for blocks, parts, and connectors.

The property *reference* stores a link to an external model

or document that covers the details of the discipline-specific element.

Figure 9.5 depicts the definitions of the SYSMOD stereotypes for discipline-specific elements: *«software»*, *«mechanical»*, and *«electrical»*. You can define our own additional stereotypes if you need more discipline-specific elements.

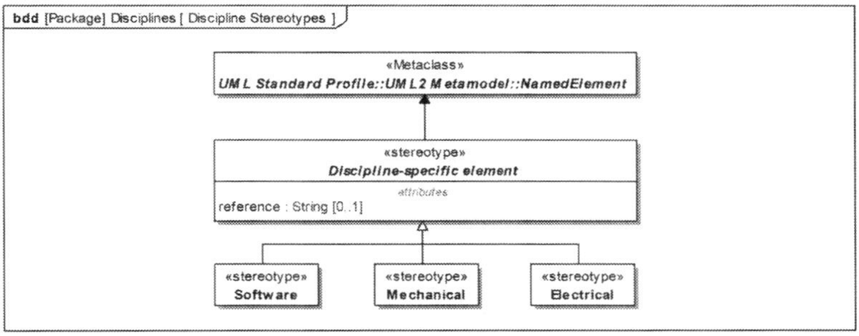

Figure 9.5: SYSMOD stereotypes for discipline-specific Elements

9.5 Relationships

The SysML relationship *Satisfy* specifies that the element at the source of the relationship satisfies the requirement at the target. It works well for one-to-one but is not precise for many-to-many relationships.

If, for example, two blocks have satisfy relationships to a single requirement in SysML (figure 9.6), it is not specified what that means. Does block A and B together satisfy requirement R42? Or each block alone and the requirement R42 is satisfied twice?

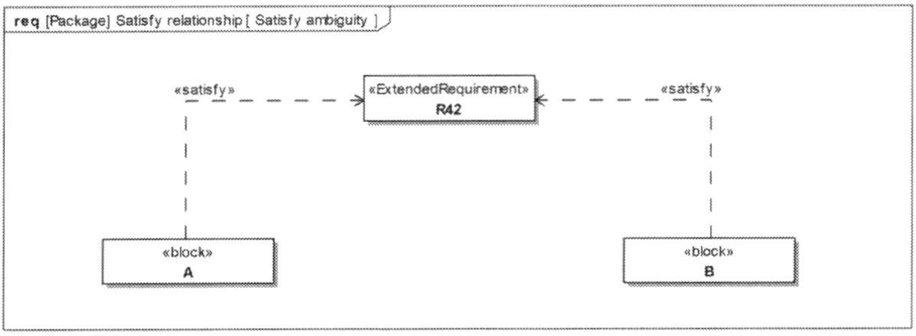

Figure 9.6: Ambiguity of the satisfy relationship

The SYSMOD stereotype *«weightedSatisfy»* adds a property to the satisfy relationship that specifies the coverage of the satisfaction. Figure 9.7 shows the same scenario of figure 9.6 with the weighted satisfy relationship. Block A satisfies 70% and block B 30% of the requirement R42.

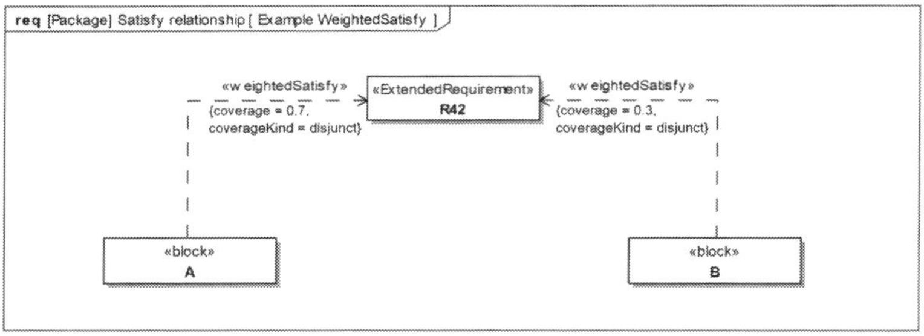

Figure 9.7: Example of SYSMOD weighted satisfy relationship

The property *coverageKind* specifies if the coverage is disjunct or overlapping. Overlapping means that the elements at the source of the *«weightedSatisfy»* relationships satisfy equal parts of the requirement. For example, if the requested feature should be implemented twice for redundancy reasons. In such a case, a satisfy coverage of 70% + 30% is not a 100% coverage of the requirement. If the property *coverageKind* is set to *disjunct*, it specifies a non-overlapping coverage. *Disjunct* is the default.

The same principle is applied to the SysML relationships *Verify* and *Allocate* by the SYSMOD stereotypes *«weighted-Verify»* and *«weightedAllocate»*.

The SysML relationship *DeriveReqt* specifies that a requirement is derived from another requirement. The SYSMOD stereotype *«exDeriveReqt»* adds a property to specify the model elements that led to the derivation, for example, architecture elements, as described in the zigzag pattern (see section 11.6). Figure 9.8 shows an example of the extended derive relationship.

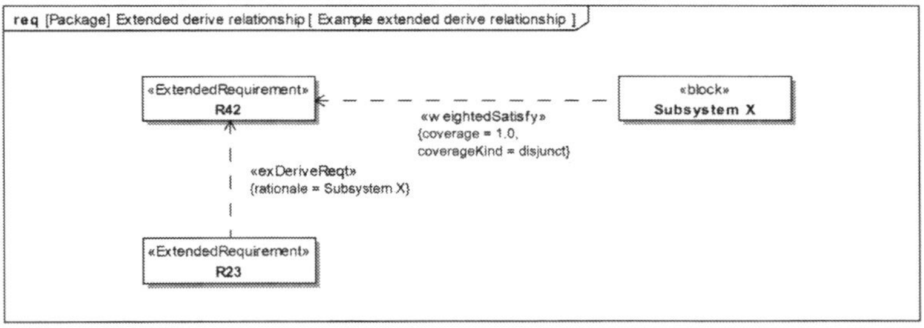

Figure 9.8: Example of SYSMOD extended derive requirement relationship

The SYSMOD stereotype *«conjugated»* is deprecated since SYSMOD v4.2 because SysML v1.6 resolved the issue that was resolved by this stereotype for older SysML versions. It is still part of SYSMOD to support models that are based on SysML < v1.6. The following paragraphs explain the issue and motivation for the stereotype.

The proxy ports of a block are typed with SysML *InterfaceBlocks*. To ensure that the block implements the features specified by its ports, it typically has a generalization relationship to the interface block (figure 9.9).

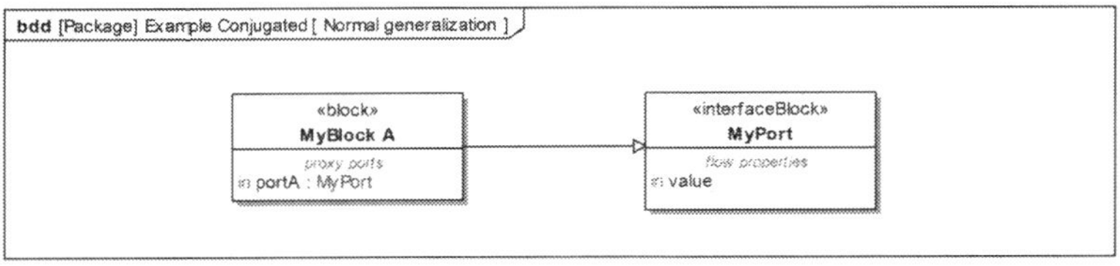

Figure 9.9: Example interface block generalization

If a proxy port is connected to another port by a connector, the connected port has typically the same type but is a conjugated port to invert the direction of the flow properties and directed features specified within the interface block (figure 9.10).

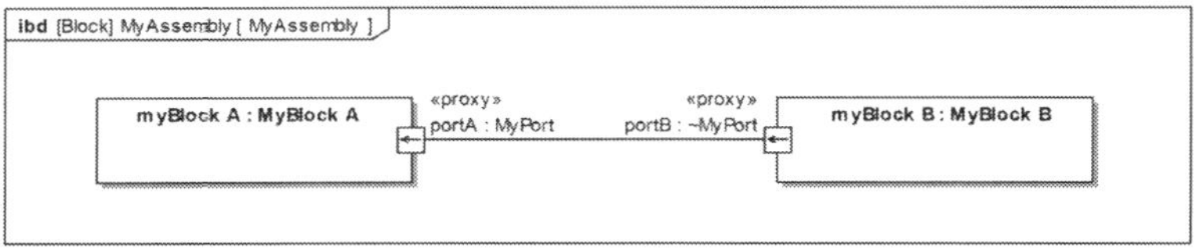

Figure 9.10: Example connected proxy ports

The block *MyBlock B* should also have a generalization relationship to the proxy port type *MyPort* to ensure that the specified features are implemented by *MyBlock B*. However, we need a conjugated type to invert the directions of the flow properties and directed features. The SYSMOD stereotype *«conjugated»* is a generalization relationship that has the same effect as the *isConjugated* property of a SysML *Port*. The direction of the inherited directed features is conjugated (figure 9.11).

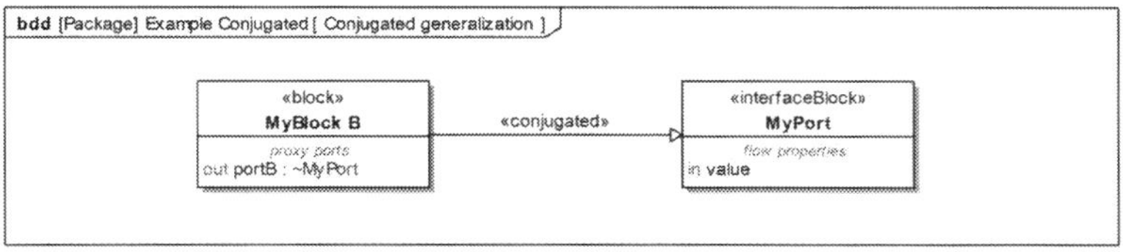

Figure 9.11: Example conjugated generalization

SysML v1.6 does not resolve the issue by a conjugated generalization relationship but by a special conjugated interface block. See section 12.6 for details about the SysML *InterfaceBlock* and *∼InterfaceBlock*.

Figure 9.12 depicts the definitions of the SYSMOD stereotypes for relationships.

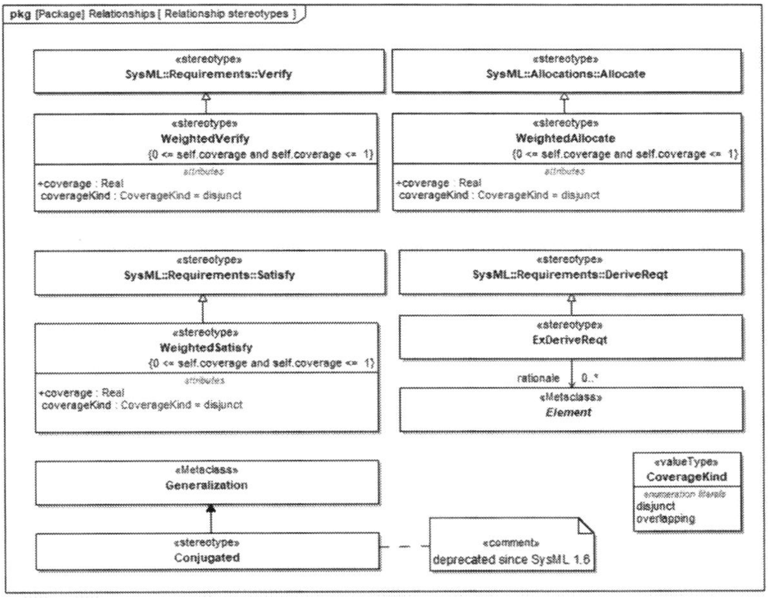

Figure 9.12: SYSMOD stereotypes for Relationships

9.6 Requirements and Risks

Figure 9.13 depicts the definition of the SYSMOD stereotypes for requirements.

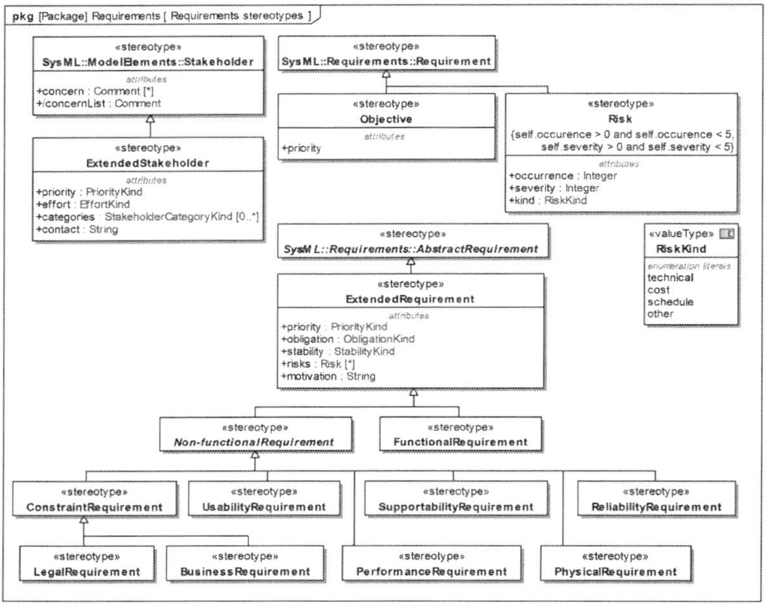

Figure 9.13: SYSMOD stereotypes for Requirements

SysML provides only a general requirement model element that covers the name, ID, and the text of a requirement. The SYSMOD stereotype *«extendedRequirement»* adds additional properties typically important for Requirements:

Priority	Specifies the importance of the requirement.
Obligation	Specifies if the requirement is optional or mandatory.

Stability	Specifies if it is likely that the requirement will change in the future.
Risk	Specifies a list of risks for the implementation of the requirement.
Motivation	Specifies why the requirement is necessary.

The SYSMOD stereotype *«extendedRequirement»* can be applied to any model element that has a name, for example, a state machine or a constraint block to designate that model element itself as a requirement. It is not necessary to translate activities or state machines that represent requirements to textual requirements.

SYSMOD provides further specializations of the stereotype *«extendedRequirement»*. They do no add more properties, but specify each a different kind of a requirement: *«functionalRequirement»*, *«non-functionalRequirement»*, *«physicalRequirement»*, *«usabilityRequirement»*, *«constraintRequirement»*, *«reliabilityRequirement»*, *«performanceRequirement»*, *«legalRequirement»*, *«businessRequirement»*, *«supportabilityRequirement»*.

The SYSMOD stereotype *«objective»* specializes the SysML stereotype *«requirement»* and represents System Objectives (section 5.6).

The stereotype *«extendedStakeholder»* extends the SysML *Stakeholder* to add additional properties that are used for the SYSMOD Stakeholder (section 5.8).

SYSMOD extends the SysML *Requirement* element to provide a model element for Risks. In the broadest sense, a Risk is a potentially undesirable situation that must be considered by the system or systems engineering project. The stereotype *«risk»* adds the following properties

occurrence	Occurrence rating of the risk, for example, 1 - 10 (10 = highest occurrence).
severity	Severity rating of the risk, for example, 1 - 10 (10 = highest severity).
kind	Classification of the risk: technical, cost, schedule, other.

Since the metaclass *NamedElement* of the stereotype *«extendedRequirement»* is abstract, you must specify a concrete model element when you apply the stereotypes. It can be any kind of a named element.

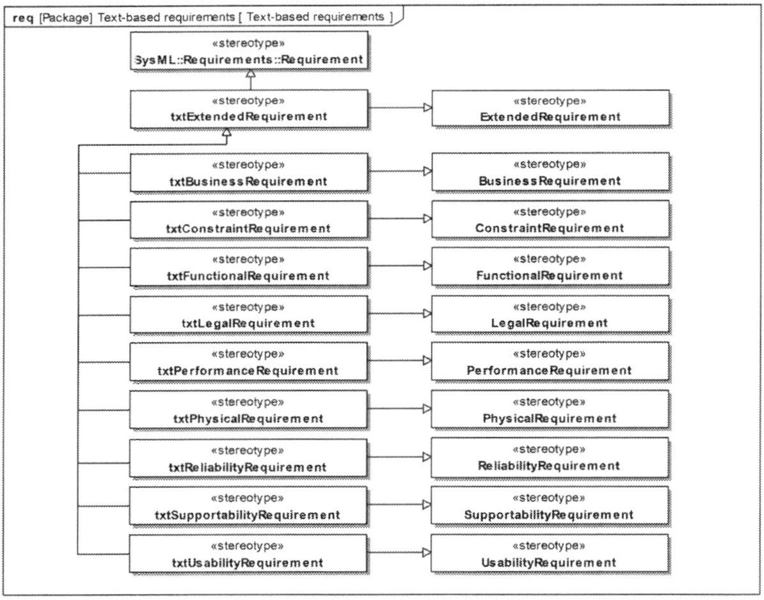

Figure 9.14: SYSMOD stereotypes for classical textual Requirements

Figure 9.14 depicts SYSMOD requirement stereotypes that specializes the concrete SysML *Requirement* instead of the abstract SysML *AbstractRequirement* element. The stereotypes for classical textual requirements have the prefix *txt*.

Figure 9.15 depicts the SYSMOD stereotype *«performance-ConstraintRequirement»* which specializes the SysML *AbstractRequirement* and the SysML *ConstraintBlock* element. Figure 8.26 shows an example of how to use it.

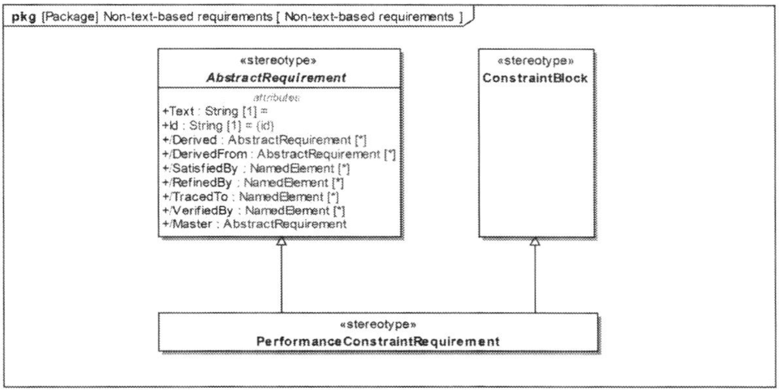

Figure 9.15: SYSMOD stereotype for parametric-based performance requirement

9.7 Test Cases

The abstract stereotype *«extendedTestCase»* specializes the SysML test case by adding the following properties. They are similar to the definitions in the UML Testing Profile [UTP13]. If you need more test modeling features, you should use the complete UML Testing Profile in addition to SysML and SYSMOD.

priority	Priority of the test case for test case management.
type	Type of the test case. The set of types is not predefined.

componentUnderTest	References the block that is tested by the test case, for example, the whole system or a subsystem.

The *priority* may be used to support test planning activities.

The *type* describes the type of the test case, for example, usability test or performance test.

The *componentUnderTest* references the block that is in the focus of the test case, for example, the whole system itself, a subsystem, or any other block of the system architecture.

The specialized stereotype *«systemTestCase»* is used to specify test cases that tests the real physical system. The stereotype *«modelTestCase»* is used to specify test cases that test the model, i.e., the specification of the system.

The following figure 9.16, depicts the definition of the stereotypes.

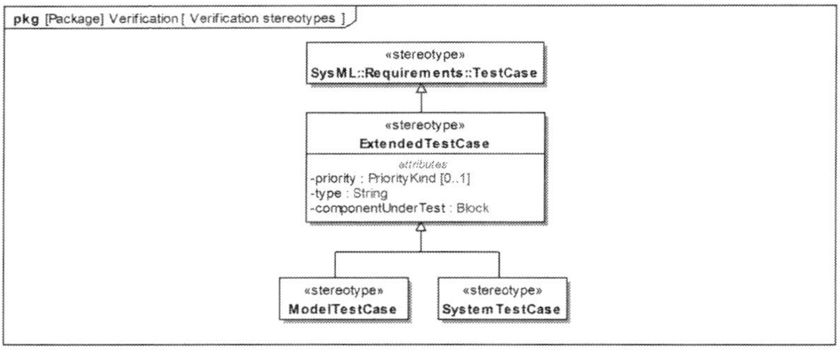

Figure 9.16: SYSMOD stereotypes for Test Cases

9.8 Use Cases

The stereotype *«systemUseCase»* adds more properties to the SysML *UseCase* element. A property to specify the trigger that starts the System Use Case, and a property for the result of the System Use Case (section 5.12).

You can specify a descriptive textual trigger, or reference a signal model element as a trigger that, for example, can be used in a state machine to trigger transitions (see figure 8.64 in section 8.18).

The stereotype *«continuousUseCase»* is a specialized *«systemUseCase»* to model a continuous behavior. A continuous use case must own a *«continuousActivity»*. The constraint is defined with OCL[1] as follows:

```
context ContinuousUeCase inv ContinuousUseCaseOwnsC\
ontinuousActivity:
self.classifierBehavior.oclIsTypeOf(SYSMOD::Activit\
ies::ContinuousActivity)
```

The SYSMOD stereotype *«systemProcess»* is applied to use cases that represent a System Process (section 5.13), that means, a specification of the logical order of execution of Use Case Activities.

Figure 9.17 depicts the definitions of the SYSMOD stereotypes for use cases.

[1]Object Constraint Language (OCL14).

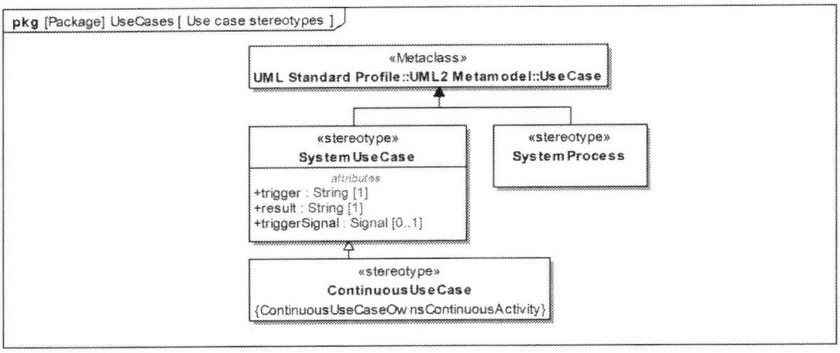

Figure 9.17: SYSMOD stereotypes for Use cases

9.9 Variants (VAMOS stereotypes)

The modeling of variants is a topic in itself. I call the method for modeling variants with SysML VAMOS (VAriant MOdeling with SysML). You find a detailed description of VAMOS and examples in the book *Variant Modeling with SysML*[2]. A brief overview is given in section 11.5.

The SYSMOD stereotypes depicted in figure 9.18 are necessary to model the variant modeling approach: *«variationPoint»*, *«variant»*, *«variation»*, *«variantConfiguration»*, *«XOR»*, *«REQUIRES»*, and the enumeration *BindingTimeKind*.

[2]https://leanpub.com/vamos

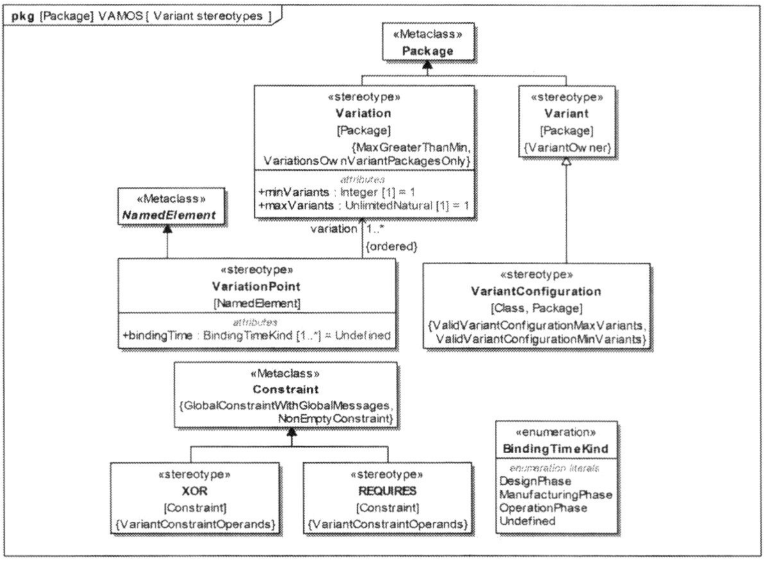

Figure 9.18: SYSMOD stereotypes for Variants

9.10 SYSMOD Enumerations

The *SYSMOD Enumerations* package contains enumeration types used by SYSMOD stereotypes: *EffortKind*, *ObligationKind*, *PriorityKind*, *RiskKind*, *StabilityKind*, and *StakeholderCategoryKind* (figure 9.19).

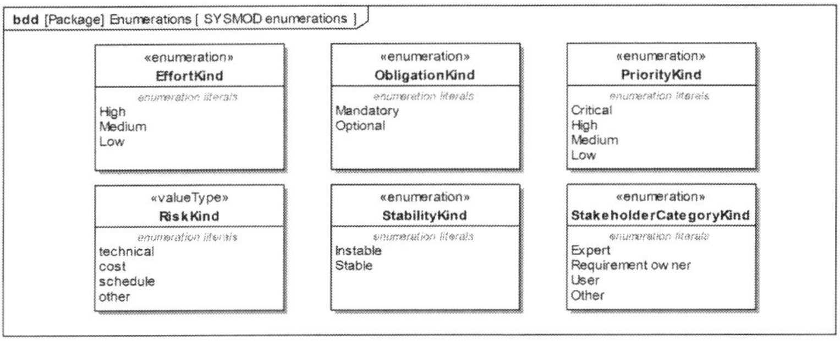

Figure 9.19: SYSMOD Profile Library: Enumerations

9.11 SYSMOD PartsCatalogue Library

The model library *PartsCatalogue* provides common model elements useful for system modeling. The library is independent of the SYSMOD profile and vice versa. The library is intended to be an example of a model library, and not to be a complete library.

The current version of the library includes four sections: Analysis, Constraints, Physics, and Units (figure 9.20).

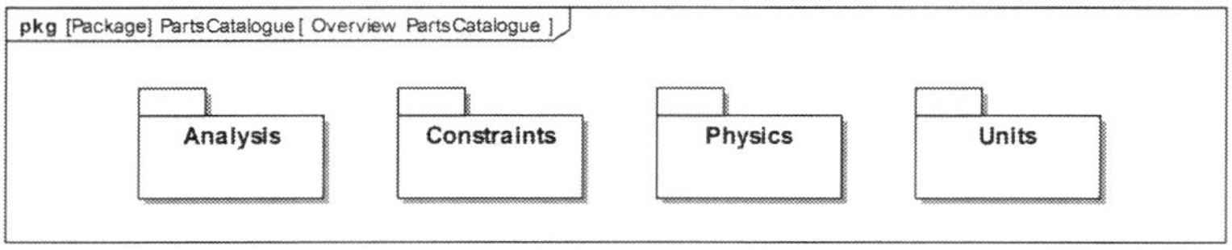

Figure 9.20: SYSMOD PartsCatalogue Library

The *Analysis* package contains an abstract block *Performance-BehaviorProperties* (figure 9.21). The properties store the minimum, maximum, and medium duration of a behavior. The appropriate derived properties *totalXXX* sum up the values of a breakdown structure, for example, an activity tree.

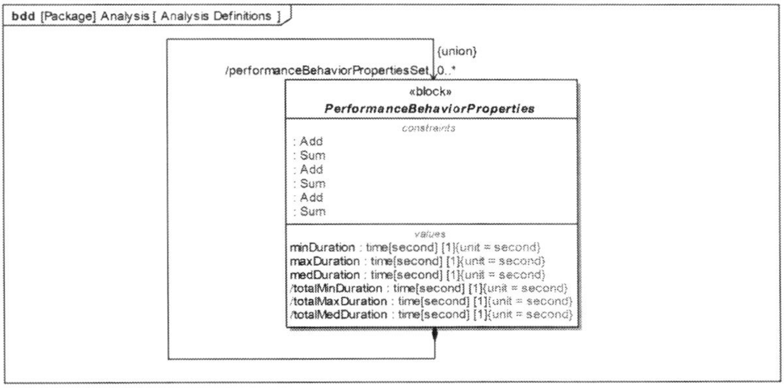

Figure 9.21: SYSMOD PartsCatalogue Library: Analysis

The calculation of the sums is performed by the constraint properties specified in the parametric diagram depicted in 9.22.

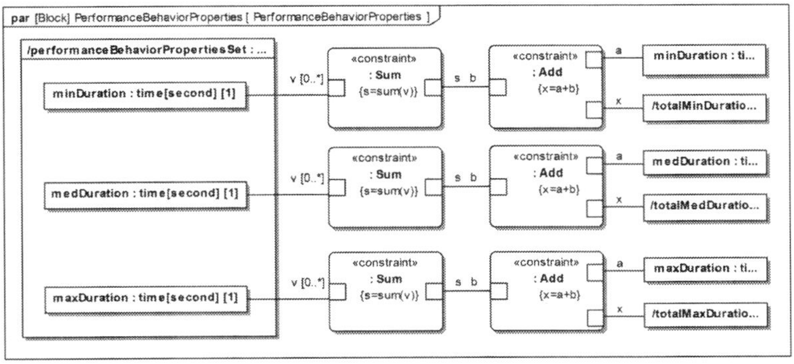

Figure 9.22: SYSMOD PartsCatalogue Library: Analysis Parametrics

The *Constraints* package includes two simple constraint blocks, *Add* and *Sum* (figure 9.23) used, for example, in the *Analysis* package above.

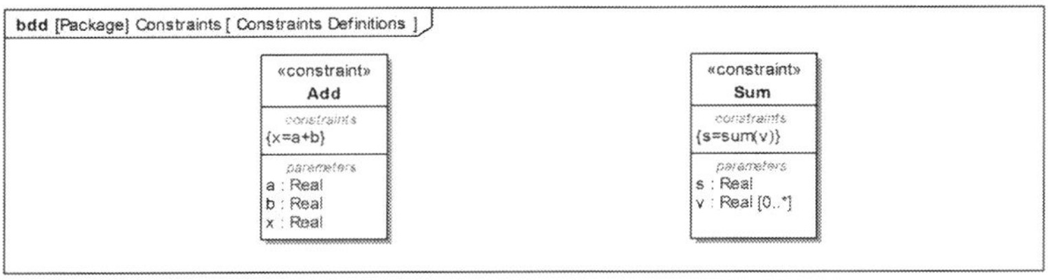

Figure 9.23: SYSMOD PartsCatalogue Library: Constraints

The *Physics* package includes an abstract block as a base block for blocks specifying physical things with a mass (figure 9.24). Similar to the *PerformanceBehaviorProperties* block in the *Analysis* package, the *PhysicalElement* provides the capability to sum up the masses of a breakdown structure.

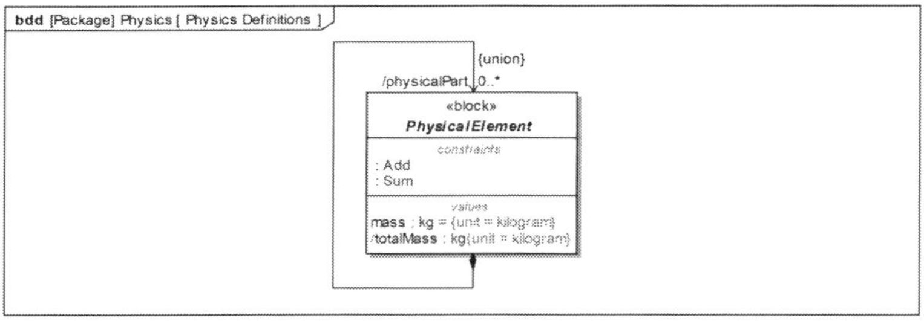

Figure 9.24: SYSMOD PartsCatalogue Library: Physics

Figure 9.25 shows an example of how to use the *PhysicalElement.* If you create an instance specification of the block *Smoke Sensor,* the value property *totalMass* has the value 0.9 kg. Of course only, if your modeling provides the necessary calculation capabilities.

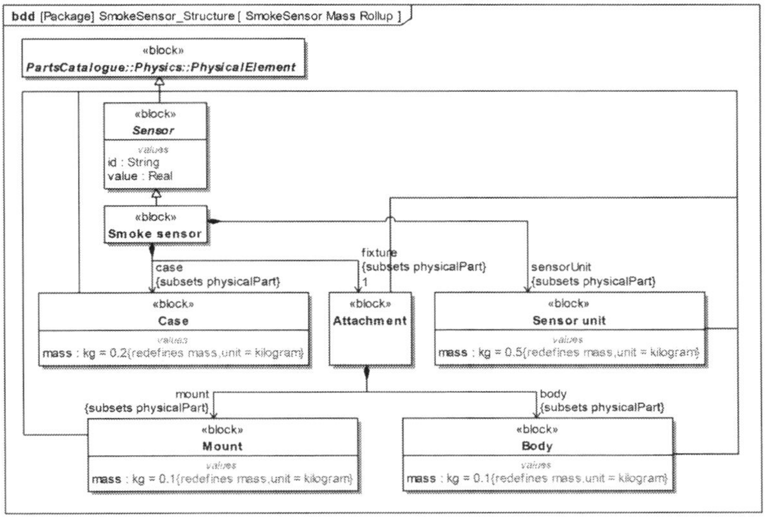

Figure 9.25: SYSMOD PartsCatalogue Library: Physics Example

The *Units* package includes only two value types specifying kilogram and timestamp values (figure 9.26). They are used in the Physics package, and the model of the FFDS.

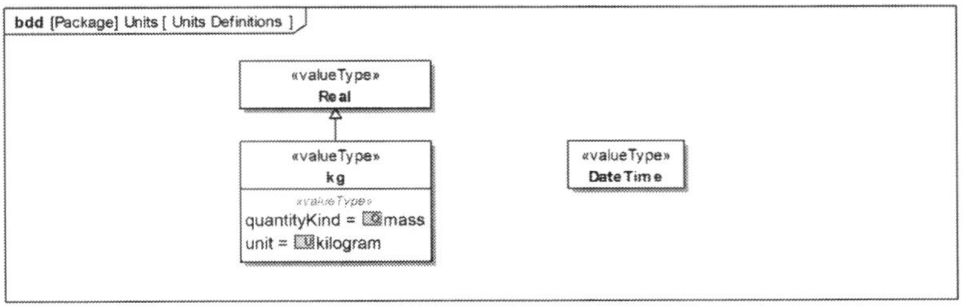

Figure 9.26: SYSMOD PartsCatalogue Library: Units

9.12 SYSMOD Simulation Library

The *SYSMOD SimLib* library provides some elements useful to create an executable model (figure 9.27). The library is only a simple example of a model library. Typically, you need many more additional elements to create an executable system model.

The library also includes a profile with the stereotype *«simElement»* to tag elements in the model that only exists to enable the model execution, for example, an action in an activity that was modeled just for executability (see figure 8.54).

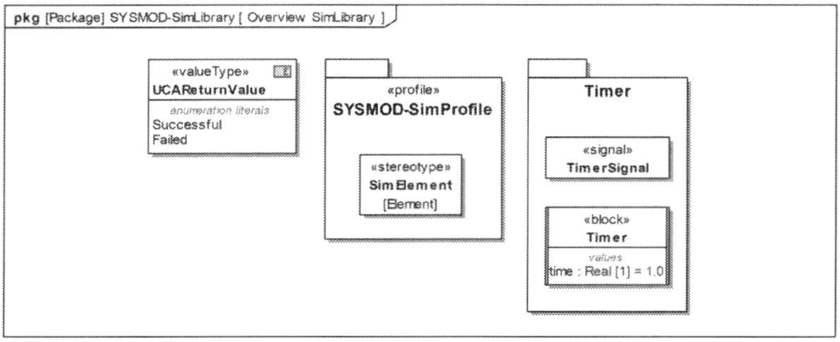

Figure 9.27: SYSMOD Simulation Library

9.13 SYSMOD Engineering4Planet Library

The SYSMOD *Engineering4Planet* Library provides two elements to model sustainability aspects (figure 9.28); see also section 2.

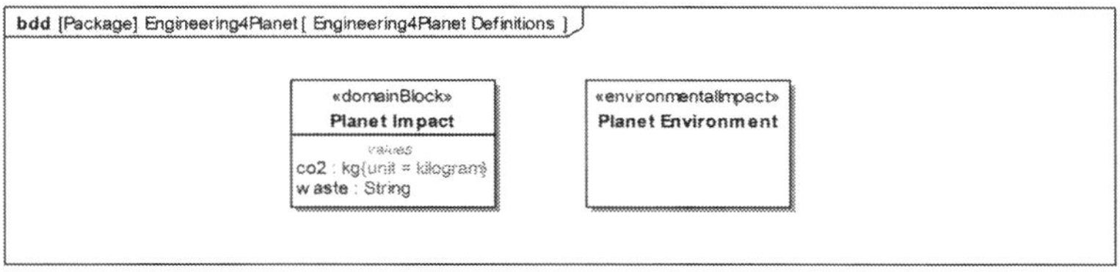

Figure 9.28: SYSMOD Engineering4Planet Library

PlanetEnvironment is an actor that, typically, should be considered in any system context.

PlanetImpact is a type of an item flow to model the impact of the system of interest on the planet.

10. MBSE Adoption Process

You should not use SYSMOD or any other MBSE Methodology out-of-the-box without customization. Every organization has its own specific needs, and none methodology can satisfy them all.

The SYSMOD Processes described in chapter 3 are useful templates and starting points. Still, you must analyze whether you need all of the steps: some must be adapted to your needs, some must be executed more intensively, some less intensively, and some necessary tasks are probably not covered by the given methodology.

Before customizing the methodology, you must be clear about your needs. Start with them before thinking about the solution. You need a purpose-driven methodology. Stakeholders define the desired artifacts and views. The methodology describes how to achieve these outputs. On this basis, you can derive the languages in which the artifacts are expressed, and the tools used to create and present them. I call this query-driven modeling, i.e., the query, respectively, the request from the stakeholders determines the type of modeling (figure 10.1).

A model-based approach requires a harmonic triad of modeling: methodologies, modeling languages, and modeling tools.

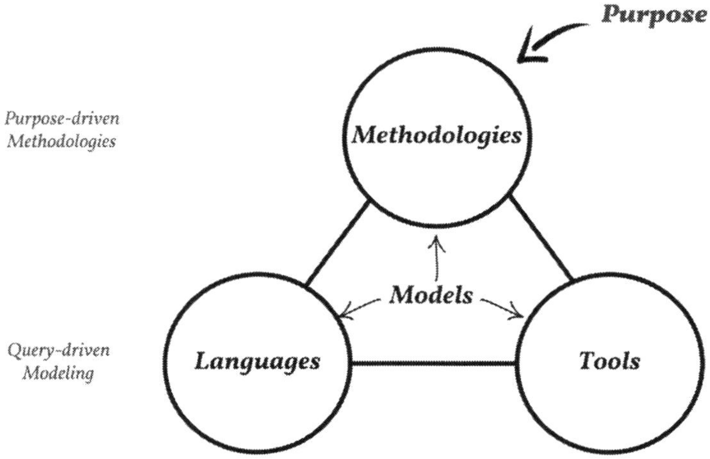

Figure 10.1: Triad of Modeling

The three domains must fit together, and to achieve this compromises must also be made in the individual areas, for example, a preset modeling tool that does not fully support the language, or methodological steps, or, conversely, offers proprietary functions that enable methodological steps and lead to a dependency of the methodology on the modeling tool.

The introduction of a new methodology into an organization is always a process of change. Rather than the technical topics of the introduction, the human factors are decisive for its success. The guidance on how to run a change project can fill a book of its own.

This book only sheds marginal light on these topics and focusses on the technical aspects of the introduction, i.e., the definition of the methodology, the languages, and the tools.

The next section 10.1 covers some challenges of the introduction of a new methodology.

Section 10.2 presents a process for defining a methodology, and section 10.3 examines the selection of the modeling language and section 10.4, the selection of a modeling tool.

The context of this chapter is based on a similar chapter about introducing modeling into an organization that I wrote for the German book “Modellbasierte Softwareentwicklung” [We18]. It includes some ideas of my co-authors Alexander Huwaldt, Jürgen Mottok, Stephan Roth, and Andreas Willert.

10.1 Resistance and Anti-Patterns

Let us assume that in the organization in which the model-based approach is to be introduced, no modeling has been carried out at all or only selectively and unplanned. So, the introduction is still at the very beginning.

There are three main interest groups within the organization regarding MBSE:

1. the initiators and drivers,
2. the organizational units that should work model-based in the future, and
3. the organizational units responsible for time, budget, etc.

All three stakeholders need to pull together to make the introduction a success - another harmonic triad.

In particular, this means that the people in the organizational unit who will use MBSE really want and support it. And that the responsible organizational unit is ready to provide the necessary money and time.

Figure 10.2 shows the percentage distribution of the degree of support among those affected by a change[Mo98]. You should concentrate on the large group of undecided (skeptics and brakepeople) and not on the small group of opponents, which is usually much louder than the other groups and, if you are not careful, ties up valuable resources.

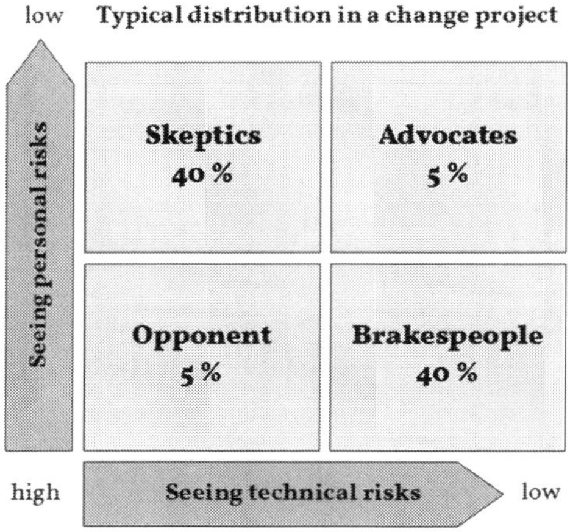

Figure 10.2: Resistance against change

An essential factor for the success of the implementation is also the support of an experienced, external expert in the project to

- transfer the new knowledge quickly and directly into the organization.
- recognize typical pitfalls, which the expert, typically, knows from his practice, at an early stage and thus to save time and not to stir up fears of a failure in the organization.
- obtain a neutral external image without operational blindness (i.e., the inability to critically reflect on oneself

as a result of working too routinely).

Make sure that the expert only supports the introduction, but does not take it over. Responsibility and tasks must remain within the organization to anchor the new approach in the long term. After a successful start, the expert should be largely superfluous and only needed selectively for specific questions or further developments.

I have seen many MBSE projects and know many typical mistakes that are made. They often happen because there is no focus on the purpose of the modeling. In this respect, knowledge of the following list of *Bad Practices* can help you to avoid errors in the first place.

Fast False Start

Full-fledged model-based specifications, traceability from requirements through architecture to implementation and back, simulation, document generation, automated analysis and verification, and more. These are all powerful tools in a model-based approach that can make projects really successful. But they are also all tools that have to be learned to use properly. To do this, you have to build up knowledge and, above all, practice a lot and gain experience.

A typical mistake is to introduce too much in one step. The probability of failure is high, and the opinion is quickly anchored in the organization that modeling does not work. Therefore, introduce a model-based methodology in several small steps. If things go well, you can increase your walking speed. If things don't go well, you have a manageable list of issues for improvement. Think big, start small!

Overmodeling

Unfortunately, overmodeling is a common phenomenon in MBSE. With SysML, almost anything can be modeled. The modeling language sets no limits and does not indicate when to stop modeling. Less is more, and just because it works, it should not be modeled.

In addition to the work of creating a model element, you also have to calculate the work that follows: changes to the definition or representations in diagrams, changes through dependencies to other elements, adjustments of simulations and automated analyses, and much more. These efforts are usually much higher than the initial effort to create the model element. An overmodeled model becomes sluggish, and the effort quickly exceeds the benefit.

Model Island

The model and associated tasks are on an isolated island and not integrated into the other development tasks. This often happens when modeling is introduced in an organization.

If the modeling is not integrated, it cannot unfold its full potential and is discarded at the latest when the project comes under pressure (which usually happens at some point).

Modeling must be an integrated and mandatory part of development from the outset, not an optional complement. Optional activities do not withstand project pressure.

Ivory Tower

The ivory tower is similar to the model island. In the tower, there are a few modelers who create very sophisticated models. The models are very detailed and use special and rare elements and rules of the modeling language. Even if the models are correct, they are only understood and used by a few project participants. Accordingly, the models (and also the modelers) are hardly integrated into development processes and have little significance and benefit for the project.

Fly out of the Learning Curve

To use modeling effectively, the modelers and the organization must also learn and gain experience. This takes time and initially runs contrary to one of the primary goals of modeling, which is to become faster and more effective.

If you do not plan the necessary times of the learning curve, it will probably carry you out of the curve at some point, and the introduction of the model-based approach can fail. This, of course, applies to the introduction of any kind of new method and is independent of modeling.

10.2 Selection of the MBSE Methodology

The SYSMOD Methodology Adoption Process (SMAP) depicted in figure 10.3 is an application of SYSMOD for developing an MBSE Methodology. You use SYSMOD itself to customize SYSMOD for the specific needs of your projects and organization.

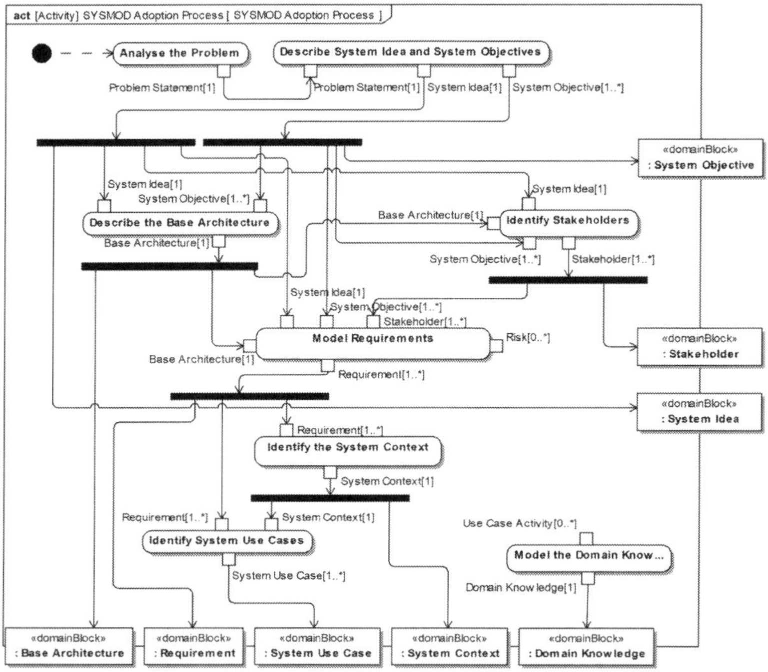

Figure 10.3: SYSMOD Adoption Process

In our fictitious organization that develops the FFDS system, the company wants to become more competitive with the introduction of the model-based approach. It is a strategic organization-wide decision and not limited to a single project. Often modeling is only introduced to solve problems in the current development project.

The first step is to describe these problems explicitly and to question whether MBSE really solves the causal problems or just symptoms. The findings then form the basis for defining the objectives of the project in the next step.

The problem analysis leads to the Problem Statement depicted in figure 10.4.

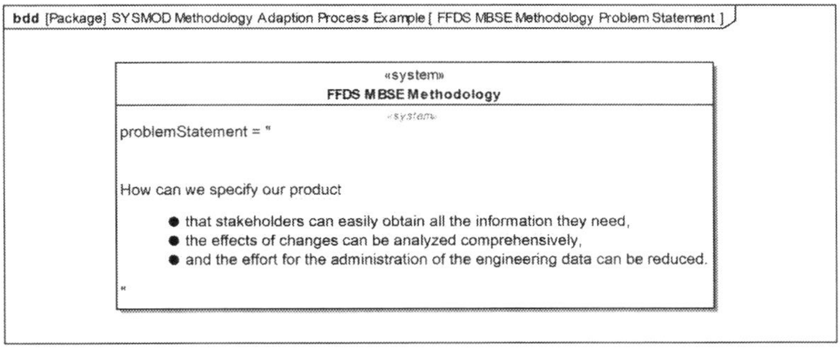

Figure 10.4: Example Problem Statement for MBSE Methodology

After the problem analysis, the company conducted a two-day workshop together with an external consultant to develop the MBSE Methodology. In the first step, the System Idea and System Objectives of the methodology were identified (figure 10.5, figure 10.6).

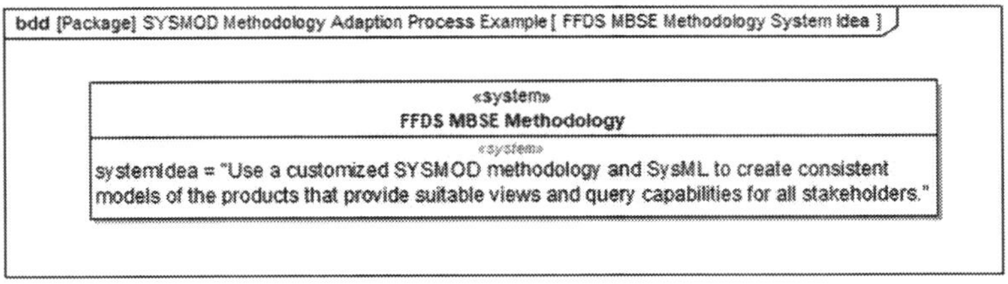

Figure 10.5: Example System Idea for MBSE Methodology

Since the concept of a "model-based approach" is broad, it is essential to describe clearly what one understands by it and how one wants to introduce it. Four objectives for the approach were derived from the identified problems (figure 10.6).

#	◇ Id	Name	◇ Text	Stakeholder
1	OBJ-M1	Redundance-free	All engineering data has exactly one defined master as single source of truth.	Head of Engineering
2	OBJ-M2	Development speedup	The development of a new product version is 40% faster than the development of products with our old methodology.	Head of Product Management
3	OBJ-M3	Error reduction	The number of errors in development, manufacturing, and operating is reduced by 70%.	Head of Engineering
4	OBJ-M4	Innovation	The development of smaller and larger innovative functions and products is increasing significantly.	CEO Vendor FFDS

Figure 10.6: Example System Objectives for MBSE Methodology

Figure 10.7 shows some typical Stakeholders of the MBSE Methodology. The direct users of MBSE, who are also stakeholders, can be found in the context diagram in figure 10.10.

#	Name	Documentation
1	CFO	The chief finance officer is responsible for the finances.
2	CIO	The chief information officer is responsible for the IT strategy.
3	Head of Engineering	The head o engineering is responsible for all engineering departments.
4	Head of Product Management	The head of product management is responsible for the product portfolio.
5	Works council	The works council of the FFDS company represents the rights of the employees.
6	CEO Vendor FFDS	The CEO of the company that develops the FFDS.
7	Systems Engineer	A systems engineer is "a person who practices systems engineering" and whose systems engineering capabilities and experience include sustained practice, specialization, leadership or authority over systems engineering activities. Systems engineering activities may be conducted by any competent person regardless of job title or professional affiliation. (SEBoK)
8	Mechanical Engineer	A mechanical engineer is works on the mechanical components of the system.
9	Electrical Engineer	A electrical engineer is works on the electrical components of the system.
10	Software Engineer	A software engineer is works on the software components of the system.
11	Human Resource	The human resource department is responsible for compliance with labor law and employment standards, administration of employees, recruitment, and training.

Figure 10.7: Example Stakeholders for MBSE Methodology

The Base Architecture represents constraint requirements for the MBSE Methodology. Here it is only that the requirements must be stored in IBM DOORS.

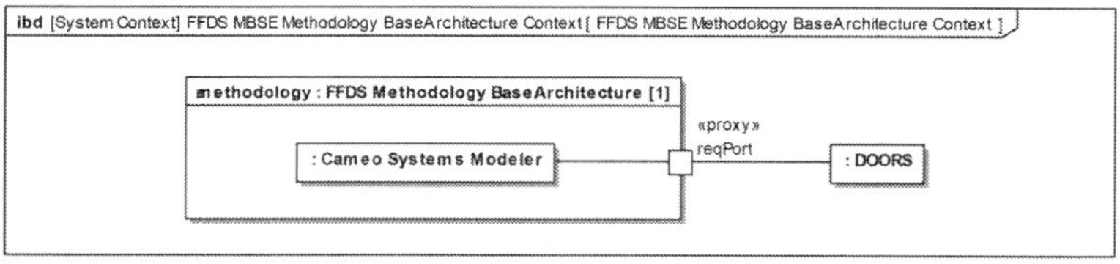

Figure 10.8: Example Base Architecture for MBSE Methodology

Some typical stakeholder Requirements can be seen in figure 10.9.

#	Id	Name	Text	Stakeholders
1	MBSE-REQ4	Measurability	KPI's and goals must be defined that objectively represent the success of MBSE.	Head of Engineering
2	MBSE-REQ3	Product Roadmap	The introduction of MBSE must not delay the planned product release roadmap.	Head of Product Management
3	MBSE-REQ1	Training	There must be a training offer for the new methods and tools on the market.	Human Resource
4	MBSE-REQ2	Employee Development	The existing employees must be trained for the new approach.	Human Resource

Figure 10.9: Example Requirements for MBSE Methodology

The methodology Context shows the users of the methodology and systems to which there are interfaces (figure 10.10). In our example, these are typical roles of the systems engineering project. The context also lists the external systems that have interfaces to the SME, which is part of the FFDS MBSE Methodology.

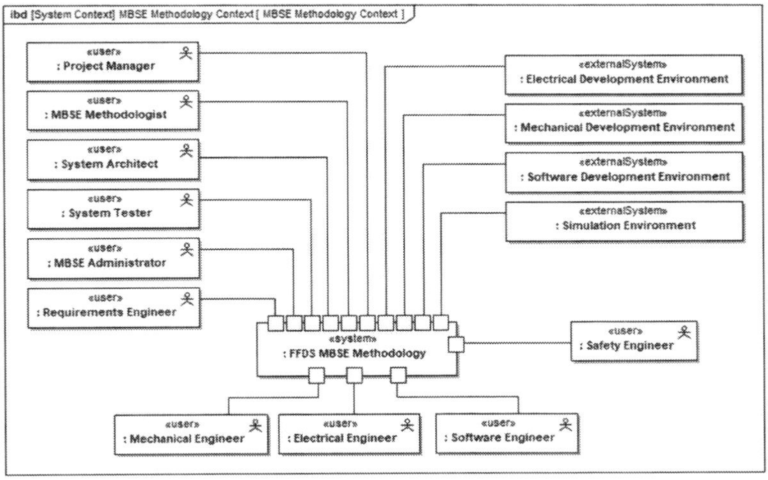

Figure 10.10: Example System Context for MBSE Methodology

To integrate the methodology into the overall engineering landscape, you need a particular focus on the interfaces, i.e., the ports in the context diagram. The ports to human actors are about views and UI needs.

The ports to external systems are about data exchange, i.e., data formats, adapter, and exchange technologies like OSLC.

The methodology Use Cases are a list of the methodological

steps required to achieve defined results of the methodology. Figure 10.11 shows some use cases of the MBSE approach and the actors involved.

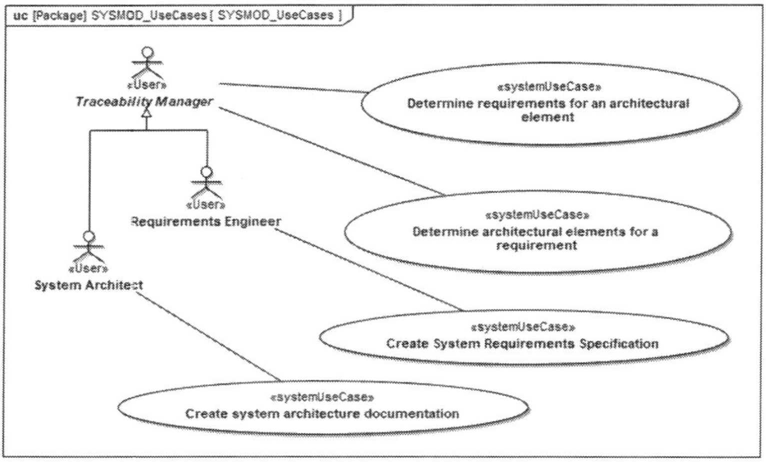

Figure 10.11: Example System Use Cases for MBSE Methodology

In contrast to the requirements analysis in systems engineering, the Use Case Activities of the MBSE Methodology are typically not described in detail. Instead, however, the incoming and outgoing objects, a short description of the use case, the interfaces to the actors, and the necessary views as well as other remarkable points are noted.

Figure 10.12 shows this as an example using the use case *Determine architectural elements for a requirement.*

Determine architectural elements for a requirement	System
Description	On the basis of the system model, the list of requirements for an architectural element is determined, which are partially or completely implemented by the architectural element.
Actorsr	Traceability-Manager
Trigger	When changes are made to the architecture, it must be checked whether all requirements have been taken into account.
Result	List of affected architectural elements in Excel format
Precondition	None
Postcondition	None

Figure 10.12: Example System Use Case Description for MBSE Methodology

The Domain Knowledge model defines the incoming and outgoing objects of the methodological steps. The diagram in figure 10.13 shows only the relationships between the objects. There are also properties and a textual description for each domain block. For example, the domain block *Requirement* also defines which requirement properties are considered and which requirement categories, such as usability requirements or performance requirements, are differentiated.

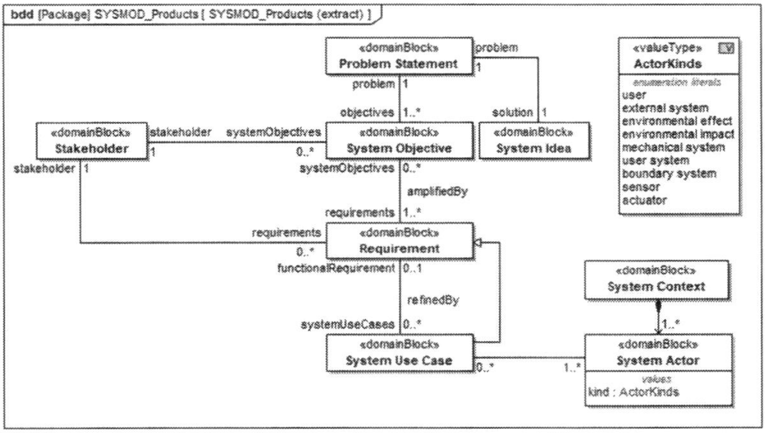

Figure 10.13: Example Domain Knowledge for MBSE Methodology

As with the development of a product, the introduction of a new methodology must be verified to ensure that it is implemented correctly and that it meets or supports the set objectives.

For verification, you look at the use cases and their associated requirements and check whether they have been implemented as planned. As a rule, this will be done by inspection. Some requirements can also be verified with tests, for example, if certain model queries or automatically generated views are implemented correctly.

For the validation, you should consider all the objectives of the methodological approach (figure 10.6) and examine whether they are met or adequately supported. If not already covered by the objectives, it must also be critically considered whether the methodological approach really brings a benefit and does not only mean additional effort. Answer honestly at least the following questions:

- Is the benefit higher than the effort minus the initial learning curve?
- Is the methodology lived by the participants or only worked through?
- Did the procedure lead to redundant work because the new ones did not replace existing steps?

From the answers and related analyses and other verification and validation, you can deduce whether the methodology is basically successful and decide whether and how it should be continued. This usually leads to adjustments in methodology. The projects certainly also regularly generate new requirements.

Overall, the adaptation and evaluation of the methodology is a continuous improvement process that must be carried out consciously.

10.3 Selection of the Modeling Languages

The main driver of the methodology is the purpose of the modeling. That, of course, must basically fit to the modeling language. If part of the purpose is *Creating a 3D specification of the mechanical parts*, SysML is not the right choice. The System Idea of SysML is

"SysML is designed to provide simple but powerful constructs for modeling a wide range of systems engineering problems. It is particularly effective in specifying requirements, structure, behavior, allocations, and constraints on system properties to support engineering analysis." [SysML19]

If that fits to your modeling purpose, SysML is an option.

Once you have selected a modeling language like SysML, you must map the outcomes of the methodology on a more detailed level to the modeling language. For example, the System Context is an outcome of the step *Identify the System Context* in SYSMOD. Figure 10.14 depicts the definition of the System Context elements in a Domain Knowledge model:

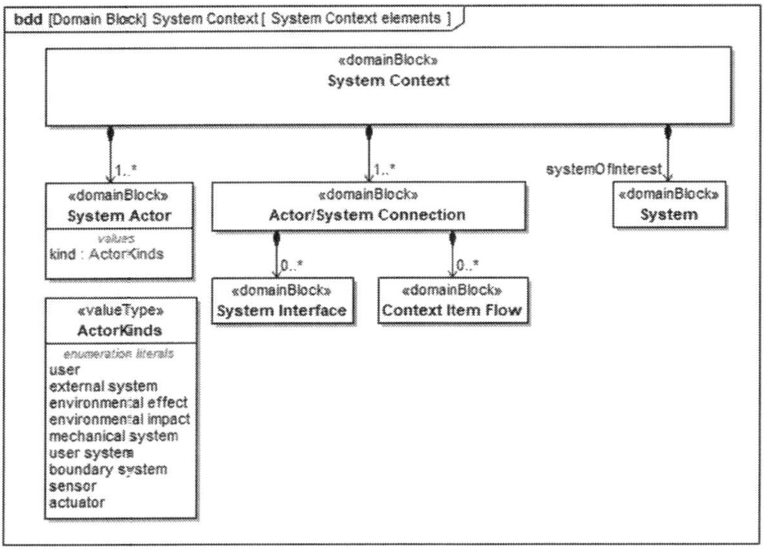

Figure 10.14: Definition of system context artifacts

The System Context includes the actors of different kinds, the connections between the system and the actors, including the interfaces and item flows, and the system of interest itself.

SysML has appropriate elements to describe these artifacts. Stereotypes can add additional properties and semantics not covered by SysML. In addition to the model elements, you must also define the views to depict the information.

The table in figure 10.15 lists the mapping of the system context concept to SysML.

Methodology Artifact	SysML Element/View
System Context	Block with stereotype «systemContext»
Actor	Actor or Block with SYSMOD actor stereotypes
Actor/System Connection	Connector
System Interface	Proxy Port, Interface Block
Context Item Flow	Item Flow, Block with stereotype «domainBlock»
View System Context	Internal Block Diagram
Documentation System Context	Automated Document Generation

Figure 10.15: Mapping Concepts/Language

An outcome of the analysis can also be that an artifact of the methodology cannot be expressed in the selected modeling language. In that case, you must find another language for this artifact, and propably also another tool, as well as a way how to link this artifact with the other elements to keep the traceability and consistency.

Based on the customized subset of SysML, you should adapt your modeling tool as much as possible to optimize the support of the subset, for example, making the model elements easily accessible in the toolbox and menus, while removing the unused model elements.

10.4 Selection of the Modeling Tools

The selection of a modeling tool directly derives from the selection of the modeling language task, which includes the set of model elements, views, and extensions (section 10.3).

The modeling language elements and views are so to say the mandatory functional requirements for the tool. In addition, you have a set of mandatory and optional quality requirements. Typical requirements are:

- Interoperability, for example, interfaces to other engineering tools, import/export formats, OSLC support
- Usability
- Support by vendor and community
- Conformance to standards
- License cost
- Extensibility, for example, support of profiles, and adaption of the UI
- Automation of modeling tasks

The set of quality requirements is different for each project or organization, and you must find your own individual set.

Figure 10.1 shows the *Triad of Modeling*. Often the modeling tool is selected early on because, for example, your own company has an agreement for licenses with the tool vendor. Ideally, however, the methodology and the modeling languages are defined first, and then the appropriate tool is selected.

11. More MBSE Tools

SYSMOD is a toolbox with some fixed core drawers for the SYSMOD Methods, Roles, Products, Modeling Guidances, and Examples.

Another drawer contains a selection of MBSE Tools that are presented in this chapter. These are not software applications, but conceptual models like the intensity model or patterns like the zigzag pattern.

Table of content of the MBSE Tools:

11.1 The Death of the Actor

I recommend not using the SysML model element *Actor*. However, I definitely recommend using the actor concept as, for example, described in the SYSMOD Method Identify System Context in section 4.11.. Instead of using the model element *Actor*, I propose to use the model element *Block* for the actor concept.

There are several good reasons to use the SysML *Block* to model an actor:

- You can switch the role of the external entity by also applying a stereotype *«system»* or *«subsystem»* without creating multiple model elements.
- You can model the internal structure of the actor, for example, to specify in detail how it is connected with the system of interest.
- You can model ports to specify the interfaces of the actors that are connected with the system of interest.

The actor concept is part of the methodology, and the SysML model element *Actor* is part of the language. You must distinguish the domains *Language*, *Methodology*, and *Modeling Tool* (figure 10.1 in chapter 10).

The term *System* is relative and depends on the viewpoint. From one viewpoint, an entity is a system; from other ones, it is a subsystem or an external system. It is the role of an entity and not an inherent characteristic. You lose the flexibility of changing the viewpoint if you model an actor with the SysML element *Actor*. By definition the model element *Actor* represents an external entity and can not be a system in another viewpoint.

Additionally, a SysML *Actor* is a black-box element, i.e., it is not allowed to model the internal structure of the actor, and it is also not allowed to define ports at the actor model element.

Therefore the SYSMOD stereotypes for actors are specializations of the SysML *Block* model element. An SYSMOD system context diagram with actors based on the model element *Block* looks almost the same as with actors based on the model element *Actor*. In addition, you gain the opportunity to model ports and parts of the actors and links between actors, for example, to get a more detailed description of the system context. See section 8.9 for an example of a System Context diagram based on a SysML internal block diagram.

11.2 Functional Architectures for Systems (FAS)

Functions are the essential core of a system. We build and operate the systems to get the functionality.

The Requirements Engineer has a focus on systems functions as functional requirements and their refinements from the viewpoint of the users and Stakeholders. The System Architect has a focus on the technical components and their specific technical functions.

The System Architect looks for functional cohesion, and the Requirements Engineer looks for user-oriented behaviors.

The Functional Architecture provides the bridge between the functional requirements and Physical Architectures. It supports the process to derive the right implementation of the system functions by a capable Physical Architecture.

The Functional Architecture consists of functions, functional interfaces and flows, and architecture decisions, and is independent of the technology that implements the functions.

The FAS method describes how to derive a Functional Architecture from Use Case Activities [We15]. The method was first presented in 2010 [LaWe10]. The latest official documentation of the FAS method is part of the book *Model-Based System Architectures* [We15]. The FAS method has proven itself to be successful in several industrial projects, for example.[DaKl14].

The FAS method is independent of SYSMOD. However, it is a perfect supplement. SYSMOD Products are inputs of the FAS method, and the Functional Architecture is helpful to derive a Physical Architecture. Figure 3.6 in chapter 3 depicts the integration of the FAS method in the SYSMOD Processes.

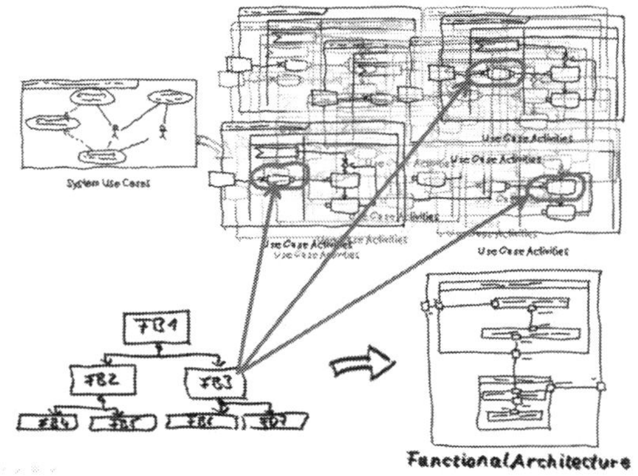

Figure 11.1: FAS Method in a nutshell

In a nutshell, figure 11.1 shows the steps of the FAS method. The Use Case Activities are the starting point. They are the set of required system functions clustered by Use Cases. This is a perfect structure for the Requirements Engineer.

The System Architect derives a new grouping of the Use Case Activities based on the criterion of functional cohesion. Functions that do similar things are members of the same functional group. The FAS method provides heuristics for the grouping. Although, finally, it is a decision of the System Architect.

Figure 11.2 shows a matrix of the functional grouping, and Figure 11.3 depicts an example of a Functional Architecture of the FFDS system.

In SysML, a group of functions in the architecture is modeled by a functional block. The groups are connected if functions in one group deliver outputs that are the input of functions in another group or vice versa. The interfaces of those connections specify the inputs and outputs. This is modeled with an internal block diagram by part properties, connectors, and proxy ports specified by interface blocks with flow properties.

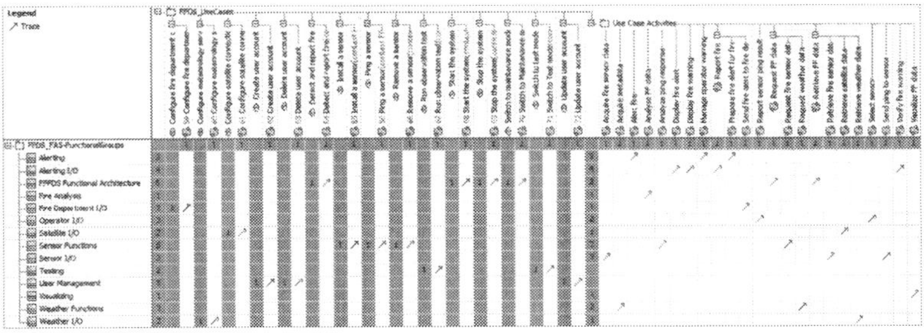

Figure 11.2: Functional Grouping based on the FAS method

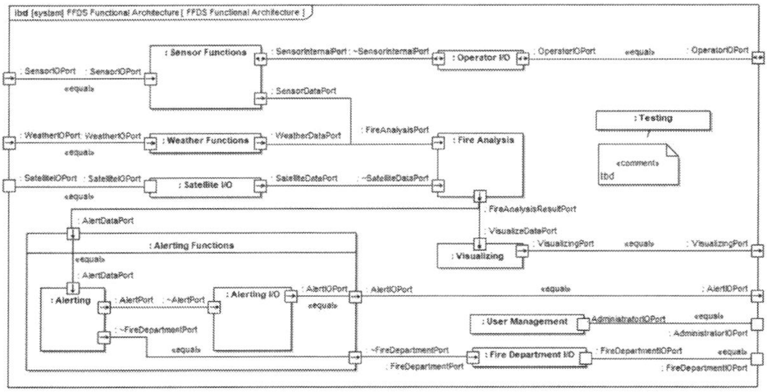

Figure 11.3: Functional Architecture of the FFDS

The elements of the Functional Architecture are allocated to a Physical Architecture. It is modeled by the SysML allocate relationship and depicted by a matrix (figure 11.4).

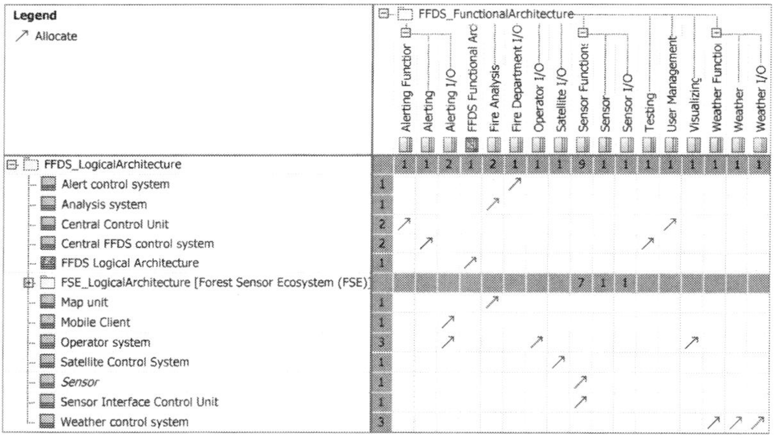

Figure 11.4: Functional to Physical allocation

You find a more detailed description of the FAS method in [We15].

11.3 Model Purpose Model

The SYSMOD Model Purpose Model is a simple description of three levels of modeling objectives. It is not intended to be a maturity model, although the levels represent increasing capabilities of modeling. In previous versions of SYSMOD, this model was named the *SYSMOD Intensity Model*.

Figure 11.5 depicts the model. It has three levels, and two add-ons. Only the third level SYSMOD3 is real MBSE with models as the primary source for the systems engineering data. The first two levels SYSMOD1 and SYSMOD2 are Model-Supported Systems Engineering (MSSE), i.e., the models support the engineering processes, but the primary source of the engineering data is in most cases documents or other elements outside of the system models.

The following paragraphs describe each level and the addons:

SYSMOD1: Purpose Communication - The objective of modeling is to improve the communication between stakeholders and other interested parties. The model and, in particular, the views on the model enable clear communication between the stakeholders and provide a holistic view of the system. The primary focus is on the views and the secondary focus on the repository. Communication and understanding are more important than formalism and completeness.

SYSMOD2: Purpose Traceability - Elements in the model are linked in a predefined manner to enable traceability queries with complete and proper results. For example, from a Requirement to all the elements in the architecture that satisfy the Requirement or vice versa to perform impact analyses. That requires a partly consistent structure of the model data in the repository. The traceability capability is independent of the graphical visualization of the model elements.

SYSMOD3: Purpose Specification - The models are the primary source of the systems engineering data for the engineering processes. Documents are only views on the model.

SYSMOD_LIB: Libraries - Common elements of the model are extracted and moved into model libraries for reuse in other projects.

SYSMOD_SIM: Simulation - The model is used to run a simulation or other automatic analysis to validate the model or to get further insights, for example, trade-off studies.

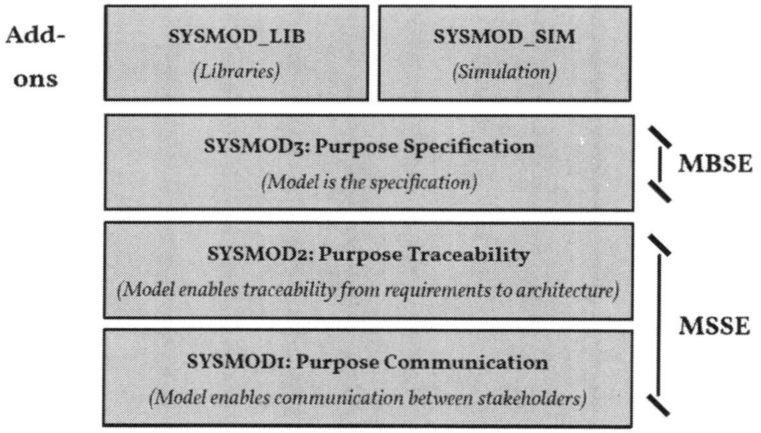

Figure 11.5: SYSMOD Purpose Model

SYSMOD1 is a low hanging fruit. You can achieve high value with low effort. SYSMOD2 requires more formalism and model queries. It is based on SYSMOD1 and has a balanced effort/value ratio. If you have achieved SYSMOD2, you still need a high effort to achieve SYSMOD3, the real MBSE level.

In return to the effort of achieving the real MBSE level you can gain lots of value out of your models. Doing things right will enable you to master complex systems with high quality and shortened time-to-market. Figure 11.6 visualizes the ratio of effort and value for the three levels assuming that you develop a complex system.

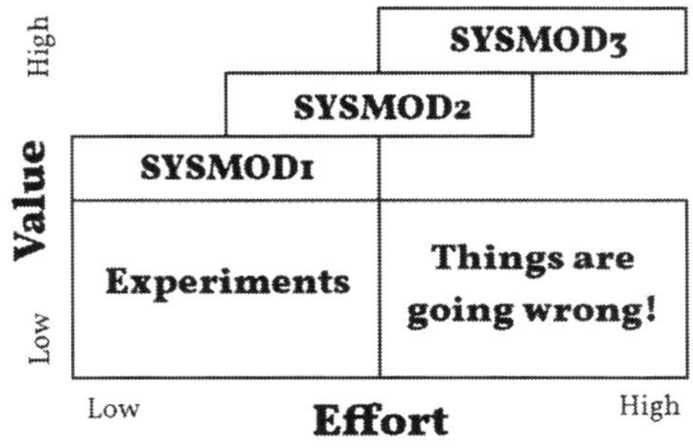

Figure 11.6: SYSMOD Model Purpose Model: Value and Effort

11.4 Proxy versus Full Port

SysML provides two different port concepts to specify the interfaces of a block: the full port and the proxy port. A SysML *FullPort* represents a real entity of the system. It is part of the bill of material (BOM) and specifies – as any other part – behavior and internal structures. The type of a full port is, typically, a SysML *Block*.

The following figure 11.7 shows an extract of the forest fire detection system (see also chapter SYSMOD Examples). The *Smoke sensor* has a full port *fixture* that specifies the attachment of the sensor to the environment. The attachment is a part of the *Smoke sensor* with its structure specified by the block *Attachment*.

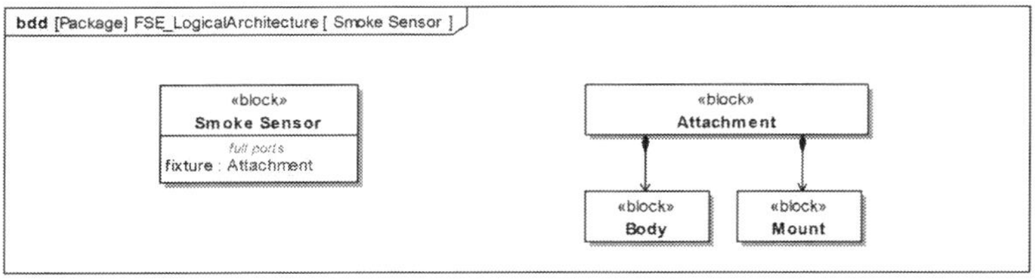

Figure 11.7: Smoke sensor with a full port

You can model the same semantics with a proxy port. The proxy port does not directly represent a real-world entity but is a proxy defining an interaction point. In the model, the proxy port is connected by a SysML *BindingConnector* with the model element that represents the real-world entity.

In figure 11.8, the attachment is now an internal part of the *Smoke sensor*. The port *fixturePort* is a proxy port and provides the relevant features of the attachment that are part of the interface specification to the outside. The features are specified by the interface block *SIF_Attachment* (SIF = System Interface).

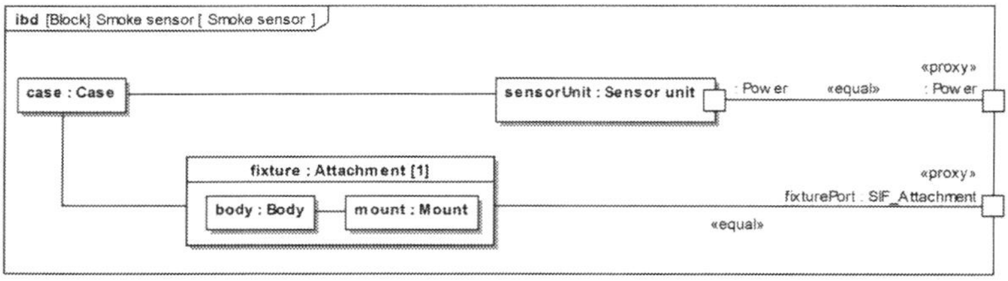

Figure 11.8: Smoke sensor with proxy port

The proxy port *fixturePort* and the appropriate internal part *fixture* are connected with a binding connector that assures that the instances of the proxy port and the part have the same value, i.e., they represent the same thing. For that reason, the types of the port and the part must be compatible, and the block *Attachment* is a specialization of the interface block

SIF_Attachment (figure 11.9).

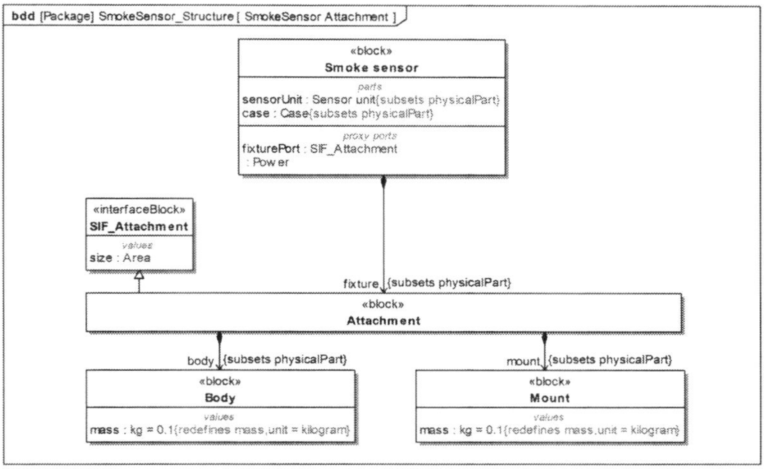

Figure 11.9: Smoke sensor with Attachment and interface definition

I recommend to use only proxy ports and to ignore the concept of full ports. In that case, all parts of the system are modeled the same way by part properties. If every port in the model is a proxy port, you can discard the stereotype notation *«proxy»*. That makes the diagrams less cluttered.

11.5 Variant Modeling

All along products exist in different variants. A product line, a customized product, or different designs for trade studies. In recent years organizations face more and more the challenge to provide a huge set of product variants. The industry moves from the phase of mass production to the phase of mass customization, i.e., mass production of customized products.

Typically, a single variant of a system varies only a few parts of the system. A car, as well as an aircraft, could be a variant of a transportation system. In most cases, it makes no sense in practice to handle a car and an aircraft as variants of a transportation system and to manage all the appropriate relationships in a single system model. The common parts of a transportation system are too abstract.

Unfortunately, you cannot measure abstraction with an objective metric. You must decide if the abstraction levels of the common parts and the abstraction level of the variant parts are close enough to be valuable for your project to be part of the same model. The benefit must be larger than the effort to manage a complex model.

The description of variants is a sophisticated task. It is already challenging to create a good description of a single system. Every variation adds another dimension to a multi-dimensional system model. For example, the engine could be a variation of a car system with three possible variants: diesel, electric, or hybrid engine. The next variation could be the chassis: small, deluxe, cabrio. Now, you can combine the variants, such as a car with a diesel engine and a small chassis or a car with a hybrid engine and a deluxe chassis, and so on. Any additional variation increases the dimension and the number of potential combinations.

The SYSMOD profile includes a set of stereotypes to model variants (section 9.9). The VAMOS approach (VAriant MOdeling with SysML) is covered in detail in the book *Variant Modeling with SysML* [We16].

The following figures show some variant modeling examples from the FFDS system model.

Figure 11.10 depicts a feature tree of the FFDS with the detection systems variation, a list of variants, and the drone variant configurations.

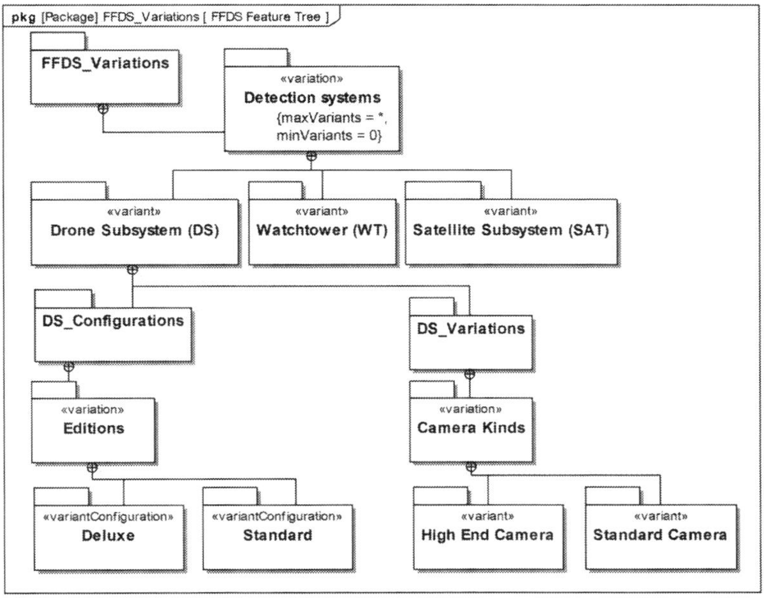

Figure 11.10: FFDS Feature Tree

Figure 11.11 shows an example of a variant configuration. The matrix depicts the import relationship between the variant configuration elements and the selected variants.

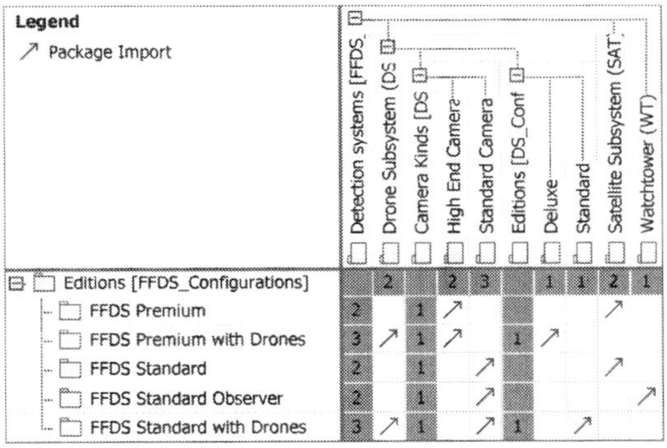

Figure 11.11: FFDS Variant Configuration Example

Figure 11.12 shows the relationship between the core element and variation point *Drone Camera* and the variant element *High-End Camera.*

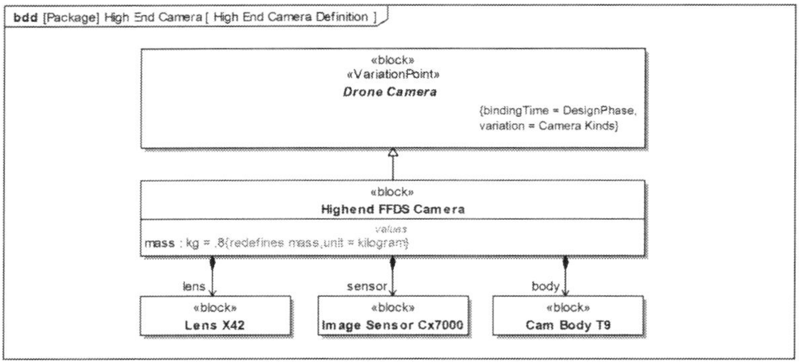

Figure 11.12: FFDS Variant

11.6 Zigzag Pattern

Requirements should not anticipate the solution. However, are your Requirements really free of any solution? Requirements describe the *What*, and the system architecture describes the *How*. Sounds easy, but.... Requirements are solution-free, and they contain solution aspects at the same time.

Let us assume that you have absolutely solution-free Requirements. Next, you derive a Logical Architecture that satisfies the Requirements, and you get the typical what/how-pair. For example, you have Requirements about a transportation system for people, and you derive a Logical Architecture that specifies a car. The solution *car* now again leads to new Requirements about aspects of the solution. For example, Requirements about the features of the engine of the car. You would not have those Requirements if your technical solution would be a ship or an aircraft.

The car engine requirements are solution-free from the viewpoint of this requirement level, but they contain solution aspects of the previous level. Again, you derive a solution from the car engine requirements, for example, a hybrid engine. That solution leads to new Requirements and so on. All in all, the steps represent a zigzag pattern (figure 11.13).

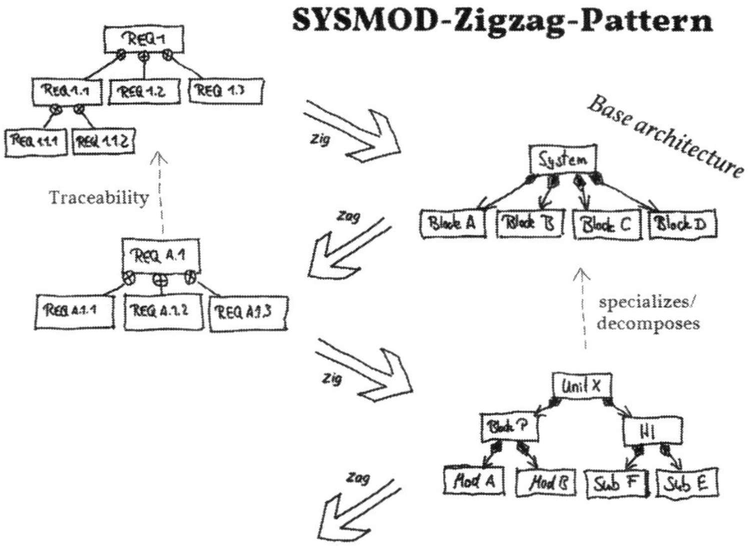

Figure 11.13: SYSMOD Zigzag Pattern

Requirements in practice always contain some solution aspects. Unfortunately, they are often implicit and are one of the causes why Requirements are a sore spot of many projects.

You should always describe the architecture that lies behind your Requirements. This architecture is the Base Architecture (section 5.7).

11.7 Coupling of System Architectures

Different kinds of System Architectures cover different aspects of the system. The Base Architecture specifies the architectural and technology decisions made upfront of the project. The Functional Architecture organizes the system functions, and the object flows between functional blocks. The Logical Architecture specifies the technical concepts and principles of the physical implementation, and the Product Architecture defines the most concrete Physical Architecture on the system level.

Conceptually, all these architectures are related, as depicted in figure 11.14.

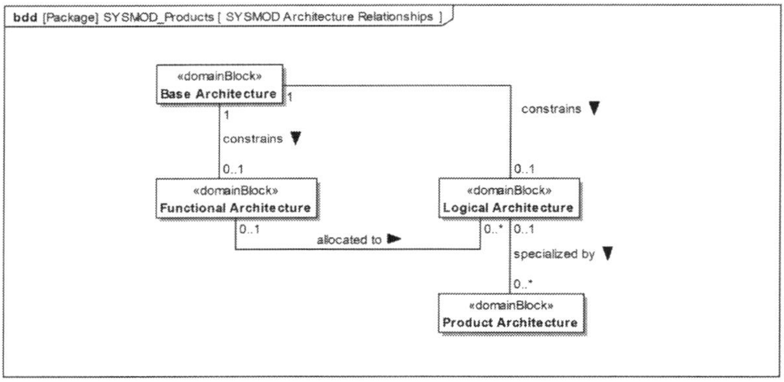

Figure 11.14: Relationships between System Architectures

The Functional Architecture and the Logical Architecture are loosely coupled by an allocate relationship (see figure 11.4 in section 11.2). All the other relationships between the architectures can be implemented by a loose or a strong coupling approach in the model.

As mentioned above, the relationship for a loose coupling between architectures is the allocation relationship. Figure 11.4 shows a matrix with the properties of one architecture as rows and the properties of the other architecture as columns, and the cells depict the allocate relationship.

A strong coupling between architectures means that a change in one architecture has a direct impact on the other architectures in the model depending on the direction of the relationship. The strong coupling relationship is the generalization relationship. Figure 8.5 in section 8.3 depicts the coupling of the root element of the Physical Architectures to the Base Architecture of the FFDS. The architecture inherits all features of the Base Architecture, can add new features, and redefine existing ones.

Both approaches - the loose and strong coupling - have their advantages and disadvantages. The loose coupling defines only a mapping between the architectures without any further impact in the model. This includes that the other architecture does not recognize a change of the leading architecture. That must be tracked manually by the System Architect. For example, a change in the Base Architecture has no impact on the Physical Architectures in the model if they are loosely coupled.

The strong coupling does not define a mapping, but a specialization of architecture elements. A change in the leading architecture is automatically forwarded to the dependent architecture. In theory, this is a straight-forward approach. In practice, the model can get very complex, and it can get hard to manage it depending on the capabilities of the modeling tool and the modelers.

11.8 Workshop Tool: Product Box

The product box is a little cardboard box that imaginary contains the system for selling purposes.

It is a tool for workshops to develop the System Idea and System Objectives. Take an unmarked cardboard box, some flipchart markers in different colors, and turn the box in an eye-catching packaging for your product.

A product box is labeled with a logo and name of the product, the objectives of the product for the customer (*"If you buy this product you will get rich, beautiful and live forever."*), and the main features. The limited space on the card box forces you to focus on the essential aspects.

Figure 11.15: Sample Product Boxes created in an analysis course (Source: oose)

The product box tool is an effective working group tool with excellent results in short times, and it makes fun. It focusses on the customer what is always a good approach. However, internal System Objectives like "This product will beat all competitors out of the market." are, typically, not written on product boxes.

Figure 11.15[1] shows some product boxes created in a course with students. They got an unmarked cardboard box and labeled it with a product name and logo as well as the idea and the main features of the system. Here, it was a system for a German car-sharing company.

11.9 Workshop Tool: Product Vision Board

The Product Vision Board is a canvas proposed by Roman Pichler [Pi16]. It provides a good overview of the main pillars of a product vision and can be used well in workshops to elaborate it.

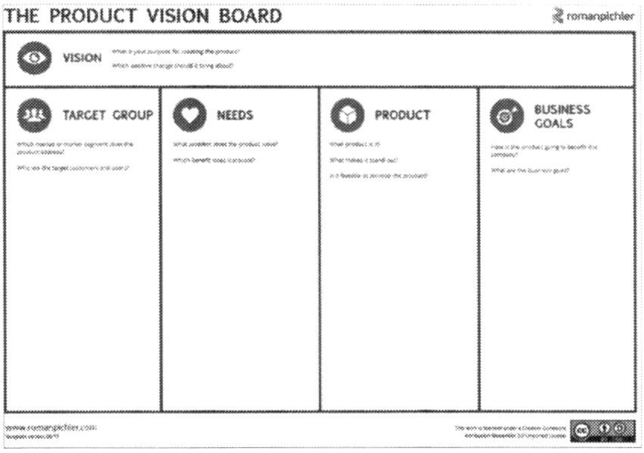

Figure 11.16: Product Vision Board

Figure 11.16[2] shows the Product Vision Board template with sections that cover System Idea and System Objectives, but also other aspects like the Stakeholders.

[1] Copyright oose Innovative Informatik eG

[2] Roman Pichler, License: https://creativecommons.org/licenses/by-sa/3.0/

11.10 Workshop Tool: SAMS Method

Walt Disney Productions developed storyboards in the 1930ies to pre-visualize motion pictures. They can also be used as a tool for the analysis of requirements.

The Storyboard Activity Modeling for Systems method (SAMS method) supports the elaboration of use cases based on storyboards [LaMe17]. The focus is on designing illustrative storyboards, deriving use cases, and establishing traceability between the storyboards and the resulting system models.

Participants of a SAMS workshop are a storyboard designer with sufficient drawing talent for achieving proper and appealing visualization together with the relevant stakeholders of the system development project. The storyboard designer visualizes the storyboards in real-time while the other participants can see the progress. The storyboard leads to new ideas or refinements of existing ideas. At the end of this iterative process, you have a set of storyboards visualizing usage scenarios of the system of interest (similar to concepts of operations (ConOps)).

The storyboards are the source to derive System Use Cases. As described in [LaMe17], the figures of the storyboards can be integrated into the model, and you can establish traceability between the storyboard snippets and the System Use Cases.

The storyboards can also be used to clarify or derive the System Idea.

11.11 Workshop Tool: 6M Method

The 6M method is a simple tool of cause and effect analysis. In the context of SYSMOD, it can be used to work out the Problem Statement.

The 6M stands for manpower, machinery, materials, methods, measurement, and mother-nature. They are categories covering potential causes leading to a problem. The diagram in figure 11.17 illustrates this relationship. It is called Ishikawa or, more general, fishbone diagram.

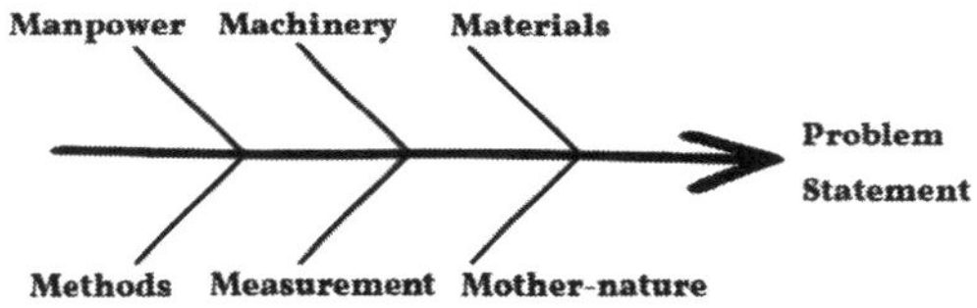

Figure 11.17: Ishikawa/Fishbone diagram for 6M method

The 6M categories are not a form sheet, but support it to broadly thinking about causes in different areas:

1. **Manpower**: Check the pains of the people doing their jobs.
2. **Machinery**: Check the pains of current products involved in the considered scenarios.
3. **Materials**: Check the pains of the used material. Are they used well? Are the supply and disposal easy?
4. **Methods**: Check the pains of workflows.
5. **Mother-nature**: Check causes coming from the environment.
6. **Measurement**: Check causes resulting from measurement issues like imprecise data.

Write down the potential causes for the problem statement at the appropriate branch in the diagram.

The 6M method can be combined with the following five whys method.

11.12 Workshop Tool: Five Whys Method

Taiichi Ohno, the mastermind behind the Toyota Production System (TPS) [Oh88], described the five whys method as the basis of Toyota's scientific approach by repeating the question why five times, because "the root cause of any problem is the key to a lasting solution" [Oh20].

The method is widespread and part of Kaizen [Im86], lean manufacturing [Wo90], and Six Sigma [Gy12].

Five whys is effective and straightforward: just ask five times "Why?". For example, a problem reported for a previous version of our FFDS system was that the fire was detected too late.

1. Why? Because the local sensor network did not work.
2. Why? An antenna in the forest was broken.
3. Why? The attachment of the antenna at the pole was broken.
4. Why? The antenna attachment was too old.
5. Why? The antenna was not maintained accordingly to the required service schedule.

Of course, you can continue asking why questions. If you think it is valuable, you should. But five questions are generally sufficient to get to the real cause.

You can create several branches of the cause-effect-chain. For example, an alternative cause to the fourth why question could be: *4. Why? The service sensor of the antenna did not report the defect.* This leads to the fifth why question: *5. Why? The service sensor does not work properly.*

The five whys cause-effect branch above can be, for example, one entry in the category *Methods* of the 6M method.

12. SysML in a Nutshell

This chapter presents the Systems Modeling Language (SysML) in a nutshell. While the previous chapters explain the MBSE Methodology and the application of SysML, this chapter describes the SysML language element by element. It provides an overview of the SysML, and explains common, but not all model elements. For a complete description of SysML, see the book We08, or the specification document [SysML19].

Section 12.4 to section 12.13 describes the SysML separated by diagram kinds and categories in the order of their appearance in the SYSMOD Processes.

12.1 History of SysML

SysML is based on the Unified Modeling Language (UML), so, the history starts with the origins of UML.

The history of UML began in the 90ies when object-oriented programming languages were a big hype. Added to this was a multitude of graphical modeling languages and methods. The multitude hindered their effective application in the industry, as there was very limited support for tools and knowledge in the form of books and the like for each modeling language.

The need for standardization was high. Finally, the Object Modeling Technique (OMT) by James Rumbaugh, the Booch method by Grady Booch and OOSE by Ivar Jacobson culminated in UML. Only the language was standardized by the UML and not the associated methods.

Grady Booch, James Rumbaugh, and Ivar Jacobson are also known as the “3 Amigos”. Today, the Object Management Group (OMG) is responsible for the UML. They provide the platform for developing and publishing UML as an OMG specification and an ISO standard ([ISO19505-1], [ISO19505-2]).

The UML 1.0 was published in 1997. It has received a great deal of attention and spread quickly worldwide. However, it should not go unmentioned that many promises were made by tool vendors and consultants about the “Weapon of Wonderment UML” that could not be kept in practice.

Simplified and slightly exaggerated: the painting of boxes and arrows could not easily replace the sophisticated art of programming. Due to the false expectations of UML, it could not fully develop its strength.

The UML was further developed with some extensions and bug fixes up to the UML 1.5 in the year 2003. Fundamental requests for change already led very early in 1999 to the fact that the OMG initiated the process for a completely new version of the UML.

Seven years later, in 2006, the UML 2.0 was officially released. In addition to some new types of diagrams and model elements, she has received a very extensive metamodel, which can be used for a much more formal description than the UML 1.x. In 2017, the latest UML 2.5.1 has been published.

The UML has 15 different diagram types, which are differentiated in structure and behavior diagrams. Figure 12.1 shows the taxonomy of the UML diagrams.

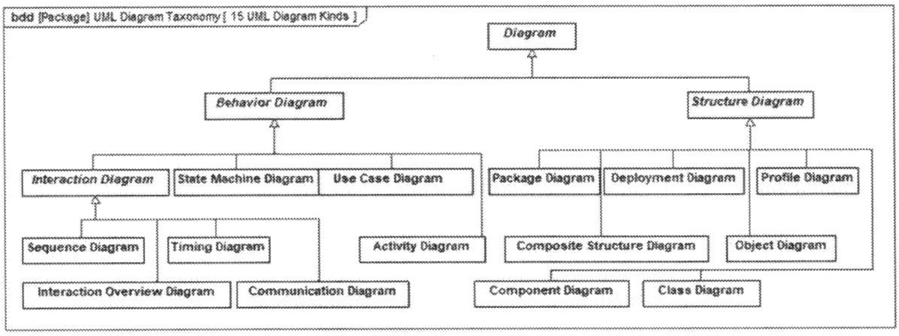

Figure 12.1: UML diagram kinds

A UML 3.0 is currently not planned but under discussion. The *3 Amigos* Booch, Rumbaugh, and Jacobson are no longer involved in the development of UML. In the working group of the OMG, people from different companies from all over the world are working, such as the company oose from Germany. The OMG also offers the certification program OMG-Certified UML Professional (OCUP) (www.omg.org/ocup-2/). With four consecutive certificates, individuals can have their UML knowledge certified.

At that time, the systems engineering discipline lacked a uniform and standardized modeling language up to SysML. What was needed was an international standard of a modeling language to describe a system that is independent of specific disciplines such as software, hardware, or mechanics.

The UML was a good candidate for this. Although it is a modeling language of software engineering, it is general enough to be used in other disciplines as well. On the one hand, UML fulfilled the essential requirements of systems engineering, and, on the other hand, it was already widely used and has been applied in systems engineering projects. Tools, literature, training offerings, and trained modelers with experience were numerous. And the extension mechanism profiles and stereotypes (section 12.11) made it possible to define an adaptation to the needs of systems engineering.

INCOSE - the worldwide umbrella organization of the system engineering discipline - had set itself the goal 2001 to establish the UML as the basis for a new modeling language of the system engineering. The new systems engineering modeling language was called Systems Modeling Language or SysML for short.

Some people think that UML is already very extensive. This is a common criticism of the language. And now, SysML adds more elements. However, elements of UML that are not needed in systems engineering were explicitly excluded. These include, for example, the components that are too software-biased for systems engineering, some rather exotic elements of class modeling such as power types, and some diagram kinds. Overall, the SysML is smaller than the UML.

In September 2007, SysML version 1.0 was released as an official standard. Thus, the development of SysML was not over. Just as the UML has evolved from version 0.9 to 1.5 to 2.5, there are also follow-on versions of SysML.

The SysML Revision Task Force is currently working on version 1.7. The working group includes companies and people from different fields. It is managed by Yves Bernard from Airbus and myself as representative of the company oose.

Due to the close relationship of SysML to UML, the structure and concepts are very similar. Figure 12.2 shows the different diagram kinds of SysML.

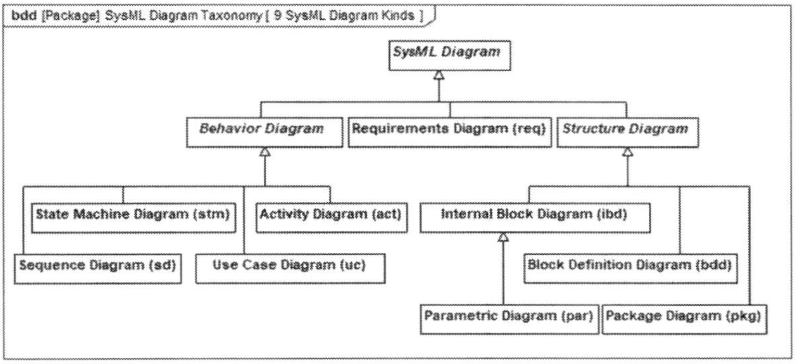

Figure 12.2: SysML diagram kinds

12.2 Structure and architecture of the SysML

The foundation of SysML is the UML. The language elements of UML are defined by three components:

- Concrete syntax
- Semantics
- Abstract syntax

The concrete syntax is the notation. For example, a use case is represented as an ellipse, or an association as a solid line, and an actor as a sticky figure.

The semantics defines the meaning of the model element. It is primarily a textual description, supplemented with constraints that are partly formally defined with the Object Constraint Language (OCL) [OCL14].

The concrete syntax and semantics are the well-known components of UML. You can find them in many books about the UML.

Much more significant, but less well-known, is the abstract syntax. It defines the structure of the language and is defined by UML with elements of the Class diagram. Put simply, it is the data model of the SysML language.

It seems strange at first glance that the UML is defined with elements of UML. But, for example, English is also not defined by a foreign language, but by English itself.

Figure 12.3 shows a simplified part of the abstract syntax, the so-called metamodel.

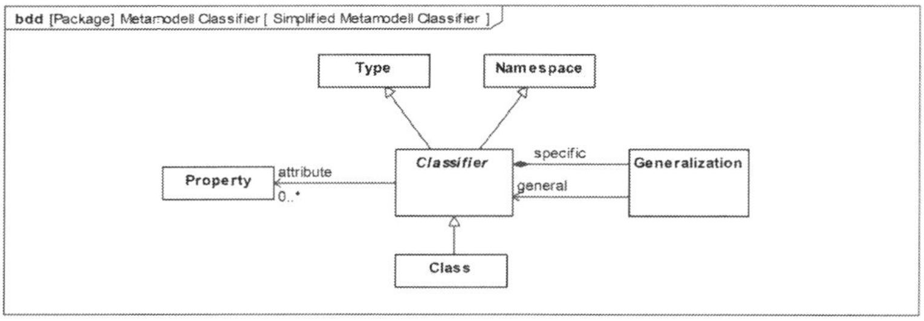

Figure 12.3: Simplified metamodel of the Classifier

In figure 12.3 you can see

- that a class is a special classifier.
- that there can be a generalization relationship between classifiers, where the specific classifier is the owner of the relationship.
- that classifiers are special types and namespaces.
- that classifiers can have attributes.

Every model element of UML is defined by a metaclass, and commonalities are extracted in generalized abstract meta-classes. All in all, the metamodel is a huge class model. A concrete user model is an instantiation of the metamodel.

Figure 12.4 shows a simple user model on the left and the instance specifications of the appropriate metamodel classes on the right. The underlying metamodel is simplified to keep the example small.

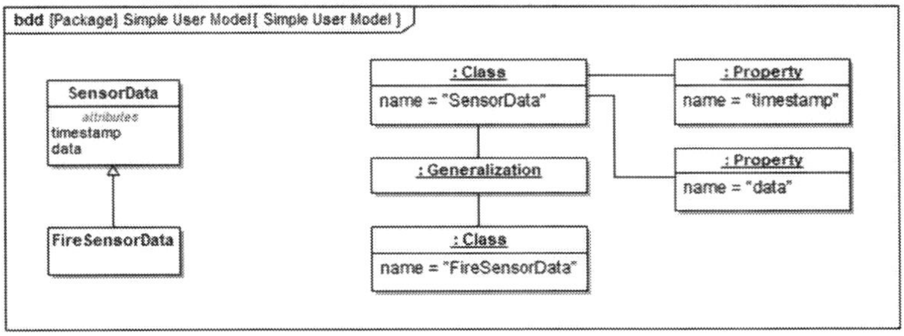

Figure 12.4: Simple user model

The language architecture of UML consists of 4 layers, called M0 - M3. The UML metamodel is layer M2, and the user model is M1. Layer M0 is the instantiation of the user model, for example, an instance specification of class *FireSensorData.*

Layer M3 is the metamodel of M2, i.e., it is the meta-meta-model that specifies the structure of M2. The metamodel of the UML metamodel is the Meta Object Facility (MOF) [MOF16].

Figure 12.5 depicts the 4-layer architecture of UML. The arrows are instance-of relationships.

Conceptually, SysML is a modeling language on its own. Technically, it is a profile of UML (see section 12.11 about profiles and stereotypes).

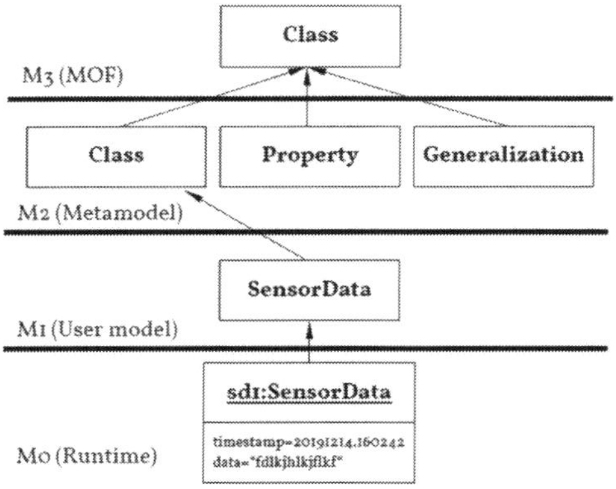

Figure 12.5: UML 4-Layer Architecture

For example, a SysML *Block* is a stereotype applied to the UML *Class*, as is the SysML *Requirement*. SysML does not extend the UML *UseCase* element. Therefore it is used directly in SysML without a definition of any stereotype.

This language architecture will change with SysML v2. Then, the UML is no longer the foundation of SysML. SysML v2 has its own metamodel independent of UML but based on MOF.

12.3 Minimal SysML

For some people, the SysML is too complex. This is based on a common misunderstanding that it is considered necessary to know and apply all elements of SysML.

Typically, a modeling project will use only a subset of the SysML. Just as you probably only use a subset of the English language every day.

It is not possible to generally specify the minimal subset of SysML to describe a system. Nevertheless one finds publications about it. Mostly the subset is defined by the diagram types. Some suggestions include the state diagrams, but not the activity diagrams. In other proposals, it is the other way round. Here, different approaches and requirements meet. This shows that it depends precisely on the very different requirements of the projects which language elements are useful and which are not. You should not select according to diagram types, but according to model elements. For example, if one includes the activity diagrams, one certainly does not mean that all model elements from this area should be used. There are a lot of them, and some are exotic and unsuitable for most projects.

First, think about what you want to describe, then look into the SysML and choose the model elements and diagram kinds you need. You can then ignore the rest of the SysML. Chapter 10 describes how to identify the subset of SysML needed by a project.

12.4 Package Diagram

The package diagram shows the structure and relationships of the packages of a model. The packages organize the model similar to folders that organize files on a storage medium.

Figure 12.6 shows a package diagram of frequently used elements, which are explained below.

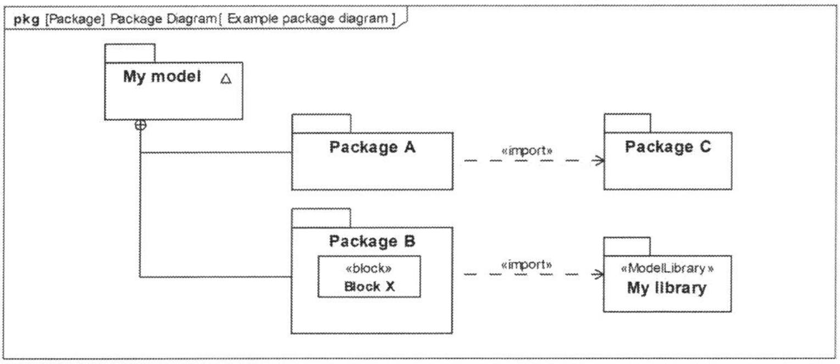

Figure 12.6: Example Package Diagram

Package, model, and model library

A package groups model elements and defines a namespace. Within a package, the model elements must have unique names and thus be referenced model-wide via their so-called qualified name. For example, the qualified name of block X in Figure 12.6 is *My model::Package B::Block X.* The delimiter between namespaces in SysML is the double colon.

The well-known folder symbol represents packages. The elements contained in the package can be shown within the package symbol. The package name is then in the top left of the tab. Otherwise, the name can also be displayed within the symbol.

The containment of elements within a namespace can also be depicted by a relationship. It is shown as a solid line and a plus sign circle on the owning namespace side.

The model element *Model* is similar to a package and represents a complete view of a system. A model is shown as a package with an additional triangle symbol.

The model library is a package that contains elements designed for reuse in several other packages or models.

Formally, it is a stereotype *«modelLibrary»*, which belongs to the standardized profile *StandardProfile* of UML that is also part of SysML.

Import packages

A package can import another package. That means that the elements of the imported package are added to the namespace of the importing package. Typically, because the elements are used in the importing package, which means that there is a unidirectional dependency between the packages. Knowing and documenting this is important for the dependency management.

The import relationship is noted as a dashed arrow with the keyword *«import»* in the direction of the imported package.

12.5 Use Case Diagram

The use case diagram shows use cases, relationships between use cases, and the actors associated with the use cases.

Depending on the methodology used, a use case itself represents a functional requirement or is a refinement of functional requirements.

Figure 12.4 shows a use case diagram with use cases, actors, and generalization relationships between actors.

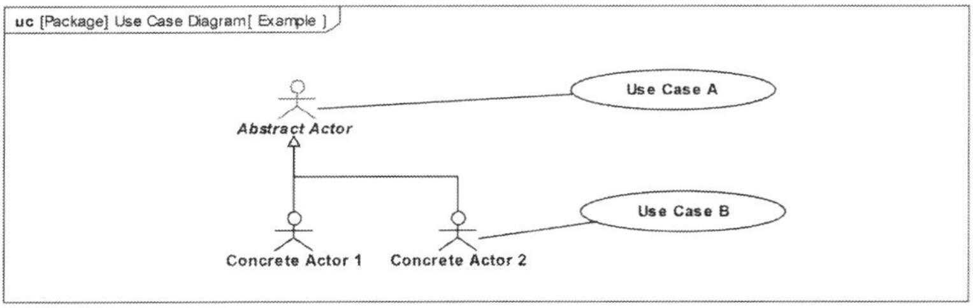

Figure 12.4: Example Use Case Diagram

Actor

The actor is a role outside of the subject that interacts with the system. The role can be taken by both a person and a subject. The subject is, typically, the system of interest.

The notation of an actor is the sticky figure. Alternatively, the actor can also be depicted by a rectangle with the keyword *«actor»*. Since not only humans can be actors, but also other systems, it makes sense to define categories with stereotypes to define new symbols and specific semantics. See section 9.2 about stereotypes for actors, and section 11.1 about a discussion about using the SysML block to model the actor concept instead of the SysML model element *Actor*.

Actors can be generalized and marked as abstract. An abstract actor only specifies common features of concrete actors, and does not directly represent an external real-world entity. Concrete actors are then modeled with a generalization relationship to the abstract actor (figure 12.4).

Use Case

A use case describes a set of actions of a system leading to an observable result, which, typically, has value to the actors or stakeholders. The use case describes a service offered by the system to its environment. The users of the service are the actors.

An actor usually triggers a use case. In most cases, the result of the use case is important for the triggering actor. In addition to these active actors, there are also passive actors who are required by the use case to perform the service. It is typical for a use case to have many actors.

A use case is noted as an ellipse. The solid line between actor and use case is an association. It means here that the actor and the system communicate with each other in the context of the use case. As described in section 12.6, the association creates a property at each association end. If you model an association between an actor and a use case, the properties are owned by the association itself.

12.6 Activity diagram

The activity diagram shows the definition of a single activity and is used to describe process-oriented behavior in contrast to the event-oriented state machine behavior (section 12.9). The activity diagram in figure 12.5 shows common elements used to model an activity.

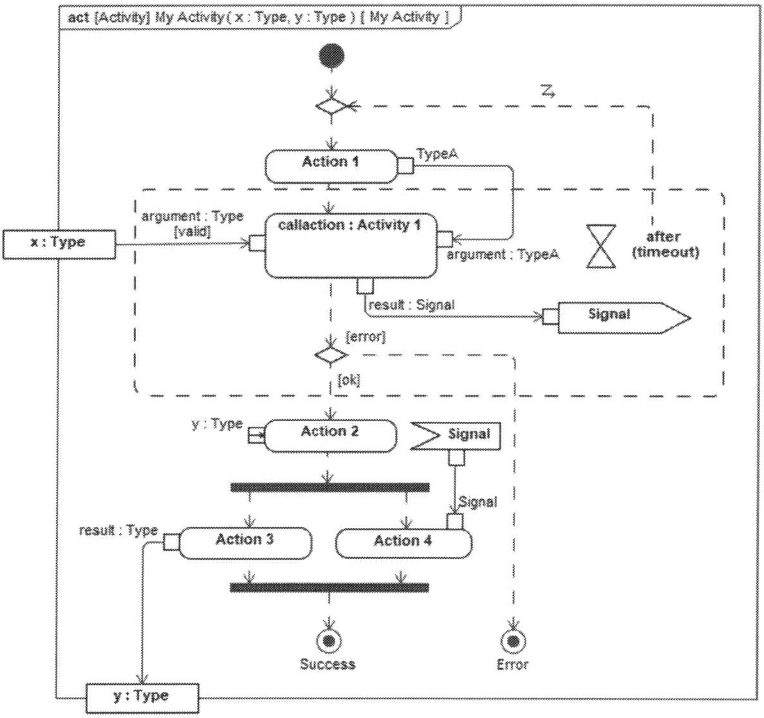

Figure 12.5: Example Activity Diagram

Activity and Activity Parameters

The activity describes processes that are composed of atomic actions. A process can be parallelized and synchronized, branched and merged based on conditions, interrupted and continued by events, and many more. Any form of a process is modelable.

The activity is a behavioral element, such as the state machine (section 12.9), interaction (section 12.8), or opaque behavior that describes a behavior specified in any language, for example, a programming language.

An activity diagram always shows just one activity. Input parameters of the activity provide input objects, and output parameters return objects after completion. Within the activity, the objects are guided to or from the pins of the actions through object flows.

The activity parameters are noted as rectangles on the edge of the activity rectangle. Inside is the name and the type of the parameter separated by a colon.

Action and Pin

The action is an atomic, executable step in an activity. The notation of an action is a rectangle with rounded corners. SysML provides a set of several action kinds. Some of the actions differ from the standard notation.

Actions can consume objects and, if necessary, return objects as a result. The pins are the holders of the incoming and outgoing objects and bind them to the parameters of the action. A distinction is made between input and output pins.

The notation of the pins is a small rectangle that is pinned to the action from the outside. If the pin is not connected to an edge, an arrow is depicted inside the pin to distinguish between an input pin and an output pin.

Next to the pin is the specification of the object that can be picked up by the pin. It is the name, the type, the multiplicity, and the state of the object specified in the syntax *<name>: <type> [<multiplicity>] [<state>].*

If the name is omitted, the type may also be displayed without a leading colon. If no multiplicity is specified, the standard multiplicity is 1..1. If the lower limit of the multiplicity is 0, then the object is optional. The *[<state>]* expression refers to a state of the type and specifies that the object flowing through this pin in this state.

In SysML, all actions are already defined independently of a special subject matter. There are about 40 predefined actions. These include actions that read and write values, compare, create and destroy objects, or invoke a behavior or operation. Each action is defined so that a runtime environment can be provided by a modeling tool as a whole. It would be beyond the scope of this book to introduce every single action. The full list of actions can be found in [UML17].

Here we limit ourselves to the so-called *CallBehaviorAction*, the *OpaqueAction* and the actions for sending and receiving signals (*SendSignalAction* and *AcceptEventAction*).

The *CallBehaviorAction* calls - as its name implies - a behavior. That can be another activity, for example. Any input pins on the action are mapped to the input parameter of the activity. Likewise, the output pins correspond to the output parameters. In the lower right corner of the action rectangle, a fork symbol is noted to symbolize the invocation hierarchy of activities. In the diagram, a distinction can be made between the name of the action and the behavior called. As with properties, the syntax is *<name>: <Behavior>*. In practice, the name is usually omitted.

The *OpaqueAction* integrates any language into the model. The language can be something executable, for example, specified in a programming language or natural language text. The selected language kind is also saved to the action for the runtime environment to respond appropriately. The purpose of *OpaqueAction* is to integrate such user-specific instructions into the overall model formally. In modeling tools, an *OpaqueAction* is often just named *Action.*

The *SendSignalAction* differs in notation from the other actions. It is an arrow that represents the sending of the signal object. The receiver of the object can not be represented in the diagram, although this information is present in the model.

The *AcceptEventAction* can receive a signal object. The notation is similar to a flag symbol. If the signal object represents an absolute or relative time, another symbol that looks like an hourglass is used.

Control and Object Flow

The control flow edge defines the execution order of actions in an activity. The object flow edge describes the flow of objects in an activity. For example, the connection that an output object of an action is the input object of another action.

The notation for the control flow is an arrow with a dashed line. The object flow arrow has a solid line. The control flow can also be depicted with a solid line, but you should avoid it to have a clear distinction between both kinds of flows.

Initial and Activity Final Node

The initial node is the starting point for an activity when the activity is called. The node is depicted as a black filled circle.

The activity final node stops the whole activity as soon as a single flow arrives at the node, regardless of how many other actions or flows are still active in the activity.

The notation for the activity final node is a black filled circle with an open outer circle.

An activity can have many initial and activity final nodes.

Decision and Merge Node

The decision node branches an incoming flow into several optional outgoing flows based on guard conditions, for example, If *XY* occurs, then do *A*, else *B*.

The notation is a diamond with one or two incoming and any number of outgoing edges, each of which has a guard condition in square brackets. Exactly one guard condition must evaluate to true. If it has two incoming edges, then one edge is the control flow, and the other is an object flow that transports the object needed for the decision.

The merge node merges several incoming flows into one outgoing flow.

The merge node has the same notation as the decision node. It is the counterpart with any number of incoming and exactly one outgoing edge. The merge does not check conditions or waits for special events.

A merge node doesn't always need to follow a decision node.

Fork and Join Node

The fork node splits an incoming flow into multiple independent outgoing flows. There is exactly one incoming and any number of outgoing edges. The fork node is shown as a black bar.

The join node synchronizes multiple independent incoming flows and merges them into a single outgoing flow. There is any number of incoming and exactly one outgoing edge. The outgoing flow does not start until all incoming flows have arrived. Like the fork node, the join node is noted as a black bar. Typically, a join node follows a fork node, but it is not mandatory.

12.7 Block Definition Diagram

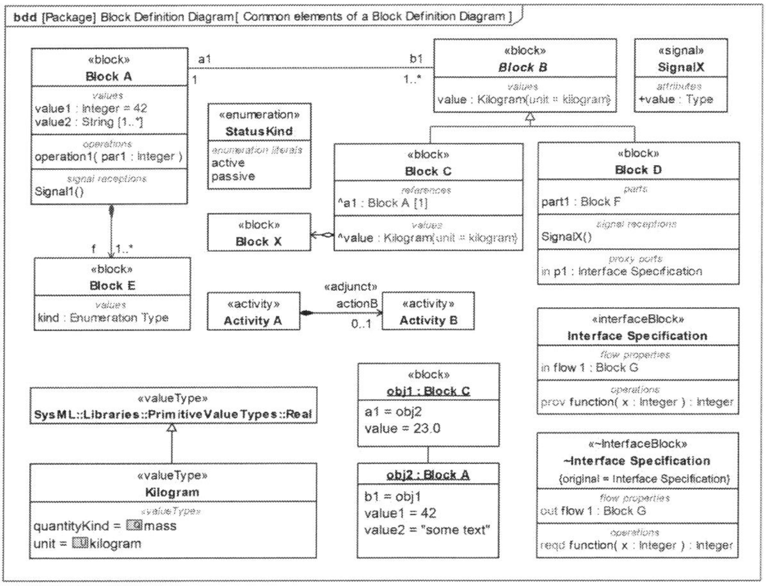

Figure 12.6: Common elements of a Block Definition Diagram

A block definition diagram depicts the definition of blocks and their relationships. The internal structure of a block is shown in internal block diagrams (section 12.7).

Figure 12.6 depicts common elements of a block definition diagram. The following sections describe the elements.

Block, Value Type, and Instance Specification

A block defines the structure and behavior of things that share the same characteristics and semantics.

The block is depicted as a rectangle divided into several compartments showing the elements of the block: name, parts, references, values, operations, constraints, proxy ports, and some more. While the name compartment must always be visible, the other compartments can be hidden in the diagram. The *«block»* keyword above the name is optional.

A block can be abstract, that means, it does not directly specifies a real-world entity, but general features of more concrete entities. Concrete sub-blocks with a generalization relationship to the abstract block inherit the general features and add new ones or redefine inherited ones. The italic spelling of the name depicts the abstract block.

A block can be marked as active. The diagram then shows the left and right sides of the rectangle with a double line. An active block defines active objects that have their own behavior that is executed independently of other behaviors, for example, in a separate process. This sounds software-specific, but actually, most components of a system have independent behaviors. This kind of modeling is, in particular, relevant if you use the SysML model for simulations.

A value type specifies a type for values. A value can only be identified by itself and cannot be referenced. SysML has some predefined value types: Real, Integer, String, Complex, and Boolean.

SysML provides the capability of modeling units and quantity kinds. They can be assigned to a value type. For example, a value type *Kilogram* with unit *kilogram* and quantity kind *mass* that specializes the SysML primitive value type *Real*.

The enumeration type is a special value type whose value range consists of a limited set of defined literals, for example, an enumeration type *StatusKind* with literals *active* and *passive.*

An instance specification specifies a concrete object at one point in time build according to the blueprint specified by the block or value type.

Instance specifications are depicted much like blocks. A colon and the type follow the name of the instance specification, and the entire text is underlined. The properties have concrete values and are called slots.

Property

A property defines a structural feature of a block or value type. The description includes a name, type, multiplicity, aggregation kind, and a default value.

The type of a property defines its blueprint. A colon behind the name separates it.

If the type is a value type, it is a value property. These properties are listed in a separate compartment with headline *values.*

If the type is a block, it is a reference property or a part property. The aggregation kind of the property sets the difference.

If it is set to *shared,* it is a reference property. That means the property holds a reference to another instance specification of a block. This is often used in the Domain Knowledge model (section 5.15). The reference property can also be modeled by an association or aggregation relationship. Actually, the aggregation relationship is an association relationship where the aggregation kind of one association end property is set to *shared.* On the other end of the association, a diamond symbol depicts the aggregation relationship. The reference properties are listed within the block rectangle symbol in their own compartment with headline *references*.

If the aggregation kind of a property is set to *composite*, it is a part property. That means the property holds an instance specification that is owned by the owning block of the property. It is a part of the block. It can also be modeled by a composition relationship, that means an association relationship with an association end property with aggregation kind set to *composite*. On the other end of the association, a filled diamond symbol depicts the composite relationship. The part properties are listed within the block rectangle symbol in their own compartment with headline *parts*.

A property can be set to be multi-valued so that it can contain multiple values of the same type. The multiplicity is depicted behind the type in square brackets. It describes an interval defining the allowed number of values, for example, [1..*] for one to many values.

The property can be assigned an initial value in the definition. Each newly created instance specification initially has this property value. It can then be changed later again.

The properties inherited from a supertype through the generalization relationship can also be listed in the list of properties of a block. In the first place before the name, the symbol ^ is then shown.

An adjunct property is a special property which values are constrained to the values of a specified principal. In 12.6, the property *actionB* must have the value of the call behavior action with the same name specified in *Activity A*. If the principal is an activity, you can use adjunct properties to create so-called activity trees representing the call hierarchy. The stereotype syntax of an adjunct property is simply *«adjunct»*.

Operation

An operation defines a behavioral feature of a block. The description includes a name, parameters, and a return type.

The implementation of the operation, called method in SysML, can be described with a behavior, i.e., an activity, a state machine, an interaction, or an opaque behavior.

The parameters of the operation are written similar to properties. Several parameters are separated by commas. The syntax of the parameter is: *<direction> <name>: <type> [<multiplicity>].*

It is defined in which direction the parameter transports its values:

- *in* = into the operation,
- *out* = out of the operation and
- *inout* = both directions.

If nothing is stated, the default is *in.* Likewise, as with the properties, an inherited operation can be prefixed with the symbol ^. Overall, the syntax of an operation is: <^> *<name> (<parameter list>): <return type>.*

Port

A port defines an interaction point of a block. Like a property, a port has a name, a type, and a multiplicity.

SysML provides two kinds of ports: proxy ports and full ports. A full port represents a real part of the owning block and is typed by a block. It is like a normal part property that also acts as an interaction point. The type of a full port is a block.

A proxy port is only a specification of the relevant features of an interaction point, but not a specification of a real-world entity. The proxy port is connected with the model element specifying the real entity or with another proxy port by a binding connector. Alternatively, the port property *isBehavior* is set to true, which specifies that the owning block of the port provides the real entity parts of the specified features (behavior port). It is like a binding connector between the proxy port and its owner. The type of a proxy port is an interface block.

The port property *isConjugated* is not used anymore in SysML 1.6 (see next section about the interface block).

The ports are listed in a compartment of the block, such as the properties and operations with headline *full ports* or *proxy ports*. In internal block diagrams, the ports are shown as rectangles on the border of the appropriate properties with name, type, multiplicity, and keyword *«proxy»* or *«full»* near or inside the rectangle.

Ports are connected by connectors, which is depicted in internal block diagrams (see section 12.7).

Interface Block

The interface block specifies operations and properties but does not have any own behaviors and no part properties. It is only the specification of an interface and is used as the type of proxy ports.

An interface block owns flow properties to specify things that flow through the appropriate interaction point. A flow property has a name, type, multiplicity, and a direction (*in*, *out*, *inout*).

The interface block can also own operations with the (functional) direction *provided*, *requested*, or *provreqd* (*provided* and *requested*).

Since SysML 1.6, the conjugated interface block stereotype *«~interfaceBlock»* is used to reverse the direction of the features of the referenced, original interface block. Before SysML 1.6, the *isConjugated* property of a port was used to model conjugation.

Association

The association is a structural relationship between blocks. It is depicted as a solid line between the blocks. At each end, there is a name and a multiplicity. The ends represent properties. If you model an association, you create three elements in the model: the association itself, and at each end, a property. Depending on the settings, the properties are owned by the blocks at the association ends, or the association itself. The properties in the model are typically created automatically by the modeling tool.

You can read associations from one block to another block using the following reading template. The resulting sentence must make sense in the context of the system:

"At any given time, each <block> has <multiplicity> <block> in the role of <role name>.

For example, in figure 12.7, you can read:

"At any given time, each Fire has exactly one Fire Location in the role of location."

Sounds a bit bumpy, and of course, you can adapt the sentence, for example, *"At any given time, each Fire has exactly one location."*

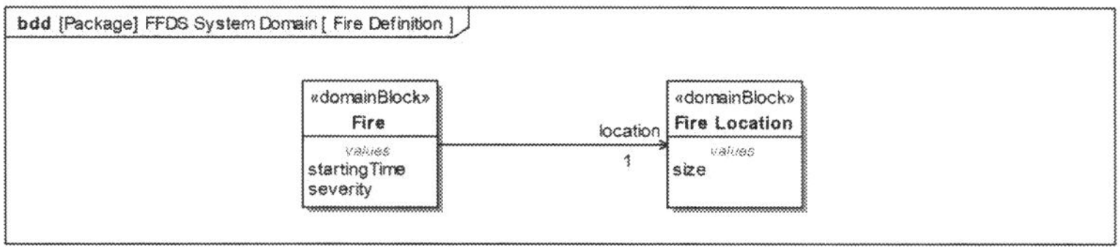

Figure 12.7: Example Association

The association defines corresponding properties in the blocks involved. If only one association direction makes sense and, accordingly, a property should also be defined in only one block, and an association end can be provided with an arrowhead. This is called navigation because you can "navigate" from one block to the other. The association owns the property at the association end without the arrowhead. Typically, it means that the property can be ignored. If no arrows are given, the convention is usually that both navigation directions are possible. Alternatively, both arrowheads can be shown.

The name of the association stands at the middle of the association line. The name can refer to a reading direction depicted by a black triangle in front of the name. Since only one association name is allowed, only one direction can be verbalized in this way, even if the other direction is valid. The association name is usually omitted and should only be used if the name really adds value to the model.

If the aggregation kind of a property at one association end is set to *shared*, the association is also called aggregation relationship, and an unfilled diamond shape symbol is shown at the opposite association end.

If the aggregation kind is set to composite, the association is also called composition relationship, and the diamond symbol at the opposite end is filled.

Generalization

The generalization is a taxonomic relationship from a special block to a general block. It is also possible to model the generalization relationship between actors, use cases, interface blocks, and behaviors like activities or state machines.

Another common but unoffical name for generalization is inheritance relationship.

The generalization is noted as an arrow with a solid line and a closed arrowhead. In the direction of the arrow, it is read as "is a kind of".

The specialized element inherits all features of the general elements, which means they are part of its definition.

Signal

The signal describes the structure of an object that can be sent from one entity to another.

The signal is a type like a block or value type and has a similar notation as the block. The keyword *«signal»* is additionally located above the name of the signal. A signal has properties and, sometimes, operations.

A block owns receptions to specify that it can react to the receipt of a signal. They are listed in a special compartment of the block with label *receptions*.

Signals are also used in activities (AcceptEventAction, SendSignalAction), and in state machines (Signal events).

12.8 Internal block diagram

The internal block diagram depicts the internal structure of a block.

Figure 12.8 shows the definition of some blocks used for the internal block diagram in the following figure 12.9.

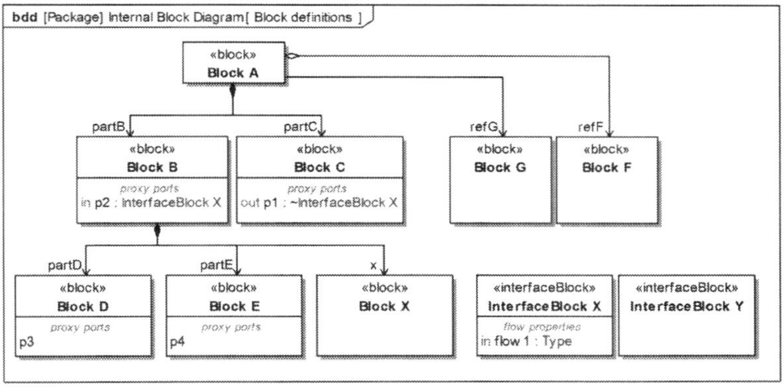

Figure 12.8: Block definitions for the internal block diagram

The block definition diagram depicts the breakdown structure of blocks, but not how the parts are connected. For example, you can not model that *partD* and *partE* in figure 12.8 communicate with each other. This relationship is modeled by a connector, which can only be shown in the internal block diagram (figure 12.9).

In figure 12.9, *partD* and *partE* are connected by a connector via the interaction points *p3* and *p4* modeled by ports.

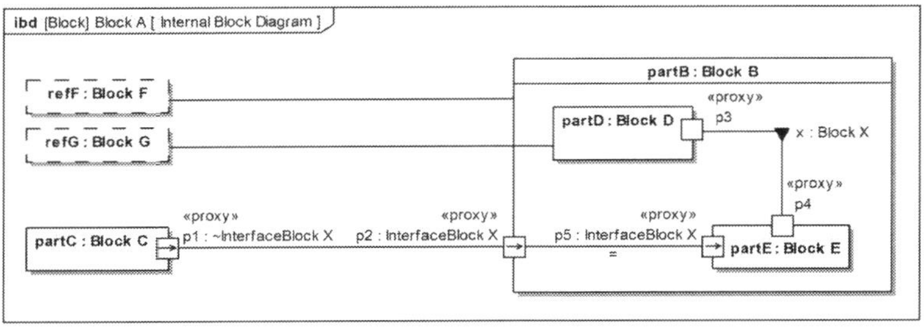

Figure 12.9: Common elements of an Internal Block Diagram

In the following, the common internal block diagram elements are described in more detail.

BindingConnector

The binding connector specifies that the elements at both ends represent the same thing.

If it is a value property, both ends have the same value. That is, typically, used in parametric diagrams (section 12.10).

A binding connector connects a proxy port with the part property that represents the real entity behind the interaction point For example, *p2* and *p5* in figure 12.9 are connected by a binding connector.

The binding connector is depicted by a solid line with attached keyword *«equal»*, or simply the equality symbol =.

Connector

The connector specifies some kind of communication between two properties. It can be a logical, software, electrical, mechanical, optical, or whatever connection.

A solid line depicts the connector. It can have a name and also a type, which is an association. The syntax *name:Association* is shown at the middle of the connector.

ItemFlow

The item flow in the internal block diagram specifies that something flows along a connector. The item is a property of the enclosing block. In figure 12.9, the property *x:BlockX* that is owned by *Bock B* flows from port *p3* to *p4* along the connector. The ports specify what is allowed to flow, the item flow specifies what really flows in the respective context.

12.9 Sequence diagram

The sequence diagrams show an interaction specifying the message exchange between elements of the system. It answers the question: "When does who call who and how?" In contrast, the activity answers the question "What happens in which order?" and the state machine "How does an object react to events in a given state?".

Figure 12.10 shows a sequence diagram with frequently used elements, which are explained in more detail below.

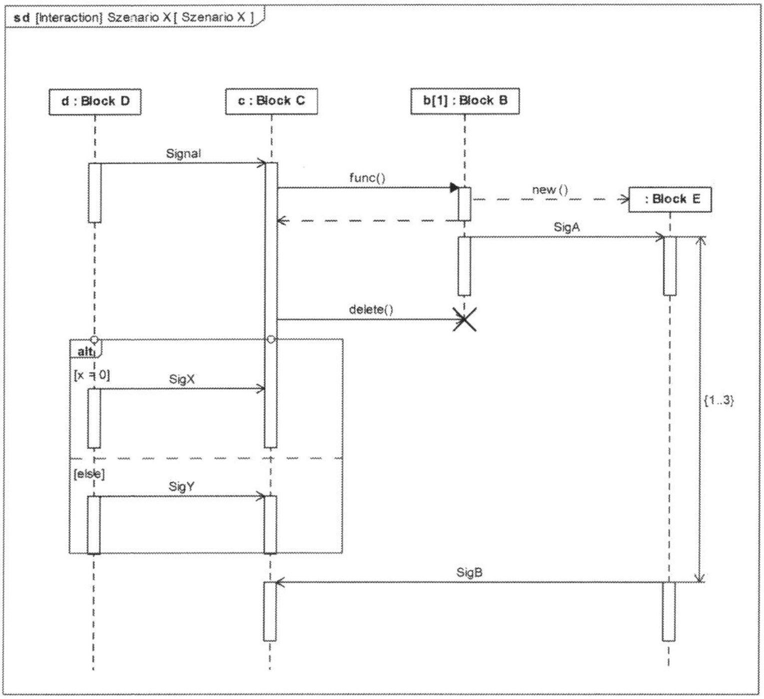

Figure 12.10: Example Sequence Diagram

Other diagrams of the UML that represent an interaction are the communication diagram, the timing diagram, and the interaction overview diagram. They are not part of SysML.

Interaction

The interaction describes communication between lifelines that represent each one partner of the communication. The communication is based on the exchange of messages in the form of operation calls or sent signals. Just like an activity or a state machine, the interaction specifies a behavior of the system.

Typically, an interaction represents one concrete scenario. Shown are the involved elements (communication partners) as well as the sequence of who sends and who receives a message. The concrete scenario does not have to be complete. Only the messages that are of interest in the context of the interaction are modeled.

The interaction does not have its own notation but, like the state machine, is represented by the entire diagram. In some cases, the diagram frame is included in the modeling, and a message can be sent to or received from the diagram frame. In that case, the sender or receiver is not shown in the diagram, but it is part of the model. Formally there is a gate element on the diagram frame. Since they are displayed as a point on the frame, the gate is not visible. But it may have a name, which is, of course, visible.

Lifeline

The lifeline represents a communication partner of an interaction. It is usually a property, i.e., it is the same model element that is also depicted in internal block diagrams (section 12.7).

A property can have multiple values if the upper multiplicity range is greater than 1. A lifeline always represents just one object. Therefore, a selector must be specified that specifies which object from the set is represented by the lifeline. The selector is an expression in any language. If the set of the object is ordered, it is typically an index value.

The head of the lifeline is noted like the corresponding property. If a selector is specified, it appears after the name in square brackets.

The dashed line of the lifeline element represents the lifetime of the object. If the object is destroyed during the interaction, the line ends, and in addition, the end of the object is displayed with a cross.

At the bottom of the interaction diagram, all the lifelines end without specifying herewith the destruction of the objects. Conversely, the head of the lifeline at the beginning of the interaction does not mean that the associated objects are generated at this point.

If an object is created during the interaction, then the lifeline head is drawn at this point of the creation. The message that creates the object points directly to the head and is noted as a dashed arrow.

On the lifeline, bars can be used to display the places where the lifeline-related object is active. Typically, the bars are automatically set by the modeling tool on the incoming and outgoing messages.

Message

The message is a communication between two lifelines. It can be synchronous or asynchronous and can specify an operation call, the sending of a signal, and the creation or destruction of an object.

The notation of a message is an arrow from the senders' life-line to the receivers' lifeline. Different arrow shapes indicate the different characteristics of a message. The message arrow for creating objects is dashed. For all the other messages, the arrow has a solid line, but with different arrowheads.

A synchronous message has a full arrowhead. Synchronous means that the sender waits until the receiver has processed the message. The end, i.e., the return of control to the sender, is depicted by a dashed arrow. It is called the return message.

The asynchronous message has an open arrowhead. Asynchronous means that the sender does not wait for the receiver and continue processing immediately after the message has been sent. This implies that the sender and the receiver are in different execution processes. The dashed return message does not exist here accordingly.

Combined fragment

Typically, sequence diagrams represent a concrete scenario, that is, a communication of selected elements in a limited situation. Loops or conditional branches are therefore not needed as much as in activities. But it is still possible with so-called combined fragments.

A combined fragment has an interaction operator and one or more interaction fragments as operands.

The interaction operator of a combined fragment includes alternatives, loops, parallel execution, and other kinds. The operands are interaction fragments, that is, a set of messages between lifelines.

The combined fragment is noted like a diagram frame: a rectangle with solid lines and a small pentagon in the upper left corner. In the pentagon, the interaction operator is noted. Dashed lines separate the interaction operands. Depending on the operator, interaction conditions are also specified. They are at the beginning of an interaction fragment near the first lifeline.

There are a total of twelve different interaction operators:

- Branches and loop: *alt, opt, break, loop*
- Concurrency and order: *seq, strict, par*
- Assertions: *critical, neg, assert, consider, ignore*

The *alt* operator describes alternative communications. In figure 12.10, an *alt* operator with two interaction operands is modeled. Any number of additional operands are possible. If *x > 0*, the signal *SigX* is sent. In all other cases, it is the *SigY*.

A complete description of all interaction operators can be found in [UML17].

12.10 State machine diagram

A system or a component of the system is always in a state that abstracts a combination of conditions that exist in the system. Events that arrive on the system or its components lead to state-dependent reactions that can alter conditions and switch to other states.

The state machine defines this behavior. A state machine diagram shows exactly one state machine. It contains states and transitions triggered by events.

Figure 12.11 shows a state diagram with frequently used elements, which we will explain in more detail below.

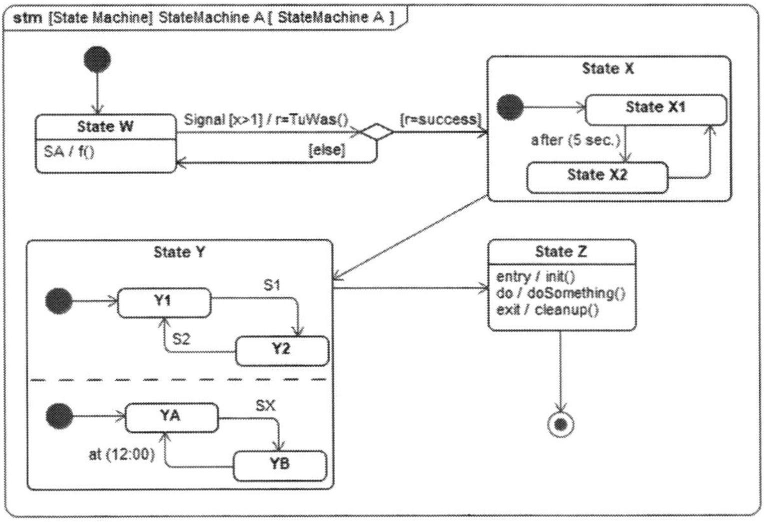

Figure 12.11: Example State Machine Diagram

State machine

The state machine describes an event-oriented behavior of an element. The element is usually a SysML *Block*. It represents the context object of the state machine.

The state machine does not have its own notation. It is represented by the entire state machine diagram. The diagram frame thus forms the boundary of the state machine.

The state machine has a queue for events that are consumed by the states and transitions according to the order of their occurrence. The so-called run-to-completion semantics applies, which means that the next event is only consumed once all actions of the previous event have been completed. An exception is the state behavior (do behavior), which need not be completed to process the next event. An event that can not be consumed, for example, because there is no suitable transition, is discarded.

State

The state represents a condition of the associated context object. It has a name and possibly internal behaviors, which are executed based on defined events.

States are represented by rounded rectangles. The name of the state is in the rectangle. In another compartment are the internal behaviors, which are triggered by events as in transitions, but does not lead to leaving the state.

In addition to the internal behavior, a state can also have three special behaviors that are triggered by predefined events:

- The entry behavior is always performed immediately after entering the state.
- The exit behavior is always executed immediately before leaving the state.
- The state behavior (do behavior) is carried out while the state is active. This behavior is interruptible.

A state can be further detailed by substates. It is a so-called composite state that contains a region with states and transitions.

It is also possible for several substates to be active at the same time. The upper state is called the orthogonal state. It is divided into any number of independent regions, each separated by a dashed line. In each region, exactly one state is active. There must be no transitions between states in different regions.

The more deeply nested transitions have a higher priority than the external transitions. If an event matches multiple transitions, the lowest transition is chosen, of course, only if the source state is active.

Transition

The transition specifies a transition from one state to another. It is a directed relationship between two states, and defines triggers and a guard condition, as well as an effect behavior that is performed during the transition.

The notation of the transition is an arrow with a solid line and an expression in the following syntax: *trigger1, trigger2, ...[guard condition] / effect behavior.*

The trigger is the link between event and behavior in the model. Notated at a transition, this means that the transition is activated by the trigger when the event occurs.

There are five types of events that can trigger a transition:

1. The call event occurs when an operation is called.
2. The change event occurs when a given Boolean expression specifying the change evaluates to true.
3. The signal event occurs when a signal has been received.
4. The time event is further differentiated. The relative time event occurs when the state from which the associated transition originates has been active for a certain time (*after (<time>)*). The absolute time event occurs when the specified absolute time occurs (*at(<time>)*).
5. The any receive event occurs both when an operation is called, or when a signal is received. In addition, it also specifies the reception of non-signal objects.

The guard condition is a Boolean expression specified in any language, such as OCL [OCL14], a programming language, or a natural language such as German or English. It depends on the runtime environment in which the state machine is executed: human or machine.

Especially in orthogonal states, the behavior within one region is often affected by which state is active in another region. You can check the condition whether or not a state is active in another region (*[in <state>]*).

A transition without trigger and condition is automatically activated as soon as the source state is completed. It is also called a completion transition.

Initial and Final state

A state machine or composite state has a beginning and may have one or more defined ends. The initial state indicates the beginning. It is a pseudo-state, i.e., it only controls the state machine and does not describe a real state of the context object. The transition starting from the initial state points to the true initial state. Triggers and conditions are not allowed on it. An effect behavior may be defined.

In contrast to the initial state, the final state is a real state, i.e., the context object can be in this state. Unlike the "normal" states, a final state, of course, has no outgoing transitions, no internal behavior, and can not be described by decomposition in more detail. If no other regions of the state machine are active, the final state terminates the state machine.

The initial or final state is noted like the initial and activity final node of the activity as a black ball, respectively, a black ball with an outer circle.

Pseudostate

The pseudostate is a state machine control that affects the behavior of a state machine. It is not a real state.

There are ten different pseudostate kinds. The initial state described above is one of them. The remaining nine pseudostates are listed below.

- Flat history
- Deep history
- Junction
- Choice
- Termination
- Fork
- Join
- Entry point
- Exit point

Figure 12.11 depicts a choice pseudostate, which is similar to the decision node in activities (section 12.5).

A detailed description of the pseudostates can be found in [UML17].

12.11 Parametric diagram

The parametric diagram is a special version of the internal block diagram (section 12.7).

Figure 12.12 shows a parametric diagram with nested value properties and a constraint property, which is a property typed by a constraint block. The constraint parameters are connected by binding connectors with the value properties. The keyword *«equal»* or the = sign at the binding connector can be omitted in a parametric diagram.

A nested property can be depicted by showing the nested structure like *number:Integer* nested within *bb* and *assembly*, or by the dot notation like *assembly.ba.ba1.value1:Integer* that is nested within *ba1*, *ba*, and *assembly*.

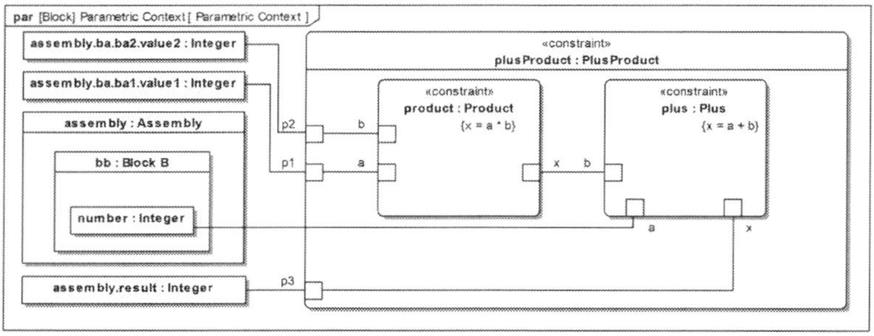

Figure 12.12: Example Parametric Diagram

Figure 12.13 depicts the definition of the properties in the parametric diagram, including the constraint blocks.

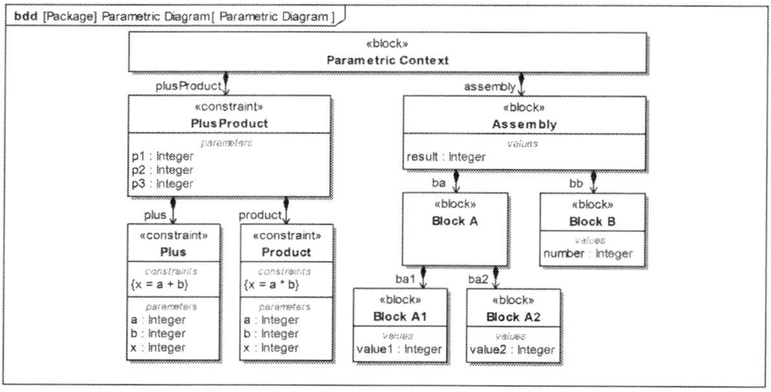

Figure 12.13: Example Constraint Block Definition

Constraint Block

Constraint blocks enable engineering analysis in a SysML model. They define a network of expressions that constrain properties of the system.

A constraint block defines a constraint and its parameters that can be used in multiple contexts. The constraint parameters are the value properties of the constraint block. The constraint block can also own constraint properties, i.e., properties typed by a constraint block, to composed constraint expressions.

The notation is similar to a block but with the keyword *«constraint»*, and a constraint and parameter compartment.

In a parametric diagram, the usage of a constraint-block-typed property (=constraint property) is depicted like a part property. The parameters are shown similar to ports, but the tiny parameter rectangles are attached to the constraint property boundary from the inside.

12.12 Profiles and Stereotypes

You cannot use naked SysML out-of-the-box. SysML is too general to be an effective language for a concrete project. For example, SysML provides the model element *Block*, but no specific model elements for system hierarchies like *subsystem*, *module*, *segment*, *unit*, *component*, and so on.

Another example is the SysML model element *Requirement*. It provides the three properties *name*, *ID*, and *text*. But no properties like *priority*, *risks*, or requirements categories like *functional* or *non-functional*.

In a project, you need more specific model elements to add domain-specific semantics and properties to the modeling language. SysML provides an extension mechanism to define a specific modeling vocabulary. A new model element is defined by a stereotype. For example, figure 12.14 depicts the definition of the SYSMOD stereotype *«systemUseCase»*.

The term *stereotype* implies that there are two types involved. You cannot define new model elements completely independent of existing SysML elements. You must take an existing SysML element (type 1) that is extended with a more detailed semantic, further properties, and new concrete syntax, i.e., an icon (type 2).

In figure 12.14, the existing element is the metaclass *UseCase*. The stereotype *«systemUseCase»* defines a new name, the SYSMOD SystemUseCase semantic, and the additional properties *trigger*, *result*, and *triggerSignal*. The relationship between stereotype and metaclass is an extension relationship that is only used for the specification of stereotypes. Do not mix it up with the generalization relationship. That is used as a relationship to specialize stereotypes, for example, between *ContinuousUseCase* and *SystemUseCase* in figure 12.14.

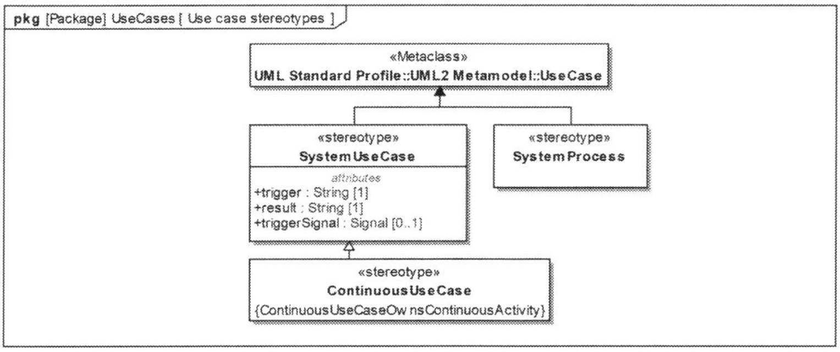

Figure 12.14: SYSMOD stereotypes for actors

You must know the architecture of the language SysML to be able to define stereotypes. Figure 12.15 depicts the relationship between SysML and the Unified Modeling Language (UML) [UML17].

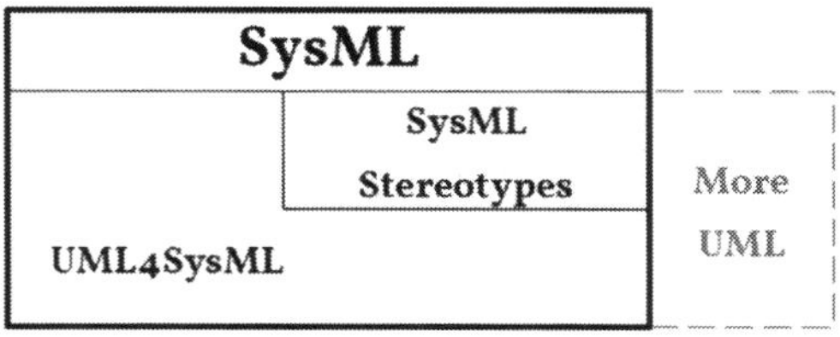

Figure 12.15: SysML Language Architecture

SysML is based on a subset of UML that is called UML4SysML. Some of the UML elements like the *UseCase* are directly a part of SysML. Other UML elements are always extended by SysML stereotypes. For example, the SysML *Block* is a stereotype that always extends the UML *Class*. The Class itself without the applied SysML stereotype *«block»* is not allowed in SysML.

The set of stereotypes is bundled in a profile. A profile is a package-like element that is linked to a model by a profile application relationship to make the stereotypes available in the model (figure 12.16).

The OMG provides many standardized profiles. For example, the UML itself also contains a standardized profile called StandardProfile, which includes, besides others, the stereotype *«modelLibrary»*. There are also standalone profiles like the OMG standards *UML Profile For MARTE: Modeling And Analysis Of Real-Time Embedded Systems*, the *UML Testing Profile (UTP)*, and the *Safety and Reliability Profile*.

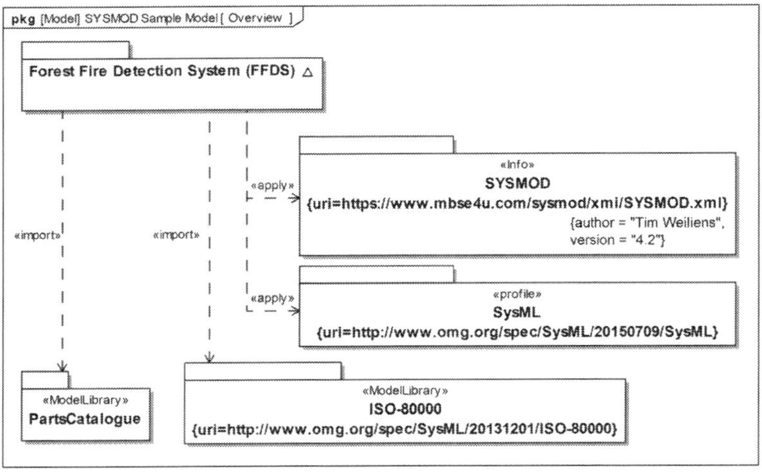

Figure 12.16: Profile application

Interestingly, the SysML is formally also "only" a profile of UML. It is, however, regarded as an independent modeling language.

12.13 Requirements diagram

Figure 12.17 shows a requirements diagram with frequently used elements, which are explained in more detail below.

Typically, requirements and their relationships are not depicted by diagrams, but by tables and matrices.

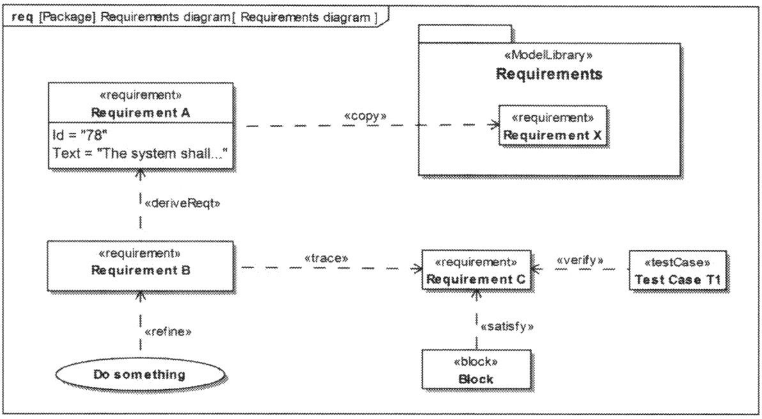

Figure 12.17: Example Requirements Diagram

Trace

The trace relationship establishes a traceability path between any two elements. There is no other semantics except the trace.

The trace relationship is shown as a dashed arrow with the keyword *«trace»*.

DeriveReqt

The derive relationship specifies that a requirement is derived from another requirement by some analysis. For example, a system requirement is derived from stakeholder requirements (see also the zigzag pattern in section 11.6).

The derive relationship is shown as a dashed arrow with the keyword *«deriveReqt»*.

Refine

The refine relationship specifies that the source element is a refinement of the target element. For example, a use case can be the refinement of a functional requirement.

The refine relationship is shown as a dashed arrow with the keyword *«refine»*.

TestCase

A test case verifies one or more requirements, which is modeled by the SysML verify relationship. It is an operation or behavior specifying the test. Typically, it is a SysML activity.

A test case always returns a verdict of enumeration type *VerdictKind*, which defines the enumeration literals

pass	The system under test adheres to the expectations.
inconclusive	The evaluation cannot be evaluated to be pass or fail.
fail	The system under test differs from the expectation.
error	An error has occurred within the testing environment.

Verify

The verify relationship connects a test case or other model elements with a requirement specifying that they can determine whether the system fulfills the requirement.

The verify relationship is shown as a dashed arrow with the keyword *«verify»*.

Satisfy

The satisfy relationship connects a model element with a requirement to specify that the model element fulfills the requirement.

The satisfy relationship is shown as a dashed arrow with the keyword *«satisfy»*.

12.14 Allocation

Figure 12.18 depicts some applications of the allocate relationship.

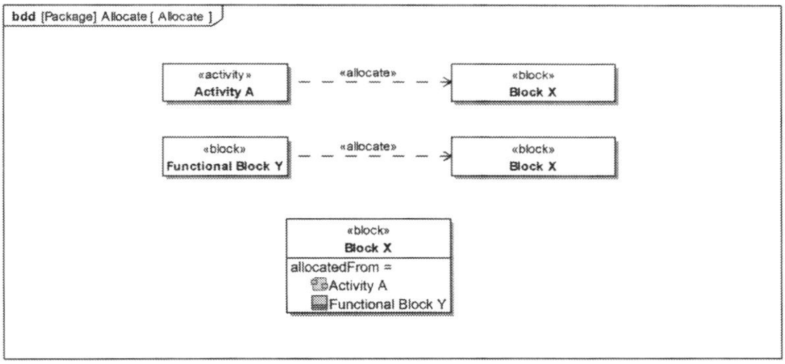

Figure 12.18: Example allocation

Allocation is a common systems engineering concept to denote the mapping of elements within various structures.

The allocate relationship defines an abstract mapping between SysML model elements without strict constrained methods on how to implement the mapping.

Typical mappings are

- from behavior elements to structural elements, for example, mapping of a functional decomposition tree (for example, use case activities) to a structural decomposition tree (for example, the logical architecture). You can model the allocate relationship from activities to blocks, or from actions to part properties. Also, you can map pins of action to ports, or object flows to item flows.
- from structural elements to structural elements, for example, mapping of one architecture kind to another (see section 11.7). You can model allocate relationships from blocks to blocks, properties to properties, or ports to ports, and so on.

The allocate relationship is always from a definition element to another definition element, or from a usage element to another usage element, for example, from an activity to a block (definition), or from an action to a part property (usage).

The allocate relationship is shown as a dashed arrow with the keyword *«allocate»*. Typically, the relationship is depicted in a matrix or table instead of showing the allocate arrows in a diagram. Alternatively, the relationship can also be depicted in a compartment (figure 12.18).

The allocation activity partition is another option to show the allocate relationship between actions and part properties (figure 12.19).

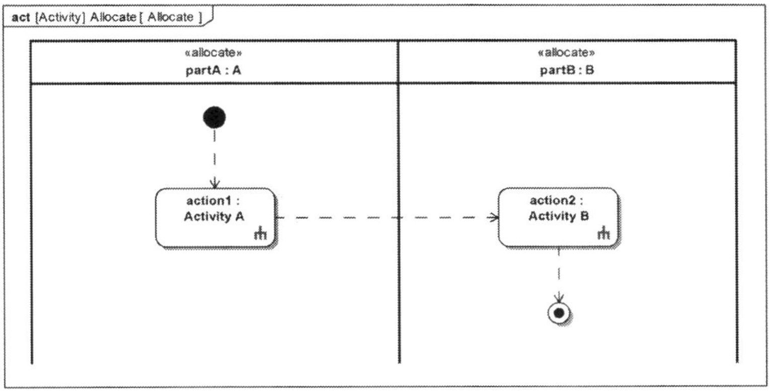

Figure 12.19: Example allocation activity partition

12.15 Cross-cutting elements

In this section, you find model elements of SysML that are independent of a diagram type. Figure 12.20 shows the cross-cutting elements comment, problem, rationale, and constraint.

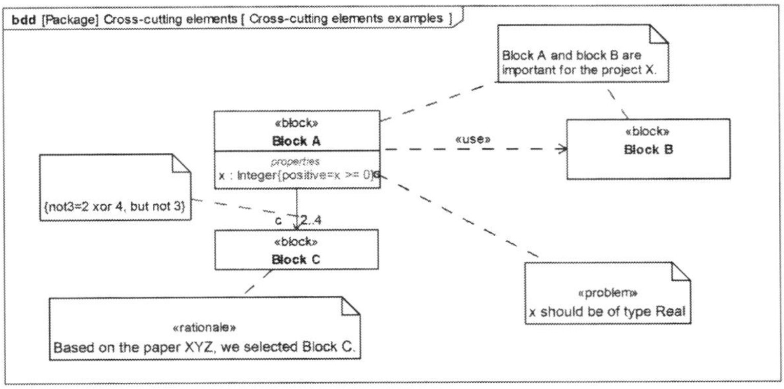

Figure 12.20: Example Cross-cutting elements

Comment

The comment is the yellow sticky note of SysML. You can comment on any model elements.

The diagram shows the comment in a box with a dog's ear corner in the upper right corner. Between the comment icon and the model elements to which the comment refers, a dashed line without arrowheads is drawn.

Problem

The problem element is a special comment representing an issue, failure, or another undesired outcome that is described by the text.

The problem is depicted like a comment with the keyword *«problem»*.

Rationale

A rationale documents the justification for a model element. It can be a text or include a reference to an external, more detailed document of the rationale.

The rationale is depicted like a comment with the keyword *«rationale»*.

Constraint

The constraint is a Boolean expression that refers to model elements and must always be true. It assures that this condition is valid at all times in the context of the model. For example, in figure 12.20, after the x property, there is a constraint expression that says x is always greater than or equal to 0.

The syntax of an constraint is *{<name>: <condition>}*. The name is optional. The condition is noted in any language that can be evaluated by a machine or a human to true or false.

The constraint can be noted directly on some model elements like properties or as a comment symbol.

Usage

The usage relationship connects an element with another element that is required by it for its full implementation. It is a special kind of a dependency relationship.

The usage relationship is depicted as a dashed arrow with open arrowhead and the attached keyword *«use»*.

Appendix A: Mapping ISO 15288 to SYSMOD

The following list shows a mapping of the ISO 15288 processes [ISO15288] to the SYSMOD Methods whereby the mapping makes no distinction between full or partial coverage:

A.1 ISO 15288: Technical Processes

ISO 15288	*SYSMOD*
Business Mission Analysis: Defines business or mission problem and characterize the solution space.	4.5 Analyze the Problem, 4.6 Describe the System Idea and the System Objectives, 4.7 Describe the Base Architecture, 4.8 Identify Stakeholders, 4.11 Identify the System Context

ISO 15288	***SYSMOD***
Stakeholder Needs and Requirements Definition: Define the stakeholder requirements.	4.8 Identify Stakeholders, 4.10 Model Requirements, 4.11 Identify the System Context, 4.12 Identify System Use Cases, 4.13 Identify System Processes, 4.14 Model Use Case Activities, 4.15 Model the Domain Knowledge, 4.21 Define System States
System requirements definition: Transform the stakeholder-oriented desired capabilities into a technical view of a solution.	4.10 Model Requirements, 4.12 Identify System Use Cases, 4.13 Identify System Processes, 4.14 Model Use Case Activities, 4.15 Model the Domain Knowledge, 4.21 Define System States
Architecture Definition: Create system architecture alternatives and select the most appropriate one(s).	4.11 Identify the System Context, 4.17 Model the Functional Architecture, 4.18 Model the Logical Architecture, 4.20 Revise an Architecture with Scenarios, 4.21 Define System States

ISO 15288	*SYSMOD*
Design Definition: Provide detailed information about the system for implementation aligned with the architecture.	4.19 Model the Product Architecture, 4.20 Revise an Architecture with Scenarios, 4.21 Define System States
System Analysis: Provide data to aid decision-making.	not explicitly covered
Implementation: Realize a specified system element.	not explicitly covered
Integration: Synthesize a set of elements into a realized system.	not explicitly covered
Verification: Provide evidence that a system fulfills its requirements.	4.16 Specify Test Cases, 4.22 Model the Test Architecture
Transition: Transfer of custody of the system from development to operation organizational entities.	not explicitly covered
Validation: Provide evidence that a system fulfills its intended use.	4.16 Specify Test Cases, 4.22 Model the Test Architecture
Operation: Perform operation of the system.	not explicitly covered

ISO 15288	***SYSMOD***
Maintenance: Perform maintenance to sustain the system services.	not explicitly covered
Disposal: End the existence of a system.	not explicitly covered

A.2 ISO 15288: Technical Management Processes

ISO 15288	*SYSMOD*
Project Planning: Produce and coordinate project plans.	not explicitly covered
Project Assessment and Control: Assess and control the plans.	not explicitly covered
Decision Management: Provide a framework for decisions.	not explicitly covered
Risk Management: Identify and manage risks.	4.9 Model Risks
Configuration Management: Manage system elements and configurations over the life cycle.	not explicitly covered
Information Management: Perform and coordinate communication of information with the stakeholders.	not explicitly covered
Measurement: Obtain objective data to support the quality management of the system.	not explicitly covered

ISO 15288	*SYSMOD*
Quality Assurance: Ensure the application of the organization's quality management process.	not explicitly covered

A.3 ISO 15288: Agreement Processes

ISO 15288	*SYSMOD*
Acquisition: Obtain a product or service.	not explicitly covered
Supply: Provide a product or service.	not explicitly covered

A.4 ISO15288: Organizational Project-Enabling

ISO 15288	*SYSMOD*
Life Cycle Model Management: Manage life cycle models, processes, and policies.	not explicitly covered
Infrastructure Management: Provide infrastructure and services to projects.	4.1 Tailor the MBSE Methodology, 4.2 Set up and maintain the SME, 4.3 Deploy the MBSE Methodology

ISO 15288	*SYSMOD*
Portfolio Management: Initiate suitable projects to meet the strategic objectives of the organization.	not explicitly covered
Human Resource Management: Provide the necessary human resources.	4.4 Provide MBSE Training and Coaching
Quality Management: Assure that the quality management process meets organizational and project quality objectives.	not explicitly covered
Knowledge Management: Create the capability to re-apply knowledge.	not explicitly covered

Bibliography

[Ar65] Bruce L. Archer. Systematic Method for Designers. Council of Industrial Design. H.M.S.O.. 1965.

[Bl56] Benjamin S. Bloom. Taxonomy of educational objectives: The classification of educational goals. Handbook I. David McKay. 1956.

[Br09] Tim Brown. Change by Design: How Design Thinking Transforms Organizations and Inspires Innovation. HarperBusiness. 2009.

[Cr81] Philip B. Crosby. The Art of Getting Your Own Sweet Way. McGraw-Hill. 1981.

[DaKl14] Matthias Dänzer, Sven Kleiner, Jesko G. Lamm, Georg Moeser, Fabian Morant, Florian Munker, Tim Weilkiens. Funktionale Systemmodellierung nach der FAS-Methode: Auswertung von vier Industrieprojekten. Tag des Systems Engineering (TdSE) 2014. Bremen. 12. – 14. November 2014.

[De10] John Dewey. How we think. D.C. Heath & Co. 1910.

[Es08] Jeff A. Estefan. Survey of Model-Based Systems Engineering (MBSE) Methodologies. INCOSE MBSE Initiative. 2008.

[Gy12] Craig Gygi, Bruce Williams, Neil DeCarlo, Stephen R. Covey. Six Sigma For Dummies. 2nd Edition. 2012.

[Ha19] Reinhard Haberfellner, Olivier de Weck, Ernst Fricke, Siegfried Vössner. Systems Engineering - Fundamentals and

Applications. Birkhäuser Basel. 2019.

[Im86] Masaaki Imai. Kaizen: The Key to Japan's Competitive Success. McGraw-Hill/Irwin. 1986.

[ISO15288] ISO/IEC/IEEE 15288:2015. Systems and software engineering — System life cycle processes. 2015.

[ISO195051] ISO/IEC 19505-1:2012. Information technology — Object Management Group Unified Modeling Language (OMG UML) — Part 1: Infrastructure. 2012.

[ISO195052] ISO/IEC 19505-2:2012. Information technology — Object Management Group Unified Modeling Language (OMG UML) — Part 2: Superstructure. 2012.

[ISO42010] ISO/IEC/IEEE 42010:2011. Systems and software engineering – Architecture description. 2011.

[LaWe10] Jesko G. Lamm, Tim Weilkiens. Functional Architectures in SysML. In M. Maurer and S.-O. Schulze (eds.). Tag des Systems Engineering 2010. pp. 109–118. Carl Hanser Verlag. Munich. Germany. November 2010.

[LaWe14] Jesko G. Lamm, Tim Weilkiens. Method for deriving functional architectures from use cases. Systems Engineering. 17(2):225-236. 2014.

[LaM17] Jesko G. Lamm, Andreas Mettauer, Georg Moeser, Tim Weilkiens, Albert Albers. Storyboards in der Systementwicklung: eine neue Methode und ihr Zusammenspiel mit der FAS-Methode. In S.-O. Schulze (eds.). Tag des Systems Engineering 2017. pp. 105–114. Carl Hanser Verlag. Munich.

[Le18] Michael Lewrick, Patrick Link, Larry Leifer. The Design Thinking Playbook: Mindful Digital Transformation of Teams, Products, Services, Businesses and Ecosystems. Wiley.

2018.

[Ma96] James N. Martin. Systems Engineering Guidebook: A Process for Developing Systems and Products. CRC Press, Inc.. 1996.

[MBSECook] Robert Karban, Tim Weilkiens, et al.. MBSE Cookbook. http://mbse.gfse.de

[Mo98] Niko Mohr, Jens Marcus Woehe. Widerstand erfolgreich managen: Professionelle Kommunikation in Veränderungsprojekten. Campus Verlag. 1998.

[MOF16] Object Management Group. Meta Object Facility, Version 2.5.1. formal/19-10-01.

[OCL14] Object Management Group. Object Constraint Language, Version 2.4. formal/14-02-03.

[Oh88] Taiichi Ohno. Toyota Production System: Beyond Large-Scale Production. Cambridge, MA: Productivity Press. 1988.

[Oh20] Taiichi Ohno. "Ask 'why' five times about every matter". https://www.toyota-myanmar.com/about-toyota/toyota-traditions/quality/ask-why-five-times-about-every-matter. Retrieved February 2020.

[Os14] Alexander Osterwalder, Yves Pigneur, Gregory Bernarda, Alan Smith. Value Proposition Design: How to Create Products and Services Customers Want. John Wiley & Sons. 2014.

[Pi16] Roman Pichler. Strategize: Product Strategy and Product Roadmap Practices for the Digital Age. Pichler Consulting. 2016.

[SE16] BKCASE Editorial Board. 2016. The Guide to the Systems Engineering Body of Knowledge (SEBoK), v. 1.6. R.D.

Adcock (EIC). Hoboken, NJ: The Trustees of the Stevens Institute of Technology. Accessed August 2016. www.sebokwiki.org.

[SysML07] Object Management Group. OMG Systems Modeling Language (OMG SysML), Version 1.0. formal/2007-09-01.

[SysML19] Object Management Group. OMG Systems Modeling Language (OMG SysML), Version 1.6. formal/19-11-01.

[UML17] Object Management Group. Unified Modeling Language (UML), Version 2.5.1. formal/17-12-05.

[UTP13] Object Management Group. UML Testing Profile (UTP), Version 1.2. formal/2013-04-03.

[We08] Tim Weilkiens. Systems Engineering with SysML/UML. Morgan Kaufmann. 2008.

[We14] Tim Weilkiens. Systems Engineering mit SysML/UML. 3rd edition. dpunkt. 2014.

[We15] Tim Weilkiens, Jesko G. Lamm, Stephan Roth, Markus Walker. Model-Based System Architecture. Wiley. 2015.

[We16] Tim Weilkiens. Variant Modeling with SysML. MBSE4U. 2016.

[We18] Tim Weilkiens. Alexander Huwaldt. Jürgen Mottok. Stephan Roth. Andreas Willert. Modellbasierte Softwareentwicklung für eingebettete Systeme verstehen und anwenden. dpunkt. 2018.

[Wo90] James P. Womack, Daniel T. Jones, Daniel Roos. Machine that Changed the World. Rawson Associates. 1990.

Index

A

B

C

D

T

Printed in Poland
by Amazon Fulfillment
Poland Sp. z o.o., Wrocław

28113324R00215